Soviet and Post-Soviet Politics and Society
ISSN 1614-3515

General Editor: Andreas Umland,
Stockholm Centre for Eastern European Studies, andreas.umland@ui.se

Commi...
London, ...

EDITORIAL COMMITTEE*

DOMESTIC & COMPARATIVE POLITICS
Prof. **Ellen Bos**, *Andrássy University of Budapest*
Dr. **Gergana Dimova**, *Florida State University*
Prof. **Heiko Pleines**, *University of Bremen*
Dr. **Sarah Whitmore**, *Oxford Brookes University*
Dr. **Harald Wydra**, *University of Cambridge*

SOCIETY, CLASS & ETHNICITY
Col. **David Glantz**, *"Journal of Slavic Military Studies"*
Dr. **Marlène Laruelle**, *George Washington University*
Dr. **Stephen Shulman**, *Southern Illinois University*
Prof. **Stefan Troebst**, *University of Leipzig*

POLITICAL ECONOMY & PUBLIC POLICY
Prof. **Andreas Goldthau**, *University of Erfurt*
Dr. **Robert Kravchuk**, *University of North Carolina*
Dr. **David Lane**, *University of Cambridge*
Dr. **Carol Leonard**, *University of Oxford*
Dr. **Maria Popova**, *McGill University, Montreal*

FOREIGN POLICY & INTERNATIONAL AFFAIRS
Dr. **Peter Duncan**, *University College London*
Prof. **Andreas Heinemann-Grüder**, *University of Bonn*
Prof. **Gerhard Mangott**, *University of Innsbruck*
Dr. **Diana Schmidt-Pfister**, *University of Konstanz*
Dr. **Lisbeth Tarlow**, *Harvard University, Cambridge*
Dr. **Christian Wipperfürth**, *N-Ost Network, Berlin*
Dr. **William Zimmerman**, *University of Michigan*

HISTORY, CULTURE & THOUGHT
Dr. **Catherine Andreyev**, *University of Oxford*
Prof. **Mark Bassin**, *Södertörn University*
Prof. **Karsten Brüggemann**, *Tallinn University*
Prof. **Alexander Etkind**, *Central European University*
Prof. **Gasan Gusejnov**, *Free University of Berlin*
Prof. **Leonid Luks**, *Catholic University of Eichstaett*
Dr. **Olga Malinova**, *Russian Academy of Sciences*
Dr. **Richard Mole**, *University College London*
Prof. **Andrei Rogatchevski**, *University of Tromsø*
Dr. **Mark Tauger**, *West Virginia University*

ADVISORY BOARD*

Prof. **Dominique Arel**, *University of Ottawa*
Prof. **Jörg Baberowski**, *Humboldt University of Berlin*
Prof. **Margarita Balmaceda**, *Seton Hall University*
Dr. **John Barber**, *University of Cambridge*
Prof. **Timm Beichelt**, *European University Viadrina*
Dr. **Katrin Boeckh**, *University of Munich*
Prof. em. **Archie Brown**, *University of Oxford*
Dr. **Vyacheslav Bryukhovetsky**, *Kyiv-Mohyla Academy*
Prof. **Timothy Colton**, *Harvard University, Cambridge*
Prof. **Paul D'Anieri**, *University of California*
Dr. **Heike Dörrenbächer**, *Friedrich Naumann Foundation*
Dr. **John Dunlop**, *Hoover Institution, Stanford, California*
Dr. **Sabine Fischer**, *SWP, Berlin*
Dr. **Geir Flikke**, *NUPI, Oslo*
Prof. **David Galbreath**, *University of Aberdeen*
Prof. **Frank Golczewski**, *University of Hamburg*
Dr. **Nikolas Gvosdev**, *Naval War College, Newport, RI*
Prof. **Mark von Hagen**, *Arizona State University*
Prof. **Guido Hausmann**, *University of Regensburg*
Prof. **Dale Herspring**, *Kansas State University*
Dr. **Stefani Hoffman**, *Hebrew University of Jerusalem*
Prof. em. **Andrzej Korbonski**, *University of California*
Dr. **Iris Kempe**, *"Caucasus Analytical Digest"*
Prof. **Herbert Küpper**, *Institut für Ostrecht Regensburg*
Prof. **Rainer Lindner**, *University of Konstanz*

Dr. **Luke March**, *University of Edinburgh*
Prof. **Michael McFaul**, *Stanford University, Palo Alto*
Prof. **Birgit Menzel**, *University of Mainz-Germersheim*
Dr. **Alex Pravda**, *University of Oxford*
Dr. **Erik van Ree**, *University of Amsterdam*
Dr. **Joachim Rogall**, *Robert Bosch Foundation Stuttgart*
Prof. **Peter Rutland**, *Wesleyan University, Middletown*
Prof. **Gwendolyn Sasse**, *University of Oxford*
Prof. **Jutta Scherrer**, *EHESS, Paris*
Prof. **Robert Service**, *University of Oxford*
Mr. **James Sherr**, *RIIA Chatham House London*
Dr. **Oxana Shevel**, *Tufts University, Medford*
Prof. **Eberhard Schneider**, *University of Siegen*
Prof. **Olexander Shnyrkov**, *Shevchenko University, Kyiv*
Prof. **Hans-Henning Schröder**, *SWP, Berlin*
Prof. **Yuri Shapoval**, *Ukrainian Academy of Sciences*
Dr. **Lisa Sundstrom**, *University of British Columbia*
Dr. **Philip Walters**, *"Religion, State and Society", Oxford*
Prof. **Zenon Wasyliw**, *Ithaca College, New York State*
Dr. **Lucan Way**, *University of Toronto*
Dr. **Markus Wehner**, *"Frankfurter Allgemeine Zeitung"*
Dr. **Andrew Wilson**, *University College London*
Prof. **Jan Zielonka**, *University of Oxford*
Prof. **Andrei Zorin**, *University of Oxford*

* While the Editorial Committee and Advisory Board support the General Editor in the choice and improvement of manuscripts for publication, responsibility for remaining errors and misinterpretations in the series' volumes lies with the books' authors.

Soviet and Post-Soviet Politics and Society (SPPS)
ISSN 1614-3515

Founded in 2004 and refereed since 2007, SPPS makes available affordable English-, German-, and Russian-language studies on the history of the countries of the former Soviet bloc from the late Tsarist period to today. It publishes between 5 and 20 volumes per year and focuses on issues in transitions to and from democracy such as economic crisis, identity formation, civil society development, and constitutional reform in CEE and the NIS. SPPS also aims to highlight so far understudied themes in East European studies such as right-wing radicalism, religious life, higher education, or human rights protection. The authors and titles of all previously published volumes are listed at the end of this book. For a full description of the series and reviews of its books, see www.ibidem-verlag.de/red/spps.

Editorial correspondence & manuscripts should be sent to: Dr. Andreas Umland, Department of Political Science, Kyiv-Mohyla Academy, vul. Voloska 8/5, UA-04070 Kyiv, UKRAINE; andreas.umland@cantab.net

Business correspondence & review copy requests should be sent to: *ibidem* Press, Leuschnerstr. 40, 30457 Hannover, Germany; tel.: +49 511 2622200; fax: +49 511 2622201; spps@ibidem.eu.

Authors, reviewers, referees, and editors for (as well as all other persons sympathetic to) SPPS are invited to join its networks at www.facebook.com/group.php?gid=52638198614 www.linkedin.com/groups?about=&gid=103012 www.xing.com/net/spps-ibidem-verlag/

Recent Volumes

273 Winfried Schneider-Deters
Russia's War in Ukraine
Debates on Peace, Fascism, and War Crimes, 2022–2023
With a foreword by Klaus Gestwa
ISBN 978-3-8382-1876-2

274 Rasmus Nilsson
Uncanny Allies
Russia and Belarus on the Edge, 2012-2024
ISBN 978-3-8382-1288-3

275 Anton Grushetskyi, Volodymyr Paniotto
War and the Transformation of Ukrainian Society (2022–23)
Empirical Evidence
ISBN 978-3-8382-1944-8

276 Christian Kaunert, Alex MacKenzie, Adrien Nonjon (eds.)
In the Eye of the Storm
Origins, Ideology, and Controversies of the Azov Brigade, 2014–23
ISBN 978-3-8382-1750-5

277 Gian Marco Moisé
The House Always Wins
The Corrupt Strategies that Shaped Kazakh Oil Politics and Business in the Nazarbayev Era
With a foreword by Alena Ledeneva
ISBN 978-3-8382-1917-2

278 Mikhail Minakov
The Post-Soviet Human
Philosophical Reflections on Social History after the End of Communism
ISBN 978-3-8382-1943-1

279 Natalia Kudriavtseva, Debra A. Friedman (eds.)
Language and Power in Ukraine and Kazakhstan
Essays on Education, Ideology, Literature, Practice, and the Media
With a foreword by Laada Bilaniuk
ISBN 978-3-8382-1949-3

280 Paweł Kowal, Georges Mink, Iwona Reichardt (eds.)
The End of the Soviet World?
Essays on Post-Communist Political and Social Change
With a foreword by Richardt Butterwick-Pawlikowski
ISBN 978-3-8382-1961-5

281 Kateryna Zarembo, Michèle Knodt, Maksym Yakovlyev (eds.)
Teaching IR in Wartime
Experiences of University Lecturers during Russia's Full-Scale Invasion of Ukraine
ISBN 978-3-8382-1954-7

UNIVERSITY OF PALERMO
Faculty of Political Science and International Relations
Centre of Advanced Studies "A.S. Cent"
NATIONAL ACADEMY OF SCIENCES OF UKRAINE
Volodymyr Koretsky Institute of State and Law
KYIV NATIONAL UNIVERSITY OF TRADE AND ECONOMICS

Oleksiy V. Kresin

THE UNITED NATIONS GENERAL ASSEMBLY RESOLUTIONS
Their Nature and Significance in the Context of the Russian War Against Ukraine

Edited by William E. Butler

Bibliografische Information der Deutschen Nationalbibliothek
Die Deutsche Nationalbibliothek verzeichnet diese Publikation in der Deutschen Nationalbibliografie; detaillierte bibliografische Daten sind im Internet über http://dnb.d-nb.de abrufbar.

Bibliographic information published by the Deutsche Nationalbibliothek
Die Deutsche Nationalbibliothek lists this publication in the Deutsche Nationalbibliografie; detailed bibliographic data are available in the Internet at http://dnb.d-nb.de.

ISBN-13: 978-3-8382-1967-7
© *ibidem*-Verlag, Hannover • Stuttgart 2024
Alle Rechte vorbehalten

Das Werk einschließlich aller seiner Teile ist urheberrechtlich geschützt. Jede Verwertung außerhalb der engen Grenzen des Urheberrechtsgesetzes ist ohne Zustimmung des Verlages unzulässig und strafbar. Dies gilt insbesondere für Vervielfältigungen, Übersetzungen, Mikroverfilmungen und elektronische Speicherformen sowie die Einspeicherung und Verarbeitung in elektronischen Systemen.

All rights reserved. No part of this publication may be reproduced, stored in or introduced into a retrieval system, or transmitted, in any form, or by any means (electronic, mechanical, photocopying, recording or otherwise) without the prior written permission of the publisher. Any person who commits any unauthorized act in relation to this publication may be liable to criminal prosecution and civil claims for damages.

Printed in the EU

Dedicated to the memory of the outstanding Polish diplomat and scholar **Krzysztof Skubiszewski** (1926-2010), the author of a landmark study on this issue,

and **Kostiantyn Oleksandrovych Savchuk** (1976-2023), a talented Ukrainian international legal scholar

Contents

Preface by *William E. Butler* 11
Introduction 13

I Nature of Powers and Acts of United Nations General
   Assembly: Evolution of Their Interpretation 19
   1.1. Charter of United Nations 19
   1.2. San Francisco Conference (1945) 22
   1.3. Interpretation of Competence of General Assembly 24
   1.4. "Uniting for Peace" Resolution (1950) 37
   1.5. Practice of the International Court of Justice 42

II United Nations General Assembly Resolutions in the
   Doctrine of International Law 49
   2.1. General Overview 49
   2.2. Recommendatory Acts with Vague Moral and Political
        Significance 51
   2.3. Political Acts Containing Standards of Proper and
        Lawful Behavior 52
   2.4. Drafts of Future Law, Soft Law, Auxiliary Source of
        International Law 59
   2.5. Role in Formation of Customary International Law 61
   2.6. International Quasi-Legislation 63
   2.7. Unilateral Acts of States or International
        Organizations 64
        2.7.1. Unilateral Acts of States 64
        2.7.2. Unilateral United Nations acts 65
   2.8. Problem of Nature of Qualifications Contained in
        Resolutions 65
   2.9. Dependence of Normative Impact of Resolutions on
        their Types and Circumstances of Adoption 70

2.10. Peculiarities of Resolutions within Framework of "Uniting for Peace" Mechanism 71

III Content, Nature, Legal and Political Significance of General Assembly Resolutions on Countering Aggression of Russian Federation against Ukraine in 2014-2023 79

3.1. Territorial Integrity of Ukraine in Resolution of 2014 79

3.2. Human Rights Protection in Crimea and Other Temporarily Controlled or Occupied Territories of Ukraine in Resolutions of 2016-2023 84

    3.2.1. Resolution 71/205 (2016) 84
    3.2.2. Resolution 72/190 (2017) 86
    3.2.3. Resolution 73/263 (2018) 87
    3.2.4. Resolution 74/168 (2019) 88
    3.2.5. Resolution 75/192 (2020) 90
    3.2.6. Resolution 76/179 (2021) 91
    3.2.7. Resolution 77/229 (2022) 93
    3.2.8. Resolution 78/221 (2023) 94

3.3. Condemnation of Russian Aggression at Sea and Militarization of Crimea in Resolutions of 2018-2021 97

    3.3.1. Resolution 73/194 (2018) 97
    3.3.2. Resolution 74/17 (2019) 100
    3.3.3. Resolution 75/29 (2020) 101
    3.3.4. Resolution 76/70 (2021) 102

3.4. Complex of Resolutions of the 2022-2023 Emergency Special Session 104

    3.4.1. Eleventh Emergency Special Session of General Assembly 104
    3.4.2. Resolution "Aggression against Ukraine" 105
    3.4.3. Resolution "Humanitarian Consequences of Aggression against Ukraine" 109
    3.4.4. Resolution on Suspension of Membership of Russian Federation in the United Nations Human Rights Council 113

    3.4.5. Resolution "Territorial Integrity of Ukraine: Defending the Principles of the Charter of the United Nations" 115

    3.4.6. Resolution "Furtherance of Remedy and Reparation for Aggression against Ukraine" 118

    3.4.7. Resolution "Principles of the Charter of the United Nations Underlying a Comprehensive, Just and Lasting Peace in Ukraine" 122

IV Perspectives 129

Sources and Literature 155
Appendices 173
    1. Territorial integrity of Ukraine. Resolution 68/262, adopted by the General Assembly on 27 March 2014 ... 173
    2. Problem of the militarization of the Autonomous Republic of Crimea and the city of Sevastopol, Ukraine, as well as parts of the Black Sea and the Sea of Azov. Resolution 76/70 adopted by the General Assembly on 9 December 2021 176
    3. Situation of human rights in the temporarily occupied territories of Ukraine, including the Autonomous Republic of Crimea and the city of Sevastopol. Resolution 78/221 adopted by the General Assembly on 19 December 2023 184
    4. Aggression against Ukraine. Resolution ES-11/1 adopted by the General Assembly on 2 March 2022 206
    5. Humanitarian consequences of the aggression against Ukraine. Resolution ES-11/2 adopted by the General Assembly on 24 March 2022 211
    6. Territorial integrity of Ukraine: defending the principles of the Charter of the United Nations. Resolution ES-11/4 adopted by the General Assembly on 12 October 2022 217

7. Furtherance of remedy and reparation for aggression against Ukraine. Resolution ES-11/5 adopted by the General Assembly on 14 November 2022....................... 220
8. Principles of the Charter of the United Nations underlying a comprehensive, just and lasting peace in Ukraine. Resolution ES-11/6 adopted by the General Assembly on 23 February 2023 223

Preface

As the United Nations approaches eight decades of existence, greatly increased in membership, issues that vexed or divided the founding countries continue to challenge the international community. The preferential status of the five permanent members of the United Nations Security Council, as reflected both in their permanent status and their veto power, is among these. Although much criticized by a membership which has nearly quadrupled since 1945, a seismic change will be required in the international order for one or more of the Great Powers to surrender this preferential position.

The principle of a veto power being vested in the five permanent members was accepted at the time: the issue was a veto precisely over what. A basic agreement reached at the Yalta Conference was imprecise in a number of respects, and the Soviet Union took the position that the veto power should extend even to the question of whether the Security Council might discuss an issue. An "immediate breakup" of the San Francisco Conference was at risk, only averted by a direct appeal to Joseph Stalin (1878-1953) by the American diplomats then in Moscow, Ambassador William Averell Harriman (1891-1986) and Harold "Harry" Lloyd Hopkins (1890-1946) on 6 June 1945 under instructions from the President of the United States. Stalin and Viacheslav Mikhailovich Molotov (1890-1986) agreed to withdraw their interpretation as "an insignificant matter" and the American position was accepted. (For details, see Ruth B. Russell, *A History of The United Nations Charter: The Role of the United States 1940-1945* (1958), esp. pp. 713-749.) The outcome preserved the "freedom of discussion" for the Security Council, but the principle of unanimity of the Great Powers, already under strain at San Francisco, has severely curtailed the effectiveness of the United Nations when such unanimity is absent.

On a more constructive note, the phrase "acts of aggression" was included in the United Nations Charter "as the result of a Soviet proposal at Dumbarton Oaks". (For the history of this provision, see L. M. Goodrich, Edvard Hambro, and Anne P. Simons,

Charter of the United Nations: Commentary and Documents (3d rev. ed.; 1968), pp. 298-300.)

The practice of the General Assembly of that Organization to assume "residual responsibility" for performing functions arising out the Purposes of the United Nations to, *inter alia*, maintain international peace and security when the Security Council is unable to do so by reason of the lack of unanimity among the permanent members has been an important and perhaps unforeseen at the time expansion of United Nations competence. In this timely study, Professor Dr. Oleksiy V. Kresin explores the course of General Assembly resolutions, voting patterns, and substantive developments between 2014 and 2023 with reference to the various actions of the Russian Federation against Ukraine, commencing with the annexation of the Autonomous Republic Crimea down to the present time. These collectively represent both an exercise and an extension of General Assembly powers in the domain of the maintenance of international peace and security of consideration interest beyond the conflict itself. This is an important addition to the repertoire of United Nations practice that enriches the literature on international organizations — their limitations, their successes, and sometimes their lack of success. They are not autonomous actors in international affairs, but an extension of their ultimately human creators, who via human-created States seek to bring a modicum of decency and order to their relations *inter se*.

William E. Butler
Penn State Dickinson Law

Introduction

Ukraine's new national liberation war against the Russian Federation has continued for more than a decade. The reasons for Russian aggression are of concern or threat to many neighboring and distant States. This threat to international peace and security requires strategic responses not only on the battlefield, but also by the States of the world and authoritative international organizations. As the High Representative for Foreign Affairs and Security Policy of the European Union, Josep Borrell, noted, "Russia has never been able to become a nation. It was always an empire with the tsar, with the Soviets, and now with Putin. It is a constant of Russia, and its political identity, and as a result a threat to its neighbors — and particularly to us".[1]

The new stage of aggression of the Russian Federation against Ukraine in 2022 actualized, *inter alia*, the need for lawyers to turn to all available tools and levers of international law and international politics to promote victory in the struggle of Ukraine. Given the authoritative and universal character of the United Nations, the acts of this organization require meticulous analysis.

The issues of countering Russian aggression are extensively reflected in resolutions of the United Nations General Assembly. The nature of these acts is the subject of long debates and, according to scholars, changes in the evolution of the United Nations. Therefore, the research acquires not only a practical, but also a theoretical character.

Unfortunately, these acts, constantly mentioned by politicians and journalists, did not attract the attention of Ukrainian jurists. The bibliography of Ukrainian publications on international law for 2022 does not contain a single scholarly work devoted to the

---

1   P. Wintour, "EU Foreign Policy Chief Fears Rightwing Surge in June Elections", *The Guardian*. 24 December 2023 (available online).

significance of General Assembly resolutions.[2] The present author managed to find a few recent articles and scholarly commentaries, but all brief and quite general.[3]

---

2   N. Vasil'eva, I. Hula, D. Danik, M. Ivankovych, and S. Kurochka, "Вибрана бібліографія з міжнародного права за 2022 рік" [Select Bibliography on International Law for 2022], Український часопис міжнародного права [Ukrainian Journal of International Law], no. 4 (2022), pp. 123-159.

3   P. Rabinovych, "Діяльність Організації Об'єднаних Націй у протидії військовій агресії Російської Федерації проти України" [UN Activities in Counteracting Russian Military Aggression against Ukraine], in: M. Kovaliv, M. Havryltsiv, N. Lepish (comp.), "Конституційні права і свободи людини та громадянина в умовах воєнного стану: матеріали наукового семінару" [Constitutional Rights and Freedoms of a Person in Conditions of Martial Law] (Lviv, 2022); Ye. Reniov, "Щодо деяких аспектів діяльності ООН в контексті підтримки суверенітету та територіальної цілісності України" [On Some Aspects of UN Activities in the Context of Sovereignty and Territorial Integrity of Ukraine Support], *Juris Europensis Scientia*, 2022, Iss. 5; I. Todorov, N. Todorova, "ООН у протидії російській агресії в Україні" [UN in Counteraction to Russian Aggression against Ukraine], *Геополітика України: історія і сучасність* [Geopolitics of Ukraine: History and Contemporaneity], 2023, No. 1 (30); R. Topolevskyi, T. Dudash, V. Honcharov, A. Nakonechna, ed. by P. Rabinovych, "Науковий коментар [до резолюції Генеральної Асамблеї ООН, ухваленої 2 березня 2022 року, ES-11/1 "Агресія проти України"]" [Scholarly commentary to the UN GA resolution *Aggression against Ukraine*], *Право України* [Law of Ukraine], 2022, No. 8; R. Topolevskyi, T. Dudash, V. Honcharov, A. Nakonechna, ed. by P. Rabinovych, "Науковий коментар [до резолюції Генеральної Асамблеї ООН, ухваленої 24 березня 2022 року, ES-11/2 "Гуманітарні наслідки агресії проти України"]", [Scholarly commentary to the UN GA resolution *Humanitarian consequences of the aggression against Ukraine*], *Право України* [Law of Ukraine], 2023, No. 2; R. Topolevskyi, T. Dudash, V. Honcharov, A. Nakonechna, ed. by P. Rabinovych, "Науковий коментар [до резолюції Генеральної Асамблеї ООН, ухваленої 7 квітня 2022 року, ES-11/3 "Зупинення прав, пов'язаних з членством Російської Федерації в Раді з прав людини ООН"]" [Scholarly commentary to the UN GA resolution *Suspension of the rights of membership of the Russian Federation in the Human Rights Council*], *Право України* [Law of Ukraine], 2023, No. 4. To some extent, the article by O. Tymchuk is an exception, which presents a brief critical analysis of the acceptability of the oppositions "West — not West", "autocracies-democracies", "rich states — poor states" for understanding the development of support for "Ukrainian" resolutions of the United Nations General Assembly. See: O. Tymchuk, "Реакція Генеральної Асамблеї ООН на російське вторгнення в Україну" [The Reaction of UN General Assembly to the Russian Invasion to Ukraine], *Актуальні проблеми та перспективи розвитку юридичної науки, освіти та технологій у XXI столітті в дослідженнях молодих учених: збірник матеріалів доповідей учасників всеукраїнської науково-практичної конференції* [Topical Issues and Prospects for Development of the Legal Science, Education, and Technologies in 21st Century: Conference Collection], Kharkiv, 2023.

One can assume that the reasons for ignoring the resolutions of the United Nations General Assembly are primarily political — from widespread utopian imaginations in society to partially preserved ideological guidelines of the Soviet doctrine of international law among lawyers. Journalists, some politicians, and many citizens perceive the United Nations General Assembly as a kind of world parliament able to prohibit a certain State from taking certain actions by its law and to ensure that this State fully complies with such norms. The United Nations Charter is, accordingly, considered as the constitution of such a world political entity, the pinnacle of world law. To a certain extent and in certain aspects, this is close to the truth or at least to the intentions of some members of the United Nations, in some situations confirmed by practice. This point of view is also supported by those international lawyers who believe in the existence of a special supra-contractual or extra-contractual essence of a unified international law.[4]

But the world is full of contradictions, in particular between State sovereignty, realized or imagined interests of individual societies, selfish and/or ideologically determined policies of State leadership — on one hand, the same interests and policies of other societies and groups — on the other hand, or the development of societal awareness of the globality of many key problems and the need for their joint solution — from a third party. Therefore, excessive optimism in assessing the abilities of the "world parliament" is without foundation — at least immediately. Faced with serious problems and the impossibility of a quick and complete solution by the "international community" represented by the United Nations General Assembly, optimistic politicians and ordinary citizens become

---

[4] The consideration and critics of such views see in: W. E. Butler, "Сравнительное международное право" [Comparative International Law], Yu. Shemshuchenko, O. Kresin (eds.), *Ідея порівняльного міжнародного права: pro et contra:* Збірник наукових праць на честь іноземного члена НАН України та НАПрН України Уїльяма Елліотта Батлера [The Idea of Comparative International Law: Pro et Contra: The Collection Dedicated to Member of the National Academy of Sciences of Ukraine and National Academy of Legal Sciences of Ukraine William Elliott Butler], Kyiv, Lviv, 2015, pp. 114-139.

pessimists, proclaiming the inaction and uselessness of the United Nations in general and the acts adopted by its organs in particular.

This game of images, passions, and disappointments is unconstructive and even dangerous. The dialectical opposite of the insufficiently effective, according to observers, United Nations law does not constitute a more perfect universal international legal order, a coordinated sum of regional international legal orders, a worldwide network of non-contradictory international relations and treaties of States, but nihility—an international space of lawlessness and war of all against all.

On the other hand, Ukrainian legal science to a certain extent is still under the influence of the Soviet and modern Russian doctrine of international law, which is generally State-centered and takes a narrow normativist view of international law. The first involves consideration of international law primarily as a system for ensuring the sovereignty and coexistence of States (as well as the "balance of power"),[5] and the second, as a continuation of the first, is recognition of the legal character only of the sources enumerated in the Statute of the International Court of Justice (Article 38), according preference to treaties.[6] Under this approach, resolutions of the United Nations General Assembly, unless their provisions have gained recognition as part of customary international law, are perceived as exclusively political in nature.

---

[5] V. Denysov, "Міжнародне співтовариство як правова реальність функціонування міжнародних відносин" [International Community as Legal Reality of the International Relations Functioning], Правова держава [Legal State], 2017, Iss. 28, p. 373.

[6] See for example: T. Langstriom, "Россия в переходный период: эволюция международно-правовых доктрин. Сравнительный анализ учебников "Международное право" под ред. Г.И. Тункина (М., 1982) и под ред. Ю.М. Колосова и В.И. Кузнецова (М, 1995)" [Russia in the Period of Transformation: Evolution of International Legal Doctrines], Московский журнал международного права [Moscow Journal of International Law], 1999, No. 1, pp. 202-235; A. Kraevskii, "Отражение международного права и права конца 1930-х—1980-х годов" [The Contemplation of International Law in Soviet Theory of State and Law in 1930s—1980s], Право и политика [Law and Politics], 2015, No. 12(192), pp. 1765-1772.

Neither utopian optimism or pessimism nor post-Soviet legal skepticism can adequately reflect the ambiguous and dynamic realities of the development of United Nations organs and institutions and their decisions.

This book summarizes the results of research, carried out in 2022-2023, against the backdrop of the war tragedy and the Ukrainian people's resistance to the full-scale aggression of the Russian Federation. Some materials have been published previously,[7] but they are comprehensively presented here for the first time.

---

[7] O. V. Kresin, "Характер повноважень та актів Генеральної Асамблеї ООН: статутні положення та еволюція їх тлумачення" [The Character of Powers and Acts of UN General Assembly: Charter Provisions and the Evolution of their Interpretation], *Право України* [Law of Ukraine], 2022, No. 7, pp. 112-126; Kresin, "Питання щодо характеру резолюцій Генеральної Асамблеї ООН у доктрині міжнародного права" [The Issue on the Character of UN General Assembly Resolutions in the International Law Doctrines], *Право України* [Law of Ukraine], 2022, No. 11, pp. 128-147; Kresin (ed.), "Деокупація. Юридичний фронт [Електронне видання]: матеріали Міжнародного експертного круглого столу (Київ, 18 березня 2022 р.) / Державний торговельно-економічний університет, Українська асоціація порівняльного правознавства, Українська асоціація міжнародного права, Асоціація реінтеграції Криму" [De-Occupation: Legal Front [Electronic Edition]: Materials of the International Round Table], Kyiv, 2022, 224 p.; Kresin, "Новітні виклики і загрози у війні Росії проти України: правові оцінки й рекомендації (за матеріалами Міжнародного експертного круглого столу «Деокупація. Юридичний фронт»)" [New Challenges and Threats in the War of Russia against Ukraine: Legal Conclusions and Recommendations], in: S. Pyrozhkov, O. Mayboroda, N. Hamitov, and others (eds.), *Національна стійкість України: стратегія відповіді на виклики та випередження гібридних загроз*: національна доповідь / Інститут політичних і етнонаціональних досліджень ім. І. Ф. Кураса НАН України [National Resilience of Ukraine: The Strategy of Response to the Challenges and Hybrid Threats: National Report], Kyiv, 2022, pp. 509-546; Kresin (ed.), De-Occupation of Ukraine. Legal expertise [Electronic publication] / State University of Trade and Economics, Ukrainian Association of Comparative Jurisprudence, Ukrainian Association of International Law, Association of Reintegration of Crimea, Kyiv, 2022. 58 p.; Kresin, "Правові аспекти протидії російській агресії та відновлення територіальної цілісності України (за матеріалами доповіді на засіданні Президії НАН України 13 квітня 2022 року)" [Legal Aspects of Counteracting the Russian Aggression and Territorial Integrity of Ukraine Restoration], *Вісник НАН України* [Herald of the National Academy of Sciences of Ukraine], 2022, No. 6, pp. 60-65; Kresin, "Доктрина міжнародного права про характер резолюцій Генеральної Асамблеї ООН" [International Law Doctrine on the UN General Assembly Resolutions Character], in: L. Pavlyk, U. Tsmots (eds.), *Війна в Україні: зроблені висновки та незасвоєні уроки*: збірник тез

Міжнародного круглого столу (23 лютого 2023 року) [War in Ukraine: Conclusions and Lessons: Conference Collection], Lviv, 2023, pp. 105-112; Kresin, "Тлумачення характеру повноважень та актів Генеральної Асамблеї ООН Міжнародним Судом ООН" [Interpretation of UN General Assembly Powers and Resolutions Character by the ICJ], in: T. Syroid, O, Havrylenko, V. Shamraeva (eds.), *Актуальні проблеми міжнародного права*: Всеукраїнська науково-практична конференція (Харків, 10 березня 2023 року): збірник матеріалів [Topical Issues of International Law: Conference Collection], Kharkiv, 2023, pp. 16-19; Kresin, "Зміст, характер, правове і політичне значення резолюцій Генеральної Асамблеї ООН щодо протидії агресії РФ проти України у 2014—2023 pp." [The Contents, Character, Legal and Political Significance of the UN General Assembly Resolutions on Counteracting the Aggression of Russian Federation against Ukraine in 2014—2023], *Право України* [Law of Ukraine], 2023, No. 11; Kresin, "Правові засади механізму «Єднання заради миру» та його використання в умовах війни рф проти України" [Legal Grounds of *Uniting for Peace* Mechanism and its Using in Conditions of the Russian Federation War against Ukraine], *Право України* [Law of Ukraine], 2024, No. 1; and others.

I Nature of Powers and Acts of United Nations General Assembly
Evolution of Their Interpretation

1.1. Charter of United Nations

The main competence and powers of the United Nations General Assembly are set out in the Charter of the United Nations. The United Nations is a universal international organization with limited supranational powers. The United Nations Charter declared this organization to be "a centre for harmonizing the actions of nations in the attainment of ... common ends", based on the principles of sovereign equality of its member States, "equal rights of ... nations large and small" (Preamble, Articles 1, 2).

The supranational powers of the organization are manifested only in coercive actions against individual States in response to certain actions of the latter. Member States are obliged to provide assistance to the United Nations in all actions taken by it in accordance with the Charter, including actions of a preventive or coercive nature against individual States (Article 2). At the same time, intervention in "matters which are essentially within the domestic jurisdiction of any state" is not provided for by the Charter—except when the State's actions threaten international peace, violate the peace or are an act of aggression (Article 2).

The subject of constant discussion among scholars is the authority of various United Nations organs to make decisions on behalf of this organization regarding the coordination of the actions of States and the application of preventive or coercive actions against individual States, as well as the authority of States to individually and collectively implement the goals of the United Nations Charter.

All member States of the organization are directly represented in one main organ—the General Assembly. Therefore, it reflects the formula "we the peoples of the United Nations", with which the United Nations Charter begins. Only General Assembly has universal powers regarding issues covered by the United Nations Charter (Articles 10, 11).

All fundamental decisions regarding the functioning of the United Nations and possible changes in the mechanism of its activity as an organization are adopted (independently, or with the involvement of other organs, but finally) by the General Assembly itself: admission to the organization (Articles 4, 18), termination of the rights and privileges of a member State (Articles 5, 18),[8] exclusion of a member State (Articles 6, 18), formation of the composition of all other main, specialized, auxiliary bodies and institutions of the United Nations, including the Security Council (except permanent members), the Economic and Social Council, the Trusteeship Council (elected members) (Articles 18, 61, 86), coordination of the activities of all specialized United Nations agencies (Article 17), submitting recommendations to the Security Council and member states on any issues (Articles 10, 11, 13, 14), consideration of the reports of all United Nations organs (Article 15), approval of the United Nations budget and distribution of financial contributions of member States (Article 17).

The same applies to the authority, on the basis of research, to formulate recommendations for the purpose of promoting international political, economic, cultural and other cooperation, encouraging the development of international law and its codification, the realization of human rights and fundamental freedoms (Article 13), coordinating international economic and social cooperation (Article 60). That is why the General Assembly is named first among the principal organs of the United Nations (Article 7).

The General Assembly has the power: to "discuss any questions or any matters within the scope of the present Charter or relating to the powers and functions of any organs provided for in the present Charter, and ... make recommendations to the Members of the United Nations or to the Security Council or to both on any such questions or matters" (Article 10),[9] to "consider the general

---

[8] But the Security Council has the power to restore the exercise of the rights and privileges of a member State (Article 5).
[9] Except for cases when the issue of a conflict or a situation of a conflict nature is under consideration by the United Nations Security Council.

principles of co-operation in the maintenance of international peace and security, including the principles governing disarmament and the regulation of armaments, and may make recommendations with regard to such principles to the Members or to the Security Council or to both" (Article 11), to "discuss any questions relating to the maintenance of international peace and security ... and ... make recommendations with regard to any such questions to the state or states concerned or to the Security Council or to both" (Article 11), to recommend measures for the peaceful resolution of conflicts (Article 14) and for the maintenance of international peace and security (Article 18). Decisions of the General Assembly on important issues are adopted by a two-thirds majority of the members of the Assembly present and participating in the vote (Article 18).[10]

The second organ, the Security Council, as noted above, is mainly formed by the General Assembly (except for the permanent members of the Security Council determined in the United Nations Charter) and accountable to the General Assembly (Articles 15, 18, 24, and others). According to the Charter, the competence of the Security Council is granted by the member States in order to "ensure prompt and effective action by the United Nations" (Article 24), which can be considered as an additional emphasis on the accountability and subordination of this body to the General Assembly as the principal body, where these members are represented.

Nevertheless, the Security Council is the second principal organ of the United Nations. Its activity to a certain extent has an autonomous character, implements the collective will of the member States, and is focused on the maintenance of international peace and security (Articles 24, 26). Issues in the field of maintenance of international peace and security must be referred to the Security Council by the United Nations General Assembly — either after considering them and adopting a recommendation, or without such consideration (Articles 11, 12).

Decisions of the Security Council are binding on member States (Article 25). However, the adoption of decisions in the Security Council requires not only a qualified majority, but also the

---

[10] Only votes cast "for" and "against" a certain decision are counted as decisive.

consent of all permanent members (Article 27). The Security Council can consider issues at the initiative of the General Assembly, the United Nations Secretary General, and member States.

The decisions of the Security Council can be either advisory or binding (Article 39) and provide for economic, transport, and/or diplomatic preventive measures not related to the use of armed forces (Articles 41, 50), or joint international coercive actions (Articles 42-45, 48). However, the declared participation of one or another State in the implementation of Security Council decisions must be carried out on the basis of a special agreement subject to ratification by that State (Article 48). The Security Council enjoys a monopoly on the authorization of international coercive actions; regional organizations cannot undertake such actions without its sanction (Article 53).

In the context of this study, questions arise that have become almost "eternal" for international lawyers: regarding the ratio of powers and cooperation of the General Assembly and the Security Council in the field of maintaining international peace and security, regarding the nature and limits of the advisory powers of the General Assembly and, accordingly, the nature of acts of the latter. The United Nations Charter does not provide precise answers to these questions. Keys to understanding can be provided by documents on the process of its drafting, as well as the development of its interpretation in the practice of the General Assembly and the International Court of Justice.

1.2. San Francisco Conference (1945)

The United Nations Charter was drafted at the San Francisco Conference (1945), convened for this purpose. The *travaux preparatoires* recording the positions of States and intergovernmental committees help clarify the meaning of the Charter. Committee II/2 considered and rejected the proposal of the Philippines to empower the

General Assembly to adopt norms of international law with the prior approval of the Security Council.[11]

And according to the document of the Commission on the judicial organization of the United Nations San Francisco Conference No. 887 (IV/2/39) of 9 June 1945, "Interpretation of the Charter" and other decisions of this body, the right to interpret the United Nations Charter within the limits of daily activities of the organization was granted to the General Assembly, the Security Council, and the International Court of Justice. In the event of misunderstandings regarding the interpretation of the Charter between various United Nations organs or between member States, they might seek an advisory opinion from the International Court of Justice (when there is sufficient time for this), convene a special international commission of lawyers, or create a bilateral conciliation commission (in urgent cases), but the decision of any of these bodies will not be binding (if it "is not generally acceptable it will be without binding force"). In the event that an agreement cannot be reached, the interpretation of the Charter should be adopted as an addition to the latter.[12]

Proposals to render a binding interpretation of the United Nations Charter by the General Assembly or the International Court of Justice were rejected. This was consistently motivated by the need to avoid a precisely defined procedure, to maintain flexibility, to allow practice to determine appropriate approaches, and was viewed as not necessary or desirable.[13] Moreover, the proposal to

---

11 K. Skubiszewski, "The Elaboration of General Multilateral Conventions and of Non-contractual Instruments Having a Normative Function or Objective. Resolutions of the General Assembly of the United Nations", *Annuaire. Institut de Droit International*, LXI (1985), I, p. 34; R. A. Falk, "On the Quasi-Legislative Competence of the General Assembly", *American Journal of International Law*, LX (1966), p. 782.

12 Interpretation of the Charter. Doc. 887. IV/2/39. June 9, 1945. *Documents of the United Nations Conference on the International Organization*: Commission IV Judicial Organization (1945), XIII, pp. 668-669; Report of the Rapporteur of Committee IV/2, as Approved by the Committee. Doc. 933. IV/2/42 (2). June 12, 1945. *Ibid.*, pp. 709-710.

13 Revised Summary Report of Fourteen Meeting of Committee IV/2. Doc. 873. IV/2/37. June 9, 1945. *Documents of the United Nations Conference on the International Organization*. San Francisco, 1945. Vol. XIII: Commission IV Judicial Organization. London, New York: United Nations Information Organizations,

include in the Charter a provision that member States cannot evade its implementation, based on the norms of national law, was also not supported.[14] The question about the correlation of international law and the United Nations Charter with national law was not resolved.

1.3. Interpretation of Competence of General Assembly

Over time, the vision of complex aspects of the competence of the General Assembly was clarified. Although the normativity of the interpretation of the Charter by any United Nations organ has not been resolved, the Charter is an international treaty and therefore subject to the principles and rules of treaty interpretation. As the International Court of Justice noted in its 1996 advisory opinion, "the constitutive instruments of international organizations are multilateral treaties, to which the well-established rules of treaty interpretation apply".[15]

According to the 1969 Vienna Convention on the Law of Treaties, treaties must be interpreted in a context that includes "any agreement relating to the treaty which was made between all the parties in connection with the conclusion of the treaty", and special meanings of terms may result from the intentions of the participants when concluding the treaty. Additional means of interpreting the treaty are "the preparatory work of the treaty and the circumstances of its conclusion" (therefore, the documents of the 1945 San Francisco Conference, considered and approved within its

---

1945. P. 653-654; Summary Report of Twelfth Meeting of Committee IV/2. Doc. 664. IV/2/33. May 29, 1945. Ibid. P. 633-635; Summary Report of Fourteenth Meeting of Committee IV/2. Doc. 843. IV/2/37. June 7, 1945. Ibid, pp. 645-646.

14 Report of the Rapporteur of Committee IV/2, as Approved by the Committee. Doc. 933. IV/2/42 (2). June 12, 1945. Ibid, pp. 708-709.

15 Legality of the Threat or Use of Nuclear Weapons. Advisory opinion of 8 July 1996. *International Court of Justice. Reports of judgements, advisory opinions and orders*. 1996. See also: G. Distefano, "International Judicial Review of the Legality of Acts Adopted by United Nations Organs", *Journal Sharia and Law*, XXXII (2018), 73, pp. 31, 33; J. Ušiak and L. Saktorová, "The International Court of Justice and the Legality of UN Security Council Resolutions", *DANUBE: Law and Economics Review*. V, no. 3 (2014).

committees, are of great importance). Along with the context there should be taken into account: "a) any subsequent agreement between the parties regarding the interpretation of the treaty or the application of its provisions; b) any subsequent practice in the application of the treaty which establishes the agreement of the parties regarding its interpretation; c) any relevant rules of international law applicable in the relations between the parties" (Articles 31, 32).

It should also be noted that the International Court of Justice in its decisions and advisory opinions stated that the practice of the main organs of this organization should be taken into account when interpreting the provisions of the United Nations Charter (see below). Therefore, quite common references to the statutory powers of the General Assembly without referring to their later interpretation are inaccurate and not productive.

The 1947 Provisional Rules of Procedure for the General Assembly repeated the Charter provisions regarding General Assembly resolutions: the resolutions of this organ were divided into two categories — regarding important issues and others. The first category included recommendations on maintaining international peace and security, elections of non-permanent members of the Security Council, acceptance of new States as United Nations members, suspension of rights and privileges of United Nations membership, expulsion of members, and others (Articles 78 and 79). Resolutions on such issues must be adopted by at least two-thirds of the votes of the member States that were present and voting.[16] Currently, these provisions are unchanged as Articles 83 and 84 of the Rules of Procedure of the General Assembly.[17] To a certain extent, in the context of this study, it is important that draft resolutions in the field of international security must be discussed beforehand in the First Committee of the General Assembly (Article 98).

---

16   Provisional Rules of Procedure for the General Assembly (as amended during the first and second parts of the first session). Lake Success, New York: United Nations, 1947, pp. 15-16.
17   Rules of Procedure of the General Assembly (embodying amendments and additions adopted by the General Assembly up to and including its seventy-fifth session). A/520/Rev*. New York: United Nations, 2022.

A Memorandum of the Office of Legal Affairs of the United Nations Secretariat in 1962 submitted to the United Nations Commission on Human Rights indicated that in United Nations practice a declaration is a "formal and solemn instrument, suitable for rare occasions when principles of great and lasting importance are being enunciated" and the recommendation is less formal. But from the point of view of the "legal principle" there is no difference between them: they are adopted in the form of a resolution of a United Nations organ. As such, the resolution "cannot be made binding upon Member States, in the sense that a treaty or convention is binding upon the parties to it, purely by the device of terming it a 'declaration' rather than a 'recommendation'." But the declaration, taking into account the greater importance granted to it by the organ that adopted it, the corresponding expectations from the States, and in the course of the "expectation is gradually justified by State practice", can be recognized in the usual way as setting out the norms binding on the States.[18]

The 2013 Memorandum of the United Nations International Law Commission "Formation and evidence of customary international law" noted (Observation No. 13): "Under certain circumstances, the practice of international organizations has been relied upon by the Commission to identify the existence of a rule of customary international law. Such reliance has related to a variety of aspects of the practice of international organizations, such as their external relations, the exercise of their functions, as well as positions adopted by their organs with respect to specific situations or general matters of international relations".[19]

In the Conclusions of the United Nations International Law Commission in 2014, it was indicated that any act or behavior of the State, and therefore its support of the resolution of the organ of the international organization, is clear evidence of State practice, and the sum of such practices constitutes the general practice as one of

---

[18] Use of the terms "declaration" and "recommendation". Memorandum by the Office of Legal Affairs. UN doc. E/CN.4/L.610. 2 April 1962 (available online).

[19] Formation and evidence of customary international law. Elements in the previous work of the International Law Commission that could be particularly relevant to the topic. Memorandum by the Secretariat. 14 March 2013. A/CN.4/659.

two—material—elements of the identification of norms of customary international law. The document directly points to the voting for "resolutions of organs of international organizations, such as the General Assembly, and international conferences", as reliable evidence of the practice of States as general practice, as also the explanations or reservations of States attached to such acts. And, accordingly, the practice of international (intergovernmental) organizations is the evidence of the existence of norms of customary law, such as of organizations empowered by the State—if this practice concerns the organization's relations with States and other international organizations and is created by the organization's intergovernmental bodies.

And, of course, for the identification of norms of customary international law, an important role is played by the consistency of general practice, its generality (prevalence and representativeness), but the universality or duration of such practice is not required. Another, subjective element of identification of norms of customary international law, *opinio juris*, must be evidenced through the clear recognition by the State of a certain practice or norm as giving rise to legal obligations. Quantitative support for General Assembly resolutions is important in this matter (voting "against" is also evidence of recognition of the normative nature of the document), the representativeness of this support, the involvement of States in the development of the resolution and proposals regarding the text of its draft, the repeatability of the resolution, but the circumstances of each specific case must be studied.[20] Also, in the 2015-2016 Conclusions on the Identification of International Law of the United Nations International Law Commission, it was noted that the resolutions of an international organization or an intergovernmental conference do not in themselves create customary international law, but provide evidence to establish the existence and content of norms of international law.[21]

---

20 Identification of Customary International Law [Agenda item 9]. Document A/CN.4/672. Second report on identification of customary international law, by Sir Michael Wood, Special Rapporteur. 22 May 2014. pp. 175-200.
21 M. N. Shaw, *International Law* (8th ed.; 2017), p. 86.

The 2006 General Assembly Resolution "Revitalization of the General Assembly" A/RES/60/286 (also adopted in other years), which refers to a number of previous resolutions, pointed to the "central position of the General Assembly as the chief deliberative, policymaking and representative organ of the United Nations", which plays a role in the process of setting standards and codifying international law. In particular, the role and authority of the General Assembly in matters of international peace and security were confirmed, along with the recognition of the main responsibility of the Security Council in this area. The procedure for holding emergency special sessions of the General Assembly to consider these issues was mentioned.[22]

Significant in the evolution of the understanding of the powers of the General Assembly is its resolution "Standing mandate for a General Assembly debate when a veto is cast in the Security Council", dated 26 April 2022. This act is quite fresh and therefore still not well considered by researchers, but Anne Peters connected its appearance with the reaction of United Nations member States to the aggression of the Russian Federation against Ukraine.[23] The resolution emphasizes that the main responsibility for maintaining international peace and security of the Security Council was laid on it by member States, and this mission is carried out on their behalf (an unequivocal hint that all are represented only in the General Assembly). It is emphasized that the General Assembly has not lost its competence in this area, and also indicated that the existing composition of the Security Council and the decision-making procedure therein require changes, and are called into question even in the decisions of the Security Council itself (Decision 62/557 of 15 September 2008 is mentioned).[24] On the basis of all of the above, the President of the General Assembly of the United Nations is obliged

---

22 Revitalization of the General Assembly. Resolution adopted by the General Assembly on 8 September 2006. A/RES/60/286.
23 A. Peters, "The War in Ukraine and the Curtailment of the Veto in the Security Council", *La Revue Européenne du Droit*. V, no. 1 (2023), pp. 87-93.
24 Question of equitable representation on and increase in the membership of the Security Council and related matters. Decision A/DEC/62/557 adopted by UN Security Council adopted at 122nd plenary meeting. 15 September 2008.

to convene "a formal meeting"[25] of the Assembly within ten working days after each case of veto application by one or more permanent members of the Security Council—in order to consider the situation on the decision of which this veto was imposed—if the General Assembly has not already called an emergency special session regarding this situation. During such a "formal meeting", the first speech is provided for the States—permanent members of the Security Council, which used the veto. The Security Council is invited to present to the General Assembly three days before its "formal meeting" a special report on the case of the use of the veto.[26]

On the basis of this resolution, in April 2023, the General Assembly held the first discussion of the principles of the application of the right of veto in the Security Council, which reflected the full support of the resolution by almost all member States that expressed their position (except Syria), including the United States, France, and United Kingdom. A significant number of countries spoke in favor of further limiting the right of veto and pointed to its obsolescence and inconsistency with the principle of sovereign equality of States.[27]

There is a developed practice of the General Assembly establishing auxiliary bodies for the performance of its functions, provided for in Article 22 of the United Nations Charter, which indicates the development of understanding of General Assembly powers. Here we turn to the classification of such entities in the field of maintaining international peace and security proposed by Rebecca Barber: 1) fact-finding missions and investigative commissions, which can also be established by the United Nations Human Rights

---

25 This term is absent in the Rules of Procedure of the General Assembly, which provides for public and private plenary and committee meetings of this body (Articles 60, 61) in the form of regular and special sessions, including emergency special sessions (Articles 1-11, 63, etc.). See: note 17 above.
26 Standing mandate for a General Assembly debate when a veto is cast in the Security Council. Resolution A/RES/76/262 adopted by the General Assembly on 26 April 2022.
27 General Assembly Holds First-Ever Debate on Historic Veto Resolution, Adopts Texts on Infrastructure, National Reviews, Council of Europe Cooperation. Press-release of the seventy-seventh UN General Assembly session, 68th and 69th meetings. GA/12500. 26 April 2023. [available online].

Committee (of the General Assembly), the basis of which are disclosed in the 1991 Declaration on Fact-Finding by the United Nations in the Field of the Maintenance of International Peace and Security; 2) investigative (pre-prosecution) mechanisms; 3) judicial bodies (*ad hoc* tribunals) — their creation is possible, they should be based on the voluntary cooperation of States, but such practice has not yet occurred.[28]

Among the means for exercising the powers of the General Assembly, the following are singled out: preventive diplomacy, applying for advisory opinions to the International Court of Justice, recommendations to the Security Council, requests to the latter and consideration of its reports, recommended sanctions, use of military force, peacekeeping, and depriving a State representative of credentials.[29]

We consider examples of activities of the General Assembly in the maintenance of international peace and security which give deeper insight into the development of its powers:

(1) the General Assembly may apply for an advisory opinion to the International Court of Justice; for example, an appeal regarding the legal consequences of Israel's construction of a protective wall in the occupied Palestinian territories;[30]

(2) the General Assembly can revoke the credentials of a State delegation, which makes it impossible for its representatives to participate in the work of United Nations organs (including the Security Council). Oleksandr Matsuka, head of the United Nations Security Council Secretariat from 2009 to 2016, considers such a decision possible and promising.[31] A precedent for such actions was the termination (or, rather, non-recognition) of the credentials of South

---

28 R. Barber, *The Powers of the UN General Assembly to Prevent and Respond to Atrocity Crimes: A Guidance Document* (2021), pp. 26-31.
29 See for example: ibid., pp. 19-52.
30 Legal Consequences of the Construction of a Wall in the Occupied Palestinian Territory. Advisory opinion of 9 July 2004. *International Court of Justice. Reports of judgements, advisory opinions and orders*. 2004.
31 Н. Erman, "Росія стає головою Ради безпеки ООН. Як це може нашкодити Україні і як можна виключити РФ звідти?" [Russia achieving the UN Security Council. How this Could Harm Ukraine and How it is Possible to Exclude Russian Federation from There], *BBC News Ukraine* (available online).

Africa due to flagrant violations of the United Nations Charter (apartheid regime) in 1974. This action has to be renewed annually — and South Africa was thus deprived of participation in the work of the United Nations for twenty years — until 1994.[32] Nevertheless, in recent cases of unconstitutional seizure of power in Myanmar and Afghanistan, the United Nations recognized the delegations of their new governments; regarding Myanmar, this action was reinforced by the decision of the International Court of Justice in 2022;[33]

(3) the General Assembly can impose diplomatic sanctions on a certain State or subject it to a trade and transport embargo — as a recommendation to member States. For example, in 1951, in connection with the aggression against the Republic of Korea the following economic measures were applied to the People's Republic of China in order to "deny contributions to the military strength of the forces opposing the United Nations": a naval embargo on weapons and military equipment, nuclear materials, gasoline, transportation of materials of strategic importance and materials that can be used in the production of weapons and equipment, export control over all of the above. Member States were recommended to prevent by any means the circumvention of such supplies by other States;[34]

(4) the General Assembly and the Human Rights Council (an auxiliary body of the General Assembly) can create commissions to investigate violations of international law. In 2006, a General Assembly resolution established a United Nations Register of Damage Caused by the Construction of the Wall in the Occupied Palestinian Territory. This is an auxiliary body, the purpose of which is to

---

[32] M. P. Scharf, "Power Shift: The Return of the Uniting for Peace Resolution", *Case Western Reserve Journal of International Law*, LV (2023), pp. 23-24.

[33] R. Barber, "The Role of the General Assembly in Determining the Legitimacy of Governments", *International and Comparative Law Quarterly*, LXXI (2022), pp 638-639.

[34] Additional measures to be employed to meet the aggression in Korea. Resolution 500 (5) adopted by the General Assembly. 18 May 1951.

document the destruction and other damage caused to individuals and juridical persons.[35]

In 2013 the United Nations Human Rights Council established the Commission of Inquiry on Human Rights in the Democratic People's Republic of Korea. According to the Council resolution, the Commission mandate (one year with the possibility of extension) included the investigation of systematic, widespread, and serious violations of human rights in that State with the aim of ensuring full accountability, in particular for violations that may constitute crimes against humanity.[36] The Commission report emphasized the need to urgently consider the issue of the commission of these crimes, regardless of the presence or absence of DPRK consent, in the International Criminal Court (at the request of the Security Council) or in an *ad hoc* international tribunal established by a decision of the Security Council or the General Assembly. Regarding the latter option, it was noted: "In the event that the Security Council fails to refer the situation to the ICC or set up an ad hoc tribunal, the General Assembly could establish a tribunal. In this regard, the General Assembly could rely on its residual powers recognized inter alia in the "Uniting for Peace" resolution and the combined sovereign powers of all individual Member States to try perpetrators of crimes against humanity on the basis of the principle of universal jurisdiction" (paragraph 1201).[37]

In 2018 the Independent Investigative Mechanism for Myanmar was established with the mandate to collect, preserve, and analyze evidence of the most serious international crimes, prepare cases for consideration in national, regional or international courts

---

[35] Establishment of the United Nations Register of Damage Caused by the Construction of the Wall in the Occupied Palestinian Territory. Resolution ES-10/17 adopted by the General Assembly 15 December 2006.

[36] Situation of human rights in the Democratic People's Republic of Korea. Resolution 22/13 adopted by the Human Rights Council. 21 March 2013.

[37] Report of the detailed findings of the commission of inquiry on human rights in the Democratic People's Republic of Korea. Human Rights Council. A/HRC/25/CRP.1. 7 February 2014.

or tribunals, disseminate information in the interests of justice and the prevention of further crimes.[38]

On 4 March 2022, the United Nations Human Rights Council established an Independent International Commission of Inquiry on Ukraine, which consists of three human rights experts and has a one-year mandate with the possibility of extension. It should function in coordination with the United Nations Human Rights Monitoring Mission in Ukraine and the Office of the United Nations High Commissioner for Human Rights. Its mandate includes: investigating all allegations of violations of human rights and international humanitarian law and related crimes in the context of Russian Federation aggression against Ukraine, establishing the facts, circumstances, and root causes of all these violations; collection, systematization, analysis, verification, preservation of evidence of such violations and their independent documentation for future court proceedings; identification, where possible, of persons and organizations responsible for these violations, in order to ensure their responsibility; formulation of recommendations on measures to ensure such responsibility; preparation of oral and written reports for the Human Rights Council and the General Assembly;[39]

(5) the General Assembly can create peacekeeping missions, including military and police missions. General Assembly resolutions established the first United Nations Emergency Force in the Middle East in 1956, took control of United Nations operations in Congo in 1960, and authorized peacekeeping efforts during the Falklands War and in a number of other situations.[40] The General Assembly oversees United Nations peacekeeping activities through the Special Committee on Peacekeeping Operations. The latter

---

[38] Situation of human rights of Rohingya Muslims and other minorities in Myanmar. Resolution 39/2 adopted by the Human Rights Council on 27 September 2018.

[39] Situation of human rights in Ukraine stemming from the Russian aggression. Resolution 49/1 adopted by the Human Rights Council on 4 March 2022. See also: R. Topolevskyi, T. Dudash, V. Honcharov, A. Nakonechna, ed. by P. Rabinovych, "Науковий коментар" [Scholarly Commentary], Право України [Law of Ukraine]. 2022, No. 12, pp. 23-25; 52/32.

[40] V. Bruz, ООН і врегулювання міжнародних конфліктів [UN and the Settlement of International Conflicts] (1995), p. 19.

reports to the fourth General Assembly' committee (special political and decolonization issues) on each peacekeeping operation.[41]

(6) the issue of creating an international *ad hoc* tribunal on the basis of a General Assembly resolution is controversial. For example, the creation of the International Criminal Tribunal for the former Yugoslavia (ICTY) took place on the basis of a decision of the Security Council—as a coercive measure based on Article 41 of the United Nations Charter. Resolving the question of the legality of its own jurisdiction in the case of Tadic in 1995, the ICTY noted that the Security Council does not have judicial powers, nor does it delegate its existing powers to the newly created tribunal. Instead, "the Security Council has resorted to the establishment of a judicial organ in the form of an international criminal tribunal as an instrument for the exercise of its own principal function of maintenance of peace and security, i.e., as a measure contributing to the restoration and maintenance of peace in the former Yugoslavia" within the framework of Chapter VII of the United Nations Charter.

It is important that, when justifying this, the ICTY referred to the legality of the powers of the General Assembly to create military-police peacekeeping missions (in particular, in the Middle East in 1956) and its creation of the United Nations Appellate Tribunal (in 2009), the legality of which was confirmed by the International Court of Justice in the *Effect of Awards* case. However, the adequacy of the creation of the ICTY as a measure and at the same time as an auxiliary body of the Security Council was argued by its freedom of discretion to carry out "political evaluation of highly complex and dynamic situations" within the limits of its powers, without pretending to determine in advance the results of the trial.[42]

According to Michael Ramsden, there is every reason to believe that the General Assembly can also establish *ad hoc* international tribunals, using the same arguments and as an organ that has

---

41 For a detailed analysis of United Nations peacekeeping and the role of the General Assembly, see O. V. Kresin (ed.), *Peacekeeping Operations in Ukraine*, transl. and ed. W. E. Butler (2019).
42 International Criminal Tribunal for the Former Yugoslavia. Prosecutor v. Tadic. Case No. IT-94-1-I. Decision on Defense Motion for Interlocutory Appeal on Jurisdiction. 2 October 1995.

powers in the field of maintaining international peace and security. Ramsden suggests relying on Article 22 of the United Nations Charter (the right of the General Assembly to create auxiliary bodies to perform its functions).[43] But Ramsden's arguments regarding the possibility for the General Assembly to create a body with coercive and binding powers for member States are not convincing.

Nonetheless, the General Assembly can create hybrid tribunals—based on the judicial system and the law of a certain State with the involvement of international judges. From 1997 to 2005, this is how the Extraordinary Chambers in Cambodian courts were created: the law of Cambodia and the agreement between it and the United Nations.[44]

To analyze the entire practice of States with regard to United Nations resolutions, in particular, reservations when adopting them, as well as giving them legally binding force, the importance of the standard in the development of legislation, and the like are beyond the scope of the present volume. But consider the following example.[45] In its reservations to the 2007 United Nations Declaration on the Rights of Indigenous Peoples, the United States delegation argued that the Declaration was drafted as "an aspirational declaration with political and moral, rather than legal, force", is non-binding and contains only recommendations, not international legal norms, including customary ones, and cannot be used in national or international courts. In addition, taking into account a number of arguments regarding the content of the 2007 Declaration, the United States delegation declared it generally unsuitable

---

43 M. Ramsden, "Uniting for MH17", *Asian Journal of International Law*, VII (2017), 2, pp. 352-353.
44 Agreement Between the United Nations and the Royal Government of Cambodia Concerning the Prosecution Under Cambodian Law of Crimes Committed During the Period of Democratic Kampuchea. *United Nations Treaty Series*, Vol. 2329 (2005), pp. 117-128; Khmer Rouge trials. Resolution 57/228 adopted by the General Assembly. 18 December 2002.
45 О. Kresin, Корінні народи: міжнародне право та законодавство України: монографія / Інститут держави і права імені В.М. Корецького НАН України [Indigenous Peoples: International Law and Ukrainian Legislation]. Kyiv, 2021.

for improvement and unacceptable.⁴⁶ Similar reservations were expressed by representatives of many other States. But in 2010, the United States changed its position and joined the Declaration of 2007 — as having moral and political significance, but not being "legally binding or a statement of current international law", it contains the aspirations of indigenous peoples and states, and its implementation must comply with the constitution, legislation, and international obligations of the State. The corresponding document contains a number of interpretative statements that fundamentally narrow the application of the provisions of the Declaration, previously defined as unacceptable.⁴⁷ It should be added that Australia, Canada, United States, and Ukraine, which initially did not support the 2007 Declaration, later officially announced their accession and so informed the United Nations, although accession to such acts of a recommendatory nature is not provided for.⁴⁸

Another example of State practice in the context of this study is the arms re-export bill, which will be considered by the Swiss Federal Assembly and has been approved by all relevant parliamentary committees. The bill provides that the re-export of weapons to a country in a state of war is possible if a violation of international law against that country is recognized by a resolution of the United Nations Security Council or a resolution of the United Nations General Assembly adopted by a two-thirds majority of member States⁴⁹ (probably referring to a vote by a qualified majority when making important decisions in accordance with Article 18 of the United Nations Charter).

---

46 Observations of the United States with respect to the Declaration on the Rights of Indigenous Peoples.
47 Announcement of U.S. Support for the United Nations Declaration on the Rights of Indigenous Peoples. U.S. Department of State (December 16, 2010).
48 А. Pryhodko, Стандарти ООН стосовно прав корінних народів: автореф. ... канд. юрид. наук. [UN Standards on the Indigenous Peoples Rights: Abstract of Theses ... Candidate of Legal Sciences]. Odesa, 2017, pp. 9-10; B. Babin, O. Hrinenko, A. Pryhodko. Питання розвитку та реалізації міжнародних стандартів прав корінних народів: монографія [Issues of Development and Implementation of International Standards of Indigenous Peoples Rights] (2018), pp. 112-113, 120, 186.
49 "Le national enterre une initiative sur les réexportations d'armes", *L'Assemblée fédérale*, 27 septembre 2023.

1.4. "Uniting for Peace" Resolution (1950)

Perhaps one of the most important and most criticized General Assembly resolutions, which interpreted and clarified its powers, was Resolution 377(V) "Uniting for Peace", adopted 3 November 1950 (also known as the Dean Acheson resolution). It won convincing support during the voting: 52 votes "for", 5 – "against" (USSR and its allies), 2 States abstained (Argentina and India).

The Resolution reaffirmed the primary responsibility of the Security Council for the maintenance of international peace and security, but stated that the "failure of the Security Council to discharge its responsibilities on behalf of all the Member States ... does not relieve Member States of their obligations or the United Nations of its responsibility under the Charter to maintain international peace and security".

The Resolution emphasized the existence of statutory powers of the General Assembly in this area, the implementation of which should be carried out even under conditions of the inability of the Security Council to perform related actions. The General Assembly has the authority to monitor the situation, establish facts, expose aggressors, recommend urgent collective measures to member States, including authorizing the use of collective armed forces. However, it was not only about establishing the facts, but also about their legal qualification (in particular, regarding the act of aggression). In the text, the "recommendations of the Security Council or the General Assembly" in the field of maintaining international peace and security and the need for their implementation by the member States are actually equated with each other, and the provision by the States of their military contingents for operations abroad in accordance with these resolutions is defined as the realization of the right to individual or collective self-defense.

The Resolution significantly changed the Rules of Procedure of the General Assembly. It declared that in the event of the Security Council's inability to fulfill its duties in the field of maintaining international peace and security due to the impossibility of achieving unanimity of the permanent members of the Security Council, the General Assembly has the authority to immediately consider the relevant issue in order to adopt recommendations to member States regarding the listed collective measures. To consider such a question, consideration at a regular session or the convening of an emergency special session of the General Assembly within 24 hours were envisaged. The request for the latter could be submitted by the Security Council (by a qualified majority vote) or by any State, supported by the decision of a simple majority of member States, expressed during voting in the Interim (intersessional) committee of the General Assembly or otherwise. The agenda of such a session is not considered in advance by any of the committees of the General Assembly and can be supplemented according to the decision of two-thirds of the member States that were present and took part in the vote.

Pursuant to the Resolution, a permanent Peace Observation Commission was established as an association of the States defined therein, which are able to monitor the situation in any territory where there is "international tension", the continuation of which may threaten international peace and security, and are ready, by the decision of the General Assembly and upon the invitation or consent of the host State, to send their troops to it in conditions of a threat to international peace and security (provided that the Security Council is unable to adopt a corresponding decision) and would perform their tasks as United Nations units. The decision on the use of the Commission resources must be taken by a qualified majority of two-thirds of the Member States present and voting. The right to use the powers of the Commission was also granted to the Security Council within the limits of its powers in this sphere. All governments of States were recommended to assist and co-operate with the Commission and to establish permanent military rapid response contingents for this purpose. A Collective Measures Committee was also established, consisting of representatives of the States specified in the Resolution. It was supposed to receive information about ready-to-use national military contingents and create a base of military experts.[50]

---

50 Uniting for Peace. 377 A (V). 3 November 1950.

The changes provided for in the Resolution regarding the work procedures of the General Assembly the same year were enshrined in Articles 8, 9, 10, 16, 19, and 65 of the Rules of Procedure of this organ.[51] This, together with the case law of the International Court of Justice (which confirmed the powers of the General Assembly), deprived the criticism directed against the "Uniting for Peace" Resolution of any normative significance.

The "Uniting for Peace" Resolution must be understood in context. The content of some provisions is now largely confirmed, transformed, or leveled by decisions and advisory opinions of the International Court of Justice (see below), although the text of the Resolution was not directly considered by the Court.

As noted by Jean Krasno and Mitushi Das, the 1950 Resolution should also be considered in the context of the discussions during the drafting of the United Nations Charter: the unanimity voting in the Security Council (with the corresponding and directly named right of veto) was accepted by other States only together with the declaration of the right of the General Assembly to discuss any issue and adopt recommendations regarding it, if it is not currently under consideration by the Security Council (by the way, the USSR opposed the adoption of this norm at the time and insisted on its maximum mitigation).[52] This essentially clarifies the significance of such recommendations.

It is equally important that the mechanism of bypassing the Security Council veto had been tested in the General Assembly during the early years of the organization's existence and before the "Uniting for Peace" Resolution. Back in 1947, a decision was made to establish the United Nations observation mission in the Balkans; to make this possible, the relevant issue was previously removed from consideration by the Security Council itself. The observation mission worked from 1947 to 1951 and reported to the General Assembly.[53]

---

51   See note 17 above.
52   J. Krasno and M. Das, "The Uniting for Peace Resolution and Other Ways of Circumventing the Authority of the Security Council", in: B. Cronin, I. Hurd (eds.), *The UN Security Council and the Politics of International Authority* (2008), p. 176.
53   Ibid., pp. 177-178.

The mechanism provided for in the "Uniting for Peace" Resolution was first used in 1951. The Security Council, after an unsuccessful vote on the resolution concerning the aggression of the unrecognized DPRK, and in fact of the People's Republic of China, against the Republic of Korea, removed the issue from its consideration by a procedural decision, and the General Assembly adopted Resolution 498(V), which contained a condemnation of the aggression and a call to the member States to oppose it, to support the United Nations military actions in Korea to repel the aggression of the People's Republic of China, and to the Collective Measures Committee to determine possible measures and report on it to the General Assembly.[54] The issue of coercive measures, including the use of collective armed forces, as well as economic sanctions and prevention of their violation by other States, and so on, was also considered in subsequent resolutions of the General Assembly on countering aggression against the Republic of Korea.[55]

In 1956, in response to the "Suez Crisis" and the invasion of Egypt by Israel, France, and Great Britain, the General Assembly authorized the deployment of the first military observer peacekeeping mission. In the same year, the General Assembly adopted a resolution calling on the USSR to end the occupation of Hungary. In 1958, a resolution of the General Assembly established the observation mission on the border of Lebanon and Syria. In 1960, a peacekeeping operation was also launched in Congo. In 1967, debates within this mechanism led to a ceasefire in the Middle East. In 1971, the General Assembly resolved the issue of the conflict in East Pakistan (now Bangladesh), in 1980 — of the Soviet invasion of Afghanistan, in 1980-1982 — of the Israeli invasion of Lebanon, in 1981 — of sanctions against South Africa for the continuing occupation of Namibia, in 1983 — of the invasion by a group of States in Grenada, in 1989 — of the United States intervention in Panama. From 1997 to 2003, the emergency special session regarding the

---

54 Intervention of the Central People's Government of the People's Republic of China in Korea. Resolution 498 (5) adopted by the General Assembly. 1 February 1951; Scharf, note 32 above, p. 7.
55 See for example: Additional measures to be employed to meet the aggression in Korea. Resolution 500 (5) adopted by the General Assembly. 18 May 1951.

Israeli-Palestinian conflict was continued, but it was not possible to reach a solution (except an appeal for an advisory opinion to the International Court of Justice).[56]

In general, the mechanisms proposed in the "Uniting for Peace" resolution, and in particular the adoption of decisions on the maintenance of international peace and security by a qualified majority at emergency special sessions, were implemented fifteen times by 2022. In seven cases, issues for consideration by the General Assembly were directly submitted by the Security Council; in one case, the Security Council removed the issue from its agenda, opening the way for the application of the "Uniting for Peace" mechanism.

At the same time, in seven cases the mechanism was applied at the request of the member States without the relevant decisions of the Security Council: in four cases — with direct reference to the 1950 Resolution and in three cases — without formally naming it, due to the interpretation of Article 11 of the United Nations Charter or Article 15 of the Rules of Procedure of the General Assembly.[57] Most cases of recalling the mechanism were connected with the use of the right of veto by the USSR during voting in the Security Council.[58] The Peace Observation Commission provided for in the 1950 resolution existed until the 1960s.[59]

The creation of an International, Impartial and Independent Mechanism to Assist in the Investigation and Prosecution of Persons Responsible for the Most Serious Crimes under International Law Committed in the Syrian Arab Republic since 2011, with the resolution of the General Assembly 71/248 of December 21, 2016, can be considered a relatively recent application of the essence of the "Uniting for Peace" mechanism, although without reference to it.[60] At least this is how it is assessed by an authoritative scholar,

---

56 Krasno and Das, note 52 above, pp. 182-186, 189.
57 Ibid., pp. 193-195.
58 Security Council Deadlocks and Uniting for Peace: An Abridged History / Security Council Report. October 2013.
59 Tomuschat C. Uniting for Peace. Assembly resolution. (available online).
60 International, Impartial and Independent Mechanism to Assist in the Investigation and Prosecution of Persons Responsible for the Most Serious Crimes under

also emphasizing that for the first time that such a mechanism was created precisely by the resolution of the General Assembly, although commissions to investigate crimes were previously created by the United Nations Human Rights Council.[61] Such a conclusion seems strange, because the General Assembly had previously created a similar mechanism for the DPRK.

But the direct implementation of the "Uniting for Peace" mechanism in a resolution of the General Assembly, and in accordance with a decision of the Security Council, took place for the first time since the "Cold War" in the context of the aggression of the Russian Federation against Ukraine. This will be considered below.

1.5. Practice of the International Court of Justice

Questions regarding the powers of the United Nations General Assembly and the nature of its resolutions have repeatedly been directly or indirectly qualified during the consideration of cases and in advisory opinions of the International Court of Justice. As early as 1949, the advisory opinion *Reparation for Injuries Suffered in the Service of the United Nations* stated that member States should accept and implement the decisions of the Security Council, but the United Nations Charter authorizes the General Assembly to make recommendations to member States. It was noted that the Charter provisions should be considered in the general context of the principles of international law, and therefore some norms concerning the General Assembly, even not directly stated in the Charter, should be understood as a "necessary implication as being essential to the performance of its duties".[62]

In the advisory opinion *Competence of the General Assembly for the Admission of a State to the United Nations* of 1950, at the request of the General Assembly regarding the possibility for it to decide

---

International Law Committed in the Syrian Arab Republic since March 2011. Resolution 71/248 adopted by the General Assembly on 21 December 2016.
61   Scharf, note 32 above, pp. 2-3, 13-15.
62   Reparation for Injuries Suffered in the Service of the United Nations. Advisory opinion of 11 April 1949. *International Court of Justice. Reports of judgements, advisory opinions and orders* (1949), pp. 178, 182.

about the admission of new States to the United Nations in a situation where the Security Council was unable to adopt a recommendation on this matter, the International Court of Justice stated: "The General Assembly and the Security Council are both principal organs of the United Nations. The Charter does not place the Security Council in a subordinate position".

The Court also determined, on the example of the Security Council, the meaning of recommendations as acts of the United Nations principal organs:

> To hold that the General Assembly has power to admit a State to membership in the absence of a recommendation of the Security Council would be to deprive the Security Council of an important power which has been entrusted to it by the Charter. It would almost nullify the role of the Security Council in the exercise of one of the essential functions of the Organization. It would mean that the Security Council would have merely to study the case, present a report, give advice, and express an opinion. ...In the opinion of the Court, Article 4, paragraph 2, envisages a favourable recommendation of the Security Council and that only. An unfavourable recommendation would not correspond to the provisions of Article 4, paragraph 2. While keeping within the limits of a Request, which deals with the scope of the powers of the General Assembly, it is enough for the Court to say that nowhere has the General Assembly received the power to change, to the point of reversing, the meaning of a vote of the Security Council. In consequence, it is impossible to admit that the General Assembly has the power to attribute to a vote of the Security Council the character of a recommendation when the Council itself considers that no such recommendation has been made.[63]

Mutatis mutandis, the same conclusions apply to the powers and recommendations of the General Assembly.

In the advisory opinion *Certain Expenses of the United Nations* of 1962, the Court denied that the resolutions of the General Assembly in the sphere of maintaining international peace and security are purely recommendatory and do not impose obligations on member States. According to the Court, the main powers of the United Nations Security Council in this sphere are not exclusive

---

63 Competence of the General Assembly for the Admission of a State to the United Nations. Advisory opinion of March 3rd, 1950. *International Court of Justice. Reports of judgements, advisory opinions and orders* (1950), pp. 8-9.

and are entrusted to this organ precisely to ensure quick and effective actions, primarily coercive ones:

> The Charter makes it abundantly clear, however, that the General Assembly is also to be concerned with international peace and security. ... The word "measures" implies some kind of action, and the only limitation which Article 14 imposes on the General Assembly is the restriction found in Article 12, namely, that the Assembly should not recommend measures while the Security Council is dealing with the same matter unless the Council requests it to do so. Thus while it is the Security Council which, exclusively, may order coercive action, the functions and powers conferred by the Charter on the General Assembly are not confined to discussion, consideration, the initiation of studies and the making of recommendations; they are not merely hortatory.

The powers of the General Assembly to suspend the rights and privileges of a member State and to expel a member from the United Nations, carried out in cooperation with the Security Council, were qualified by the Court as "specifically related to preventive or enforcement measures". In addition, with recommendations to States and the Security Council, the General Assembly has the authority to organize peacekeeping operations at the request or with the consent of the State concerned, since these are measures, not coercive actions, under Chapter VII, which are within the competence of the Security Council.[64]

No less important is another provision formulated by the International Court of Justice in this advisory opinion. No organ of the United Nations is authorized to provide the final interpretation of the Charter of this organization, including the clarification of the ratio of powers of the General Assembly and the Security Council. Therefore, the general approach to understanding the lawfulness of the actions of these organs is the consistency of such actions with the goals of the organization. If this is so, then the actions of the organ should be considered as a decision of the whole organization: "when the Organization takes action which warrants the assertion that it was appropriate for the fulfilment of one of the stated

---

[64] Certain Expenses of the United Nations. Advisory opinion of 20 July 1962. *International Court of Justice. Reports of judgements, advisory opinions and orders* (1962), pp. 160-165.

purposes of the United Nations, the presumption is that such action is not *ultra vires* the Organization".[65]

Instead, in the decision in the *South West Africa Cases* of 1966, the International Court of Justice noted that the resolutions of the General Assembly have an exclusively recommendatory nature: "The persuasive force of Assembly resolutions can indeed be very considerable, — but this is a different thing. It operates on the political not the legal level: it does not make these resolutions binding in law".[66]

As noted in the 1986 *Nicaragua* decision, *opinio juris* regarding the customary nature of certain norms can be deduced "with all due caution" from, among other things, the attitude of States to General Assembly resolutions:

> The effect of consent to the text of such resolutions cannot be understood as merely that of a "reiteration or elucidation" of the treaty commitment undertaken in the Charter. On the contrary, it may be understood as an acceptance of the validity of the rule or set of rules declared by the resolution by themselves.

These norms should be considered separately from the United Nations Charter, although in connection with it.[67]

As Marko Divac Öberg noted, in the *Nicaragua* case of 1986, the International Court of Justice recognized that certain resolutions of the General Assembly can be considered being a reflection of customary international law, and in themselves seem to have no legal consequences. Nonetheless, the Court further noted that from the attitude of States to certain resolutions of the General Assembly as binding, the formation of *opinio juris* regarding their content can be determined as evidence of not just the existence, but the creation of international customary law. Here too it seems that the effect is

---

65 Ibid., p. 168.
66 South West Africa Cases (Ethiopia v. South Africa; Liberia v. South Africa). Second phase. Judgement of 18 July 1966. *International Court of Justice. Reports of judgements, advisory opinions and orders* (1966), pp. 50-51.
67 Case concerning military and paramilitary activities in and against Nicaragua (Nicaragua vs. United States of America. Merits. Judgement of 27 June 1986. *International Court of Justice. Reports of judgements, advisory opinions and orders* (1986), pp. 99-100.

not caused by the resolutions themselves, but by a factor external to them—the attitude of States, but in fact it comes down primarily to the fact of the resolution being approved.[68]

In the 1996 advisory opinion on the *Legality of the Threat or Use of Nuclear Weapons*, the International Court of Justice noted:

> General Assembly resolutions, even if they are not binding, may sometimes have normative value. They can, in certain circumstances, provide evidence important for establishing the existence of a rule or the emergence of an *opinio juris*. To establish whether this is true of a given General Assembly resolution, it is necessary to look at its content and the conditions of its adoption; it is also necessary to see whether an *opinio juris* exists as to its normative character. Or a series of resolutions may show the gradual evolution of the *opinio juris* required for the establishment of a new rule.

According to the Court, however, the condition for recognizing the formation of *opinio juris* is not only the consistency of the relevant provisions of the resolutions of the General Assembly (which are evidence of "the desire of a very large section of the international community"), but also the absence of a "substantial numbers of negative votes and abstentions". "The emergence, as *lex lata*, of a customary rule specifically prohibiting the use of nuclear weapons as such is hampered by the continuing tensions between the nascent *opinio juris* on the one hand, and the still strong adherence to the practice of deterrence on the other".[69]

In the advisory opinion *Legal Consequences of the Construction of a Wall in the Occupied Palestinian Territory* of 2004, the International Court of Justice confirmed the previously expressed position: the powers of the Security Council in the field of maintaining international peace and security are, although principal, not exclusive. When considering the relationship between the powers of the Security Council and the General Assembly, the Court proceeded not only from the provisions of the United Nations Charter and its

---

[68] M. D. Öberg, "The Legal Effects of Resolutions of the UN Security Council and General Assembly in the Jurisprudence of the ICJ", *European Journal of International Law*, XVI (2006), 5, pp. 896-897.

[69] Legality of the Threat or Use of Nuclear Weapons. Advisory opinion of 8 July 1996. *International Court of Justice. Reports of judgements, advisory opinions and orders* (1996), pp. 254-255.

previous decisions, but also from United Nations practice, in particular of the Security Council, deliberately removing certain issues from its agenda to enable their consideration by the General Assembly. The Court also pointed to the development of this practice and the interpretation of the United Nations Charter, the result of which is the possibility of consideration and adoption of resolutions by the General Assembly even on issues currently under consideration by the Security Council. The basis for this is the consideration of certain situations by the Security Council from the point of view of international peace and security, and by the General Assembly — more broadly, taking into account their humanitarian, social and economic aspects. The court indicated that the development of such practice does not contradict the United Nations Charter.[70] So, as Christian Tomuschat pointed out, in this advisory opinion, the ICJ recognized that the prohibition of parallel consideration of issues in the Security Council and the General Assembly, provided for by the United Nations Charter, has been changed by practice.[71]

---

70 Legal Consequences of the Construction of a Wall in the Occupied Palestinian Territory. Advisory opinion of 9 July 2004. *International Court of Justice. Reports of judgements, advisory opinions and orders* (2004), pp. 148-150.
71 Tomuschat, note 59 above.

II United Nations General Assembly Resolutions in the Doctrine of International Law

2.1. General Overview

The legal or political normativity of the United Nations General Assembly resolutions has theoretical and practical significance and has become the subject of a number of studies by international lawyers. However, the relevant fundamental works were mostly written many decades ago, often based on later unrealized optimistic interpretations and expectations and, of course, do not take into account subsequent practice and doctrine.[72] In other works, the problem is considered briefly or indirectly.

The ambiguity of the legal basis of General Assembly powers was considered above.[73] The complexity of understanding these issues is reflected in the description of General Assembly resolutions suggested by the Ukrainian international and comparative lawyer, Volodymyr Denysov (1937-2023): although they "do not have binding force for the governments of the United Nations member states, they are valid as an expression of the collective opinion of the states on important issues or as a moral sanction from the international community", and their provisions can become the basis for the formation of customary norms of the international law, provide an interpretation of international treaties, "are perceived as authoritative

---

72 See for example: Philip C. Jessup, "International Parliamentary Law". *American Journal of International Law*, LI (1957), 2, pp. 396-402; Jessup, "The U. N. General Assembly as a Parliamentary Body", *Pakistan Horizon*, XIV (1961), 1, pp. 3-9; Rosalyn Higgins, "The Development of International Law by the Political Organs of the United Nations", *Proceedings of the American Society of International Law*, LIX (1965), pp. 116-124; Higgins, "The United Nations and Lawmaking: The Political Organs", *American Journal of International Law*, LXIV (1970), 4, pp. 37-48; and others.
73 See also O. V. Kresin, "Характер повноважень та актів Генеральної Асамблеї ООН: статутні положення та еволюція їх тлумачення" [UN General Assembly Powers and Resolutions Character: Charter Provisions and the Evolution of Their Interpretation]. *Право України* [Law of Ukraine], no. 7. (2022), pp. 112-126.

evidence of international law principles in circumstances under which the conclusion of a formal treaty cannot be achieved".[74]

A fundamental study of this issue was undertaken by the Polish scholar, diplomat, and statesman Krzysztof Skubiszewski in 1985 as the head and rapporteur of a special commission created by the Institute of International Law, and later as the principal author and editor of the collective conclusions of the Commission in 1987. This study considered General Assembly resolutions as a non-contractual instruments that "explicitly lays down general and abstract rules of conduct", are external (that is, do not regulate purely internal organizational issues), and perform a normative function or have a normative purpose.[75] The nature of United Nations General Assembly resolutions was examined in detail by the Italian international lawyer Gaetano Arangio-Ruiz in 1979.[76]

There are some studies in which classification elements were proposed. Öberg classified the consequences of General Assembly resolutions into binding, other substantive (in particular, authorizing and empowering), as well as causative and modal.[77] Ramsden considered one of the key functions of the General Assembly to be collective legalization, the elements of which are: declaring international norms (quasi-legislation), applying norms to the situation (quasi-judicial), calling on States to take certain actions in accordance with international law (recommendation), legal authorization for States to act with the aim of requiring offending States to perform their obligations (authorization).[78]

There is an unsatisfied need exists to consider the evolution or periodization of the powers and nature of General Assembly resolutions. This issue has been raised by Peter Malanczuk and

---

74　V. N. Denysov, «Організація Об'єднаних Націй» [United Nations], *Енциклопедія міжнародного права* [Encyclopedia of International Law] (2019), III, p. 455; Denysov, «Резолюції Генеральної Асамблеї ООН» [Resolutions of United Nations General Assembly], ibid., III, pp. 684-685.

75　Skubiszewski, note 11 above, I, pp. 32-33.

76　G. Arangio-Ruiz, *The United Nations Declaration on Friendly Relations and the System of the Sources of International Law* (1979).

77　Öberg, note 68 above, pp. 883, 905.

78　M. Ramsden, Collective Legalization as a Strategic Function of the UN General Assembly in Responding to Human Rights Violations. p. 1 (available online).

Malcolm N. Shaw. Malanczuk noted that the real ratio of activities of the Security Council and the General Assembly changed in different periods depending on the balance of forces in these organs and the interests of large groups of States.[79] According to Shaw, the original idea when creating the United Nations was to define the General Assembly as a parliamentary advisory body (in addition to internal organizational powers), and to give the Security Council the authority to make binding decisions in a certain area. He defined the General Assembly as a parliamentary body, a chamber of debates, a forum for exchanging ideas and discussing a wide range of categories of problems. But, he noted, the adoption by the General Assembly of a large number of important resolutions changed the situation and had an impact on the direction of international law.[80]

Understanding the evolution of the competence of advisory assemblies is also relevant for other international organizations. For example, the Parliamentary Assembly of the Council of Europe has largely gone beyond the consultative status prescribed for it; its enhanced role is recognized, although not enshrined in the statutory documents of the Council of Europe.[81]

The present writer's own generalization of the positions of scholars with some elements of classification is as follows.

2.2. Recommendatory Acts with Vague Moral and Political Significance

The point of departure for the positions of some scholars is the traditional postulate regarding the inadmissibility of granting any supranational powers to international organizations; General Assembly resolutions are recommendations with a vague moral and political significance. The long-term formation of the idea that the

---

[79] P. Malanczuk, *Akehurst's Modern Introduction to International Law* (7th rev. ed.; 1997), p. 379.
[80] Shaw, note 21 above, pp. 86, 928, 930.
[81] M. Sharvtseva, «Реформирование Парламентской Ассамблеи Совета Европы» [Reformation of the Parliamentary Assembly of the Council of Europe], *Legea si Viata* (August 2015), p. 117.

international obligations of a State originate exclusively from its sovereign will, coordinated with the will of other States reflected in treaties and customs, was set forth, for example, in the *Lotus* case in the Permanent Court of International Justice in 1927. The principle was declared: "Restrictions upon the independence of States cannot ... be presumed".[82]

As Skubiszewski noted, explaining this position, unlike the realities of national law, the authority of an international organ to create law for States cannot be presumed, but must result from the unambiguous authorization by the States themselves. Absent such authorization in the founding document of the international organization, the decisions of the relevant organs are merely recommendatory.[83] Malanczuk noted that most resolutions of international organizations have nothing to do with international law, and even if they do, they mostly recommend changes, talk about what the law should be, and not what it is.[84] Similarly, Gregory G. Kerwin noted that the strength of the General Assembly as an international political body simultaneously means its weakness as a law-making body:

> The nations of the world have not yet reached the point where they will entrust their legal rights to an assembly founded on the one nation, one vote principle. ... If member nations knew they would be bound by their votes, many Resolutions would never be passed, and the General Assembly's unique function as the voice of world opinion would be undermined.[85]

2.3. Political Acts Containing Standards of Proper and Lawful Behavior

The most common and most developed is the understanding of General Assembly resolutions as political acts that reflect or create standards of proper and lawful policy acceptable for all or most States regarding a specific situation or in a specific field of activity.

---

82 Falk, note 11 above, p. 784.
83 Skubiszewski, note 11 above, I, pp. 34-36.
84 Malanczuk, note 79 above, p. 53.
85 G. J. Kerwin, "The Role of United Nations General Assembly Resolutions in Determining Principles of International Law in United States Courts", *Duke Law Journal*, XXXII (1983), 4, pp. 898-899.

According to Falk, in many contexts, "the characterization of a norm as *formally binding* is not very significantly connected with its *functional operation* as law". Formal restrictions on the status of General Assembly resolutions do not prevent many of them from "acquiring a normative status in international life". Their normativity lies in their authority, and much depends on the specific contextual conditions of the adoption of a certain resolution (expectations regarding permissible behavior, the extent and quality of consensus, the possibility of ensuring the implementation of provisions), as well as the process of implementing the resolution ("influence behavior" and recognition in legal circles, influence on the science of international law).[86]

Inis L. Claude (1922-2013) called collective legitimization the main political function of the General Assembly. Given that the relations of States are more determined and controlled by political rather than legal considerations, the General Assembly plays an important role in the formation of international consensus on the approval or rejection of demands, policies, and actions of States. This is increasing with the insufficient effectiveness of the International Court of Justice, which depends on the consent of States to consider cases, and that forces States to look for answers regarding the legality of their actions in the decisions of other bodies.[87]

According to Skubiszewski, General Assembly resolutions establish the standards of behavior for the member States. Although of a recommendatory nature, later they can be transformed into legal norms, an example being the 1948 Universal Declaration of Human Rights, which, when adopted, was considered as a "common standard of achievement".[88] As Sir Hersch Lauterpacht (1897-1960) noted, although recommendatory resolutions do not impose obligations, "on proper occasions they provide a legal authorization for Members determined to act upon them individually or collectively". Whatever the powers of the General Assembly, they are neither academic nor without consequences. Summarizing this and

---

86 Falk, note 11 above, pp. 783-784, 786.
87 Ramsden, note 78 above, pp. 2-4.
88 Skubiszewski, note 11 above, I, p. 57.

other views of scholars, Skubiszewski noted: "The resolution, without definitely deciding the issue, can serve as one of the supporting arguments in favour of lawfulness or, to put it somewhat differently, as a means of legitimizing the conduct in question".[89]

According to Skubiszewski, "Unless States decide otherwise, a principle of law stated in the resolution is directly enforceable in inter-State relations. Future elaboration of detailed rules is implicit in almost any statement or proclamation of principles, but that is not a bar to their producing regulatory effect and to their being implemented in practice".[90] In the end, Skubiszewski defined declarations of the General Assembly of general content as normative resolutions. However, he understood normativity as a broader concept than legal (binding) force. Normative resolutions are not only those that declare law, but also those that formulate a standard of behavior that seeks to acquire the status of law.[91]

In the final conclusions of the special commission of the Institute of International Law under the leadership of Skubiszewski in 1987, the following types of General Assembly resolutions were distinguished: (a) resolutions that directly formulate or repeat general and abstract norms of State behavior; (b) resolutions that are dedicated to specific situations, but which directly or implicitly affirm the existence of a general and abstract rule of conduct of States; (c) resolutions that are addressed to specific States, but which presume that compliance with the rule of conduct required of the directly named State will be required of all States. However, various provisions of the same resolution can confirm the existence of a law, crystallize or generate a new law, set standards for the application or interpretation of a law.[92]

---

89   Ibid., I, pp. 173-174; K. Skubiszewski. The elaboration of general multilateral conventions and of non-contractual instruments having a normative function or objective. Resolutions of the General Assembly of the United Nations. Definitive Report and Draft Resolution. *Annuaire. Institut de Droit International*. LXI (1985), I, p. 312.
90   Skubiszewski, note 11 above, I, pp. 231-232.
91   Skubiszewski, note 89 above, I, p. 310.
92   "The Elaboration of General Multilateral Conventions and of Non-contractual Instruments Having a Normative Function or Objective. Thirteenth

According to Malanczuk, the resolutions condemning a State for violating international law are a useful tool for putting pressure on this State in order to rethink its positions. And the resolution condemning the State for its aggression assumes legitimacy for other States to come to the defense of the victim and encourages them to do so. Therefore, the Security Council often, not being able to make a decision on an issue, intentionally removes it from its agenda in order to leave the freedom to adopt resolutions to the General Assembly.[93]

According to the authors of a modern French textbook on international law, the authorizing (permissive) force of resolutions consists of:

> If the material and formal force of the recommendation is beyond any doubt, all member states have the right to apply it. The question of their international responsibility cannot be raised if they act in accordance with the resolution, and their behavior cannot be considered unlawful in relations with other member states, for they just comply with the requirements of the founding act of the organization.

Therefore, the recommendation "gives rise to a new legal situation if the principles established by the recommendation do not coincide with the norms that have regulated relations between states earlier".[94]

Öberg sees the essence of the authorization effect of General Assembly resolutions in "generalized reciprocal obligations not to interfere with the exercise of the given right, rather than a specific reciprocal duty of action". It is rather a privilege to act, and not a subjective right, which implies positive duties of certain addressees.[95]

As stated in a modern monograph devoted to the philosophy of international law, the norms of such resolutions can be

---

Commission. Session of Cairo – 1987. Rapporteur K. Skubiszewski", in: *Institute of International Law. Compilation of Resolutions 1873 – 2017* (2018), p. 286.
93   Malanczuk, note 79 above, p. 379.
94   Nguyen Quoc dinh, Patrick Dailler, Alain Pellet. Международное публичное право [International Public Law] (Kyiv, 2000), I, pp. 230-231. (Translation from the: Nguyen Quoc dinh, Patrick Dailler, Alain Pellet. Droit international public. (6th ed.). Paris, 1999).
95   Öberg, note 68 above, p. 895.

considered coordinating; their importance is strengthened by the democratic, multilateral, and inclusive way of their creation, which can be defined as procedural legitimacy.[96] According to another international lawyer, General Assembly resolutions, besides those relating to the functioning of the United Nations, "contain recommendations, do not have legal force, but can play a certain role in the process of social regulation. These resolutions rely on the authority of the United Nations and can be voluntarily implemented by states; in addition, some of them are important for the formation of norms of customary law".[97]

As Stefan Talmon pointed out, General Assembly resolutions provide a basis for the introduction by member States of collective measures that do not involve the use of force. Following Lauterpacht, Talmon attributed this to authorizing powers: "While a recommendation by the General Assembly cannot serve as an independent legal justification of otherwise wrongful conduct, it may establish a presumption that the conduct recommended by the Assembly is lawful for other reasons". This might be the qualification of State actions as a threat to or violation of international peace and security, which, in turn, violates obligations under the United Nations Charter. In this case, the recommendation of the General Assembly also plays a coordinating function.[98]

Shaw warned against attributing a legal character to everything that comes from the General Assembly, because resolutions are often the result of political compromises and agreements, not pretending to create binding norms: one should be cautious when moving from the diversity of practice to the identification of legal norms.[99]

The authors of the modern textbook write about a broad international normative system, which includes both the proper rules of

---

96 S. Besson and J. Tasioulas (eds.), *The Philosophy of International Law* (2010), pp. 170-171, 177.
97 V. Tolstykh, Курс международного права: Учебник [Course of International Law: Textbook] (2010), p. 413.
98 S. Talmon, *The Legalizing and Legitimizing Function of UN General Assembly Resolutions*, pp. 3-10 (Bonn research papers on public international law. Paper No 8/2011, 14 October 2014).
99 Shaw, note 21 above, p. 87.

international law and other norms of a moral and political nature that can be considered as soft law: international agreements, "a means of pre-legal regulation", created through the coordination of the expression of will of States, are "considered as binding (in a non-legal sense)" and have an impact on the regulation of international relations, but when creating them, States do not intend to take on precise legal obligations to implement their provisions.[100]

As Ramsden noted, the recommendatory function of General Assembly resolutions provides for the definition and consolidation of the requirements stipulated in international law regarding the obligations of States to eliminate violations of international law, and so on. The authorizing function consists in determining measures against States that violate international law: the General Assembly provides legal powers to States to implement coercive measures that, without authorization, could violate their international obligations.[101] According to Ramsden, the collective legalization is to some extent "a symptom of United Nations institutional failure, with the many (that is, the 193 members in the Assembly) attempting to do through collective legal interpretation what the few have failed to do through Chapter VII binding decisions (that is, the fifteen members of the Security Council)".[102] The type of legal influence of the General Assembly resolutions is primarily dialogic: it consists of supporting the application of the norms of international law by its subjects, in particular through the finding or gradual formation of a consensus of States on the content of international law.[103]

Rebecca Barber considered the political normativity of General Assembly resolutions by using the example of the international sanctions. Despite the fact that, according to the United Nations Charter, the right to introduce sanctions against States belongs to the Security Council, in practice most (almost 90%) are adopted by States or groups thereof without the authorization of this organ.

---

100 R. M. Valeev and G. I. Kurdiukov (eds.), Международное право: Учебник [International Law: Textbook] (2017), pp. 51-52, 67, 69.
101 Ramsden, note 78 above, pp. 4-8, 28-31, 34.
102 Ibid., p. 9.
103 Ibid., pp. 37, 42-43.

According to Barber, the General Assembly could now play a key role in this matter, based on special studies and advisory opinions of the International Court of Justice. Moreover, the General Assembly has a rich practice of recommended sanctions, especially from the 1960s to the 1990s.[104]

Multilateral sanctions are those introduced by the Security Council on the basis of Chapter VII of the United Nations Charter. However, in practice, between unilateral (introduced by an individual State against another State) and multilateral sanctions, there is a third category — group sanctions imposed by States jointly on the recommendation of an international universal or regional organization; for example, according to a United Nations General Assembly resolution or a decision of the European Union. In this regard, some observers believe that General Assembly resolutions on sanctions have an authorization effect.[105]

Individual sanctions violate not only bilateral, but also multilateral agreements and conventions, and principles of international law. Moreover, they contradict numerous resolutions (in particular, declarations) of the General Assembly regarding the inadmissibility of interference in the internal affairs of States, particularly in the economic sphere. But, as was stated in the Report of the United Nations Secretary General in 1997 based on the conclusions of a special expert group, as well as in a special Report of the Office of the United Nations High Commissioner for Human Rights in 2012, coercive economic measures can be permissible, expedient, and legitimate if introduced in response to violations of generally accepted norms, standards, and obligations and are aimed at eliminating these violations. In fact, Barber notes, there is no contradiction here, because it is assumed and in many cases expressly stated that the recognition of relevant violations by States and the authorization to introduce coercive economic measures or countermeasures (in fact,

---

104 Barber, "An Exploration of the General Assembly's Troubled Relationship with Unilateral Sanctions", *International and Comparative Law Quarterly*, LXX (2021), pp. 344-345.
105 Ibid., pp. 347-348.

sanctions) should be carried out by the relevant United Nations organs.[106]

Thus, the General Assembly can recommend the introduction of multilateral measures to the Security Council and/or individual sanctions to member States, declare the compliance of sanctions introduced under specific circumstances with international law, or conclude that specific sanctions as countermeasures are permissible. Such recommendations can contribute to the correct direction and coordination of such sanctions.[107] According to Barber, the conclusion contained in a General Assembly resolution regarding large-scale violations of human rights and the risk of these violations continuing provides grounds for qualifying targeted sanctions as countermeasures and "could create a presumption of legality that could be difficult for the targeted individuals and/or entities to refute".[108]

Barber generally develops the presumption of implied powers which, according to the findings of the International Court of Justice, although not expressly provided in the United Nations Charter, are necessary for the performance of duties under the Charter and flow from them. Accordingly, General Assembly resolutions which generally do not go beyond its competence and correspond to the goals of the United Nations, including the measures provided for in the resolutions, may be perceived by member States as legitimate.[109]

2.4. Drafts of Future Law, Soft Law, Auxiliary Source of International Law

Many observers view General Assembly resolutions as drafts of future law (*de lege ferenda*), soft law, an auxiliary source of international law. Malanczuk states this regarding resolutions of international organizations: "in the sense of guidelines of conduct ...

---

106 Ibid., pp. 352, 356-357, 364.
107 Ibid., pp. 371-373.
108 Ibid., p. 377.
109 Barber, *The Powers of the UN General Assembly to Prevent and Respond to Atrocity Crimes: A Guidance Document* (2021), p. 11.

which are neither strictly binding norms of law, nor completely irrelevant political maxims, and operate in a grey zone between law and politics". He connected their appearance with the fact that States are not ready to bind themselves legally upon reaching an agreement, but, nevertheless, "wish to adopt and test certain rules and principles before they become law". This is what often makes consensus possible, which would be impossible in the form of "hard law". Sometimes States are willing to create international organizations to carry out international tasks without accepting legal obligations, as was the case with the Conference on Security and Co-operation in Europe in 1975 on the basis of the Helsinki Final Act. Such documents can in practice "acquire considerable strength in structuring international conduct". The difference between law and non-law at each specific moment must be clearly understood, but the recommendatory acts provide additional arguments for the courts as evidence of the direction of the development of law.[110]

As noted by Skubiszewski regarding *de lege ferenda*, "The Assembly resolutions do not limit themselves to embodying principles of positive law. They also enunciate principles of future law". The assertion of law by the General Assembly is not recommendatory in nature, but declaratory.[111] A law-declaring resolution asserts the existence of law (is a means of establishing or interpreting international law, evidence of international custom, or an exposition of general principles of law). Law-developing resolutions can be of four types: (a) those that contribute to the creation of international custom; (b) those that contribute to the emergence of general principles of law; (c) those that determine the scope of negotiations regarding a multilateral agreement or general interest (in particular, propose norms for inclusion in a future agreement); (d) those that establish policy that determines the content of future customary or treaty law.[112]

A group of Ukrainian scholars in 1997 defined the decisions of international organs and organizations as one of the auxiliary

---

110 Malanczuk, note 79 above, pp. 54-55.
111 Skubiszewski, note 11 above, I, pp. 54, 234.
112 Note 92 above, pp. 286-287.

sources of international law.¹¹³ The authors of another modern textbook refer the resolutions of the General Assembly to acts of soft law that "have a recommendatory nature or serve as program guidelines", and their norms can play "an auxiliary role in the process of contractual or customary law regulation."¹¹⁴ International lawyers note that such norms of soft law often "contribute to the maturing of actual social relations to the level required for the implementation of international legal norms" or, on the contrary, prevent the appearance of certain treaty or customary norms in international law. And at the same time, they refer the resolutions of organs of international organizations as auxiliary sources of international law.¹¹⁵

2.5. Role in Formation of Customary International Law

International lawyers consider the role of the United Nations General Assembly resolutions in the formation of norms of international customary law — as a reflection of *opinio juris* and the practice of States. This view was expressed by Arangio-Ruiz in 1979. But he emphasized that the decisive factor is not the statements of States, but their behavior, which reflects their conviction that the relevant norms are appropriate or necessary.¹¹⁶ Even earlier, Falk emphasized this caveat: "The legislative content of customary international law is the most dramatic area wherein the myth of consent is frequently supplanted by the reality of an inferred consensus".¹¹⁷

---

113 O. V. Zadorozhnyi, V. G. Butkevych, and V. V. Mytsyk, Основи теорії міжнародного права: Конспект лекцій [Bases of Theory of International Law: Conspectus of Lectures] (2001), p. 16.
114 G. V. Ignatenko and O. I. Tiunov (eds.), Международное право: учебник [International Law: Textbook] (6th ed.; 2013), p. 137.
115 Valeev, note 100 above, pp. 51-52, 67, 69.
116 G. Arangio-Ruiz, "The Concept of International Law and the Theory of International Organization", in: Arangio-Ruiz, *The United Nations Declaration on Friendly Relations and the System of the Sources of International Law* (1979), pp. 41-43. See also: S. M. Schwebel, "The Effect of Resolutions of the U.N. General Assembly on Customary International Law", *Proceedings of the ASIL Annual Meeting*, LXXIII (1979), pp. 301-309.
117 Falk, note 11 above, p. 790.

This position was supported by Malanczuk: if the resolution declares certain norms and has significant support, then this may be evidence of the existence of norms of customary law, but not the decisive one.[118]

Skubiszewski noted that resolutions declaring certain norms as rules of law can be considered as the evidence of their acceptance by member States as customary law, evidence of State practice, and/or achievement of *opinio juris* regarding them. And *vice versa*, the content of a resolution can "deprive a hitherto existing rule of its *opinio juris* and, consequently, terminate the rule's universal or general application".[119] Resolutions can also be proof of the existence of general principles of law, especially in the field of human rights.[120]

According to the authors of the French textbook, precedents created by international organizations are extremely valuable: "Due to the fact that they become known immediately and are taken into account by a large number of States, they can accelerate the process of forming international legal custom".[121]

Öberg believes that the development of customary international law is influenced, according to the International Court of Justice (*Namibia, Western Sahara, Nicaragua, Nuclear Weapons* cases), primarily by the provisions of the declarations of the General Assembly. They contain *lex ferenda* norms, which the ICJ considers as a possible source of *opinio juris*, which to some extent means their pre-substantive consequences for international law.[122]

Some international lawyers consider the traditional list of sources of international law enumerated in Article 38 of the Statute of the International Court of Justice (treaty law, customary law, general principles of law, together with auxiliary sources) to be significantly outdated. But the fact remains that international law is mainly contractual and consensual. The authors suggest that the list should be expanded. In addition to the formal sources of

---

118 Malanczuk, note 79 above, p. 53.
119 Skubiszewski, note 11 above, I, pp. 69, 95.
120 Ibid., p. 237.
121 Nguyen Quoc dinh, note 94 above, pp. 195-196.
122 Öberg, note 68 above, pp. 903-905.

international law *stricto sensu*, one can single out probationary sources—"places where one finds evidence of the outcome of the law-making process". Among them are the recommendatory resolutions of United Nations organs, which are evidence of the practice of States and *opinio juris* necessary for the creation of customary norms and can be considered to be soft law.[123]

Shaw defined *opinio juris* as the conviction that a certain activity of a State is legally binding, which turns a political or moral custom into a legal one and gives it the meaning of a norm of international law. This is revealed through the analysis of the repetition and consistency of the relevant behavior of the State. According to Shaw, the procedure and circumstances of the adoption of General Assembly resolutions testify to the practice of States and *opinio juris*, form a custom, and even make it binding on the State that supported this resolution—as evidenced by the *Nicaragua* case.[124]

Relying on the conclusions of the International Law Commission and the International Court of Justice, Barber claims that General Assembly resolutions can testify to both general practice (regardless of the vote of a specific country for a particular act) and *opinio juris*, as two elements and at the same time evidence of the existence of customary international legal norms.[125]

2.6. International Quasi-Legislation

In addition, according to some international lawyers, General Assembly resolutions play the role of international quasi-legislation as soft law. Skubiszewski argued: although international organizations do not have the authority to adopt legislation binding upon States, in their resolutions they indicate the norms of State behavior, what the law should be, and thereby influence its development. Such a role is played by resolutions not only containing general content, but also those that presuppose the existence of a principle or norm, condemning specific acts or calling on States to follow a

---

123 Besson, note 96 above, pp. 164-170.
124 Shaw, note 21 above, pp. 62-63, 86, 928, 930.
125 Barber, note 109 above, p. 12.

certain line of behavior.[126] This view is presented more categorically by Falk, who proposed to define the authority of the General Assembly to adopt resolutions of a recommendatory nature as quasi-legislative. In his opinion, this qualification is in the "middle position between a formally difficult affirmation of true legislative status and a formalistic denial of a law-creating role and impact".[127] Ramsden offered a compromise vision: the quasi-legislative function of the General Assembly is not an automatic obligation, but rather a persuasive influence on the interpretation of the norms of international law and the promotion of new norms and principles.[128]

2.7. Unilateral Acts of States or International Organizations

Some international lawyers consider General Assembly resolutions to be legally binding unilateral acts of States or the United Nations as an international organization.

2.7.1. Unilateral Acts of States

This view was supported by Skubiszewski. A resolution may be accepted as binding by individual member States, but such recognition is a fact external to the resolution, does not follow from it, and does not change its recommendatory significance. However, "Acceptance of the resolution as mandatory need not be expressed; it may reveal itself in conduct that conforms to the resolution". A State can make a resolution binding on itself by publicly recognizing it as such. But the support of a resolution by a State cannot be perceived unambiguously. A resolution does not always imply a law-affirming or law-making intention, it can reflect considerations of profitability or conformism, or be the result of a political compromise. In addition, it does not necessarily indicate the consent of

---

126 Skubiszewski, note 11 above, I, pp. 29-30, 32.
127 Falk, note 11 above, p. 782.
128 Ramsden, note 78 above, pp. 4-8, 28-31, 34.

the State to undertake obligations according to the declared norms.[129]

Some French international lawyers believe that acts of a recommendatory nature supported by a State become binding on it — the fact of voting is an expression of the unilateral will of the State. This approach, they note, was confirmed by the Permanent Court of International Justice with respect to the League of Nations.[130]

2.7.2. Unilateral United Nations Acts

The aforementioned French authors noted that "international law is not consensual law in the strict sense of the word", and considered General Assembly resolutions as unilateral acts of an international organization and sources of law, "the legal consequences of which have been proven". Such unilateral acts are legal acts. Among the acts of organs of international organizations, some are decisions in the technical sense—"authoritative unilateral acts, ... which are an expression of the will of the organization, and therefore, proceed from it and generate obligations for the object of these acts". Such is, for example, a decision of the Security Council within the limits of powers under Article 25 of the United Nations Charter. Other decisions of United Nations organs are such in the usual sense and have a recommendatory nature. The practice of international courts demonstrates that the name of acts of organs of international organizations is not of decisive importance.[131]

2.8. Problem of Nature of Qualifications Contained in Resolutions

Formally extraneous but inextricably linked to the issue of determining the nature of General Assembly resolutions is the problem of the nature of the qualifications contained in these resolutions —

---

129 Skubiszewski, note 11 above, I, pp. 167-170, 233, 239-240; Skubiszewski, note 89 above, p. 325.
130 Nguyen Quoc dinh, note 94 above, p. 232.
131 Ibid., pp. 64, 222-225.

as empirical (determining the presence of a fact that can have a causal effect) or legal (identification or interpretation of law).

Arangio-Ruiz argued that the resolutions of international organizations, including their political organs, are a reference point for legal qualifications and as such are of great importance, regardless of their role in law-making.[132] As he noted, the decisions and recommendations of the General Assembly can potentially be objected to as acts issued in excess of powers (*ultra vires*) precisely because they contain an interpretation of the United Nations Charter. But they perform the role of legal qualification, interpretation of the United Nations Charter (especially "considering the high degree of generality or imprecision of many Charter rules and principles"), and guidelines for law-making. However, "this activity is of importance whatever one believes the function of legal interpretation to be", and even if the corresponding legal qualifications are so only in a material sense and have only factual authority.[133]

According to Skubiszewski, the importance of resolutions lies in their authority — usually a State will not violate provisions of a declaration approved by the General Assembly by the majority of member States. But the nature of the norms included in a General Assembly resolution should be distinguished from the nature of the resolution itself: it is non-binding, whereas its subject-matter may already be regulated by law and constitute an obligation for States. Therefore, resolutions may contain norms of international law.[134]

These resolutions offer principles of legal interpretation. Among them are the definitions of terms provided for in treaty law. An example is Resolution 3314 (XXIX), which contains the definition of aggression — the "fundamental principles as a guide" for determining whether an act of aggression has occurred. The same applies to the definition of genocide in Resolution 96 (I), propaganda against peace in Resolution 381 (V), the proclamation of armed intervention to be a form of aggression in Resolution 2131 (XX), and others.[135] However, as Skubiszewski emphasized, the inter-

---

[132] Arangio-Ruiz, note 116 above, p. 37.
[133] Ibid., pp. 60-62.
[134] Skubiszewski, note 11 above, I, pp. 46, 181.
[135] Ibid., pp. 55-56, 70.

pretation "acquires here a meaning so broad that once again approaches the realm of law-making. In any case, there is no constitutional obstacle for the Assembly to draw normative inferences. To say that one moves here between interpretation and enactment of law is obviously true ...".[136] He noted, "A resolution is a means whereby the law can be identified in a field where it seem uncertain or controversial whenever other instruments, in particular judicial decisions and treaties, have not fulfilled that role".[137]

Malanczuk wrote that although the resolutions of the General Assembly are not binding, they have important legal consequences—as evidence of customary law or the correct interpretation of the United Nations Charter.[138] Shaw recognized this interpretation of the principles of the United Nations Charter as being authoritative.[139]

Öberg linked the causal effect of General Assembly resolutions with the legal and factual qualification contained in them. This involves the awakening of the "dormant substantive effects" through the determination of the presence or absence of a certain event or state. This fact may or may not be legally relevant. For example, the recognition of the invasion of one State by another has legal significance. The legal consequences of the recognition of facts may prevent or launch the application of certain norms—and therefore has substantive legal effects. But the International Court of Justice has determined that definitions contained in recommendatory acts are also considered to be recommendatory. In this case, according to Öberg, causal effects are optional, remaining at the discretion of the authority applying the norm. If the definitions are contained in binding acts of the General Assembly (for example, regarding trusteeship or the United Nations budget) or the Security Council (regarding international peace and security), then they are also binding. However, the International Court of Justice does not consider itself bound by the definitions of these organs, although it

---

[136] Ibid., p. 164.
[137] Ibid., p. 235.
[138] Malanczuk, note 79 above, p. 379.
[139] Shaw, note 21 above, p. 87.

takes them into account (cases *Nicaragua* 1986, *East Timor* 1991).[140] The modal effect of General Assembly resolutions consists in establishing how and when meaningful consequences should occur (usually immediately, without retroactive effect, with the possibility of subsequent changes).[141]

As Ramsden noted, because the General Assembly consists of representatives of almost all countries of the world, its resolutions are a unique tool for forming a common understanding of international treaty and customary law. In addition, the quasi-judicial function of these resolutions consists in the collective formulation by representatives of States of legal qualifications for specific situations based on the norms of international law, "denotes the mandate of a political body to monitor compliance with a set of norms or to make evidence-based factual determinations", as well as to provide them with a legal assessment.[142]

In the context of the aggression of the Russian Federation against Ukraine, Ramsden emphasized that the definition of the annexation of Crimea as illegal in General Assembly Resolution No. 68/262 became the basis for the initiation of an investigation by the prosecutor of the International Criminal Court in 2014, and the definition of a full-scale invasion of the Russian Federation into Ukraine in 2022 as aggression in Resolution ES-11/1 became the basis for the appointment of temporary protective measures by the same court. In addition, the indication in Resolution ES-11/1 that the rights and privileges of membership in the United Nations require it to fulfill its obligations in good faith "provide a hook for future claims that the Russian government has not acted in accordance with the expectations incumbent on a United Nations member state". This could, if members are willing, prevent recognition of the powers of representatives of the Russian Federation in the General Assembly. Legal qualifications in General Assembly resolutions regarding Russian aggression can become a legal justification for the introduction of various sanctions against the Russian

---

140 Öberg, note 68 above, pp. 890-891, 905.
141 Ibid., pp. 893-894, 904.
142 Ramsden, note 78 above, pp. 4-8, 28-31, 34, 62.

Federation or the approval of already introduced collective and unilateral sanctions (countermeasures) or for requiring member States to cooperate in order to stop the violation of peremptory norms of international law (in particular, the prohibition of aggression). In the same way, the legal qualifications in the resolutions of the General Assembly open the possibility for it to create inquiry commissions to investigate the war crimes of the Russian Federation.[143]

Barber pointed out that, despite the lack of judicial powers at the General Assembly, its resolutions in certain cases have the significance of qualification regarding the application of existing legal principles to a specific set of facts: for example, regarding the right to statehood, the legitimacy of a certain regime, the legality or illegality of State actions (including aggression, genocide, violation of the territorial integrity of another State, a threat to international peace and security, flagrant and systematic violation of human rights, violation of the United Nations Charter, the Geneva Conventions, international humanitarian law, international obligations), the legitimacy of holding referendums, annexations, determining the parties to the conflict and its nature. Such powers of the General Assembly in specific situations were confirmed in judgements of the International Court of Justice and used by it and by the International Criminal Court to determine general issues of international law in criminal cases, such as strengthening the evidentiary base, when determining temporary measures, determining the territorial jurisdiction of the International Criminal Court, and in other cases. In addition, General Assembly resolutions can determine the presence of humanitarian crises, an urgent need in a certain region or a certain group of the population for humanitarian aid – which, regardless of the consent of the State where such a crisis occurs, opens the possibility for the provision of such aid by other countries and international organizations freeing them, to a

---

143 Ramsden, "Uniting for Peace: The Emergency Special Session on Ukraine", *Harvard International Law Journal Online*. 1 April 2022. (available online).

certain extent, from potentially possible accusations of violation of the territorial integrity of this State.[144]

2.9. Dependence of Normative Impact of Resolutions on their Types and Circumstances of Adoption

Doctrinal writings emphasize the dependence of the normative impact of General Assembly resolutions on their types and the circumstances of their adoption. As noted by the aforementioned commission under the leadership of Skubiszewski, all resolutions formally have the same *status*, but the choice of form of the declaration emphasizes the significance of the norms embedded therein because declarations can contain a comprehensive consideration of the subject or express principles whose purpose is to influence the progressive development of international law.[145] On the contrary, Öberg considered the impact of declarations to be more limited than other resolutions because they have a pre-contentious character and are devoid of causal consequences.[146]

According to Arangio-Ruiz, the *indicators of support* for the resolution are important for its hortative or moral value, and also affect the chances of compliance by States and indirectly the prospects of their materialization as a customary norm.[147]

According to the commission headed by Skubiszewski, the unanimous adoption of a law-declaring resolution without negative votes and abstentions "creates a presumption that the resolution contains an exact statement of law" (although this presumption can be denied). Moreover, the unanimous adoption of the resolution can confirm the existence of a customary norm that originates from the practice of States and international organizations, but previously looked doubtful. If the vote for the resolution was not unanimous, its normativity directly depends on whether it was voted for by a representative majority, including "the main legal systems" (which represent the main regions of the world without

---

144 Barber, note 109 above, pp. 32-35.
145 Skubiszewski, note 92 above, p. 288.
146 Öberg, note 68 above, pp. 903-905.
147 Arangio-Ruiz, note 116 above, p. 43.

"geopolitical gaps"), as well as on the number of votes "against" and abstentions, the presence of reservations and declarations of member States narrowing or denying its normative significance, and the presence or absence of implementation procedures or supervisory mechanisms provided for in the resolution.[148]

There are different views on the significance of the *repetition* of resolutions. Arangio-Ruiz argued that the repetition of resolutions and the number of votes cast for them do not increase their influence on the formation of international customary law.[149] Skubiszewski believed that

> Unopposed repetition or re-citation of a rule which has already been laid down in an earlier resolution, if it is not merely meant to give evidence of law, is proof of the existence of a standard of conduct that could become law or be relevant to the interpretation of law. Such repetition can be a means of pressure on the opposing States to induce them to change their attitude. The voting record will show whether the pressure is effective and, consequently, the support for the repeated rule is increasing.[150]

2.10. Peculiarities of Resolutions within Framework of "Uniting for Peace" Mechanism

Few doctrinal works have been devoted to the question of the peculiarities of the nature of United Nations General Assembly resolutions adopted within the framework of the "Uniting for Peace" mechanism. In general, three views can be conditionally distinguished: (1) optimistic — the lawfulness of replacing Security Council decisions with General Assembly resolutions as a result of the delegation of powers or the development of United Nations institutional practice; (2) differentiated — the lawfulness and significance of General Assembly resolutions depend on the referral of issues to it by the Security Council, but in any case these resolutions cannot usurp the charter powers of the Security Council; (3) skeptical — the "Uniting for Peace" mechanism does not have added value

---

148 Skubiszewski, note 11 above, I, pp. 167-170, 233, 240; Skubiszewski, note 92 above, p. 289.
149 Arangio-Ruiz, note 116 above, pp. 41-43.
150 Skubiszewski, note 11 above, I, p. 233.

and does not attach any special importance to the General Assembly resolutions adopted within its framework.

"Optimists". Jean Krasno and Mitushi Das proposed a vision of the "Uniting for Peace" mechanism as a means for temporarily delegating the powers of the Security Council to the General Assembly. This mechanism is an exception that does not contradict, but affirms, the powers of the Security Council. They recognize that the General Assembly resolutions adopted in this way are not legally binding in any event. In their opinion, however, together with the last unsuccessful experience of considering the Israeli-Palestinian issue in 1997-2003, the "Uniting for Peace" mechanism lost its usefulness, turned into "yet another forum for rhetorical debate", and later was not used due to the reluctance of the member States to intervene in difficult conflict situations: "when there is no will to act, it is useless". But the mechanism itself retains potential if it is rethought as a tool for increasing the effectiveness of the United Nations.[151]

As Scharf pointed out, in connection with the war in Syria and the invasion of the Russian Federation in Ukraine, the United Nations "wiped the dust" from this mechanism ["Uniting for Peace"], and its new use marked "a shift in power away from the Security Council and to the General Assembly, with potentially broad and long-term implications". According to Scharf, the General Assembly resolution regarding Syria played the role of authorizing collective force measures (the bombing of chemical weapons production plants in Syria by American, British, and French aircraft); they were qualified as humanitarian intervention in connection with the principle of "responsibility to protect" declared in 2005.[152] Regarding the full-scale aggression of the Russian Federation against Ukraine and the prospects for using the United Nations General Assembly, Scharf noted: "the General Assembly, through diplomatic practice and International Court of Justice decisions, had slowly amassed the power to act on matters of which the Security Council was

---

[151] Krasno and Das, note 52 above, pp. 173, 186, 190-191.
[152] Scharf, note 32 above, pp. 1, 4, 17-21, 27. The principle "responsibility to protect" was proclaimed in the 2005 World Summit Outcome (Resolution 60/1 adopted by the General Assembly, 16 September 2005).

seized. This amassed power allowed the General Assembly to recommend imposition of sanctions, and to create investigative bodies and hybrid tribunals without invoking the Uniting for Peace resolution".[153]

Ramsden noted that, apart from the debate about the legal nature and binding nature of General Assembly resolutions, as well as the lack of formal advantages of resolutions adopted during emergency special sessions of the General Assembly convened within the framework of the "Uniting for Peace" mechanism, these sessions are symbolic, because they call attention to shocking events that require an urgent response and give a solemn meaning to this response through the "crystallising a series of legal claims by the community of nations that can be used to support future actions" and the implementation of "collective legal interpretation".[154]

Henry Richardson noted that the "Uniting for Peace" mechanism should be considered not as a one-time formulation, but as a part of a long process of gradual acquisition by General Assembly resolutions of its current significance (with a further prospect of development) in the context of the law-declaring intentions of the majority in this organ, the emergence or fixation of a rule of customary international law, and/or the formation of institutional precedential practice in the General Assembly—based on the evolving interpretation of the United Nations Charter. And *vice versa*—this mechanism cannot be considered unsuitable or inconsistent with the United Nations Charter on the basis of the unfounded presumption of the absolute nature of the right of veto of the permanent members of the Security Council—because it is precisely the interpretation of the right of veto, being unlawful and inconsistent with the United Nations Charter, the intentions when it was written and adopted, and the goals of the organization, that led to appearance of the "Uniting for Peace". Based on the need to temporarily replace the Security Council in case of paralysis and the responsibility of the General Assembly in the field of maintaining international

---

153 Ibid., p. 28.
154 Ramsden, note 143 above.

peace and security, the powers of the General Assembly within the framework of the "Uniting for Peace" mechanism should be considered broadly, and taking into account the development of international law, including the possible recommendation of coercive measures. The General Assembly cannot be considered as an organ inferior to the Security Council—because it reflects the goal of the United Nations to represent the interests of all or almost all States and all or almost all the world's population.

According to Richardson, the "Uniting for Peace" mechanism should be perceived not as something extraordinary, but as part of the charter powers of the General Assembly in their modern interpretation, including the possible use of coercive measures, and regardless of the authorization of this mechanism by the Security Council or even the presence of a reference to it. In cases of the inability of the Security Council to implement its primary responsibility for maintaining international peace and security provided for by the United Nations Charter, the General Assembly acquires the authority of "collective power" in this area, which can authorize member States to implement collective coercive measures.[155]

Nanda believed that all provisions embodied in the "Uniting for Peace" Resolution have their source in the United Nations Charter. Although the powers of the General Assembly to recommend the use of military force are ambiguous, the possibility of recommendations for the use of other measures is not in doubt. And the very ambiguity regarding military force can only be about its mandatory character, whereas the General Assembly recommendation of its collective use by member States can be legitimate within the framework of collective self-defense. According to Nanda, it is the indication of this power in the "Uniting for Peace" Resolution that

---

155 Henry Richardson, "Comment on Larry Johnson, 'Uniting for Peace'". *American Journal of International Law Unbound*, CVIII (2014), pp. 135-140. See also: F. L. Kirgis, "He Got It Almost Right", *American Journal of International Law Unbound*, CVIII (2014), pp. 116-117; B. N. Mamlyuk, "Uniting for 'Peace' in the Second Cold War: A Response to Larry Johnson", *American Journal of International Law Unbound*, CVIII (2014), pp. 129-134.

makes this act still relevant, especially in the context of the "responsibility to protect" principle.[156]

Other international lawyers offer a more *differentiated view*. For example, Andrew Carswell noted that the act

> revealed the latent powers of the General Assembly existing within the UN Charter to make recommendations in lieu of a blocked [Security] Council, up to and including the use of force. However, it went too far when it assigned to the Assembly a role that effectively usurped the primary role of the Security Council in the maintenance of international peace and security. When P5 members [of the Security Council] realized that it potentially restricted their respective sovereign interests, it [the resolution] was relegated to obscurity. Nevertheless, read down to reflect a constitutional balance between the UN's primary organs, the resolution represents a viable tool capable of overcoming the worst effects of a veto exercised in circumstances that cry out for an international response.

Carswell emphasized that further use of the experience with the 1950 Resolution is relevant, but "the key to maintaining both the credibility and constitutionality of this process is ensuring that the Security Council plays the central role conferred upon it by the Charter". The General Assembly cannot determine the inability of the Security Council to perform its duties and usurp the latter's functions.[157]

However, the recommendations of the General Assembly within the framework provided by the 1950 Resolution can be considered as collective self-defense. But, as Carswell pointed out, the question arises about such a recommendation conflicting with the principle of refraining from the threat or use of force (Article 2(4), United Nations Charter). The resolution of this conflict is possible only if the actions of States can be qualified as actions of the United

---

156 Ved P. Nanda, "The Security Council Veto in the Context of Atrocity Crimes, Uniting for Peace and the Responsbility to Protect", *Case Western Reserve Journal of International Law*, LII (2020), 1, pp. 136, 139-140. See also N. Ahmad, "The Erosion of the Prohibition on the Use of Force in the Face of United Nations Security Council Inaction: How Can the United Nations General Assembly Maintain International Peace?", *Chicago Journal of International Law Online*, I (2002), 2, pp. 81-98.
157 A. J. Carswell, "Unblocking the UN Security Council: The Uniting for Peace Resolution", *Journal of Conflict & Security Law*, XVIII (2013), 3, pp. 453, 455-456, 476, 478-479.

Nations—and therefore, whether General Assembly resolutions are decisions not only of the organ, but also of this organization as a whole. The auxiliary charter competence of the General Assembly in the field of maintaining international peace and security was confirmed in the advisory opinion of the International Court of Justice on *Certain Expenses* (1962), but the limits of such competence were not defined. According to Carswell, there is nothing preventing General Assembly recommendations to member States being considered as delegating them its powers in this area on behalf of the United Nations, similar to how the Security Council does this. But the relevant General Assembly resolutions "must clearly define the objective and scope of the use of force, and should specify the time frame", and also be adopted after the Security Council has referred the matter to this organ for consideration. As Carswell noted, through such a transfer,

> the Council does effectively activate the Assembly's secondary role in the realm of collective security, eliminating any controversy concerning the qualification of the matter as a threat to the peace, breach of the peace or act of aggression demanding the attention of the United Nations Organization. Most importantly, a referral from the Council bestows a degree of moral legitimacy on that secondary role.

Thus, the General Assembly resolutions created on this basis are adopted on behalf of the entire organization, and the measures implemented by the member States in accordance with these resolutions do not violate the principle of non-use of force or the threat of force.[158]

Barber noted that regardless of the disputes about whether the "Uniting for Peace" Resolution fully complies with the United Nations Charter, this mechanism currently "serves as a valid interpretation by the UNGA of its own powers", which on many occasions the International Court of Justice has not denied and, on the contrary, affirmed in essence. Nevertheless, in order to avoid disputes regarding "constitutionality", it is better that the use of this mechanism will involve a request of the Security Council to the General

---

158 Ibid., pp. 460, 463-467.

Assembly or the removal of the issue from consideration by the Security Council.[159]

A *skeptical position* exists about the suitability of the "Uniting for Peace" mechanism. Larry Johnson (former assistant of the United Nations Secretary-General for legal affairs) offered a number of conclusions about the long-standing practice of its application. He believed that with the change in the work schedule of the General Assembly and the disappearance of long breaks between regular sessions, the need to hold emergency special sessions has disappeared, unless there is a desire to impart political emphasis to the importance of a certain situation. Doubts that the General Assembly and the Security Council can consider the same issues also disappeared, and the International Court of Justice recognized that this practice is not contrary to the United Nations Charter. The General Assembly both before and after 1950 introduced voluntary collective measures against various States regardless of the "Uniting for Peace" mechanism. Moreover, outside this mechanism, based on the right to individual and collective self-defense (Article 51, United Nations Charter), the General Assembly can recommend coercive or forceful measures. Therefore, taking into account the development of the practice of interpretation and application of the United Nations Charter, the appeal to the mentioned mechanism, in the opinion of Johnson, has become unnecessary.[160]

Some international lawyers offer an even more skeptical view of the problem. For example, the authors of a French textbook on international law believe that the "Uniting for Peace" mechanism does not comply with the United Nations Charter, especially in those cases when the General Assembly acts without a prior request from the Security Council.[161]

To some extent, a new stage of understanding the "Uniting for Peace" mechanism has begun in connection with the large-scale invasion of the Russian Federation into Ukraine and the convening of the eleventh emergency special session of the General Assembly in 2022.

---

159 Barber, note 109 above, pp. 14, 16.
160 L. D. Johnson, "'Uniting for Peace': Does It Still Serve Any Useful Purpose?", *American Journal of International Law*. CVIII (2014). pp. 108-115.
161 Nguyen Quoc dinh, note 94 above, II, p. 166.

III Content, Nature, Legal and Political Significance of General Assembly Resolutions on Countering Aggression of Russian Federation against Ukraine in 2014-2023

3.1. Territorial Integrity of Ukraine in Resolution of 2014

The first and basic resolution of the General Assembly which reflected the position of the majority of the United Nations member States in relation to Ukraine as a victim of Russian aggression was "Territorial Integrity of Ukraine", adopted 27 March 2014. Cautious in formulation, the Resolution called for the "de-escalation of the situation" and for "inclusive political dialogue" within Ukrainian society. The "referendum" of 16 March 2014 in the Autonomous Republic of Crimea and the City of Sevastopol was qualified as "having no validity"; its results should not be recognized and cannot serve as a basis for altering the status of these administrative-territorial units. It contained a call to "all states" to refuse and refrain from actions aimed at violating the national unity and territorial integrity of Ukraine, as well as a call to "all parties" to immediately start the search for a peaceful solution to the "situation with respect to Ukraine" through direct political dialogue. The need was emphasized to continue the efforts of the United Nations and the OSCE to assist Ukraine in protecting human rights, including rights of persons belonging to minorities. The commitment of United Nations members to the independence and territorial integrity of Ukraine was confirmed. The Resolution emphasized such principles as refraining from the threat or use of force against any State; non-recognition of territorial changes resulting from such threats or use of force; and the settlement of international disputes with peaceful means.[162]

---

162 Territorial integrity of Ukraine. Resolution 68/262, adopted by the General Assembly on 27 March 2014.

Opening the discussion on the draft Resolution, the representative of Ukraine, Andrii Deshchytsia, referred to the principles of the territorial integrity of States and of refraining to use force to resolve disputes. He stated that the draft Resolution "does not break any new legal or normative ground. Yet it sends a crucial message that the international community will not allow what has happened in Crimea to set a precedent for further challenges to our rules-based international framework". Although the events were generally defined by him as a "situation" that flagrantly violates international law, the speech directly pointed to the military occupation and forceful annexation of Crimea and the existing and potentially possible wider aggression of the Russian Federation against Ukraine.[163]

It should be noted that within the discussion the representative of the Russian Federation, Vitaly Churkin, asserted that during the "referendum" on 21 March 2014, the population of Crimea expressed their will for "reunification" with the Russian Federation and thereby exercised their right to self-determination, an act of "historical justice" because "Crimea was an integral part of our country for several centuries". This population, he said, is a part of the Russian people and shares a common history and culture with it. The 1954 decision to transfer Crimea to the Ukrainian SSR was called arbitrary and unnatural, but carried out "in the framework of a single state". Churkin stated that the dissolution of the former USSR cut off Crimea from the Russian Federation, and this was never accepted by the population of the peninsula. This non-acceptance grew in the context of the "deep political crisis in Ukraine" caused by the adventurous actions of political forces that "sought to break the centuries-old ties of Russia and Ukraine". The Revolution of Dignity was characterized by Churkin as violent attacks by "well-trained and equipped units of militants" against law enforcement officers, which led to the overthrow of the legitimate government in the State. He said that the cancellation of the official status of the Russian language and the threat to the population of the

---

[163] United Nations General Assembly. Sixty-eight session. 80th plenary meeting. Official records. A/68/PV.80. 27 March 2014.

southern and eastern regions of Ukraine led the Crimeans to "take a decision on self-determination and reunification with Russia". Churkin opposed the adoption of the Resolution, contending that it "seeks to put into question the meaning of the referendum that took place in Crimea", posing a challenge for it (its results).[164]

The initiators and "sponsors" of the resolution became 47 States (including all 28 European Union members),[165] and during the voting it was supported by 100 States. Eleven countries voted against: Armenia, Belarus, Bolivia, Cuba, DPRK, Nicaragua, Russian Federation, Sudan, Syria, Venezuela, and Zimbabwe. Fifty-eight countries from Africa, Asia, and Latin America abstained from voting, including China, India, South Africa, Kazakhstan, Uzbekistan, and others. Twenty-four States (among them Iran, Israel, Kyrgyzstan, Tajikistan, Turkmenistan, Serbia, UAE) did not participate in the vote.[166]

Before and after the vote, representatives of the European Union and several dozen States decided to explain the reasons for their decision.[167] The expressed positions and reservations cannot be fully reduced to the voting results. They reveal more complex and contradictory motives of the United Nations members and deserve special attention. Several conditional types of such positions can be identified:

(1) Unequivocal condemnation of the Russian aggression, occupation, and annexation of Crimea, as well as the declaration of the legal nullity of the Crimean "referendum", were contained in the speeches of the representatives of Canada, Japan, Turkey, Costa Rica, Georgia, Iceland, Norway, Singapore, and Moldova. The representative of Norway indicated the absence of any impartial testimony regarding alleged violations of the rights of the Russian-speaking population in Ukraine which could be taken into account by the United Nations. Azerbaijan, Malaysia, Honduras, and Cape Verde expressed unequivocal support for the Resolution, but

---

164 Ibid.
165 Territorial integrity of Ukraine. Draft resolution A/68/L.39. 24 March 2014.
166 United Nations General Assembly. Sixty-eight session. 80th plenary meeting. Official records. A/68/PV.80. 27 March 2014.
167 Ibid.

without clearly condemning the actions of the Russian Federation, only making a general reference to the principles of international law.

(2) Some United Nations members expressed unequivocal condemnation of the aggression of the Russian Federation, while at the same time drawing attention to internal Ukrainian causes of the crisis, including political opposition and fears regarding observance of minority rights. The representative of the European Union, Thomas Mayr-Harting, declared the illegality of the "referendum" of 21 March 2014, condemnation of "acts of aggression by the Russian armed forces", non-recognition of the annexation of Autonomous Republic Crimea and the City of Sevastopol, and strong support for the territorial integrity of Ukraine within its internationally recognized borders. He called on Russia to "take steps to de-escalate the crisis, immediately withdraw its forces back to their pre-crisis numbers and garrisons in line with its international commitments, and avail itself of all relevant international mechanisms to find a peaceful and negotiated solution", in accordance with its bilateral and multilateral commitments to respect Ukraine's sovereignty and territorial integrity. The Russian Federation and Ukraine were urged to "start a meaningful dialogue as soon as possible and without preconditions". However, support was indicated also for multilateral initiatives aimed at "fostering peace, stability and security, and respect for human rights in Ukraine", especially regarding monitoring of compliance with OSCE principles and standards in Ukraine: "monitor the current situation throughout the country so as to help investigations, prevent further violations and verify the truth with regard to the human rights situation". Mayr-Harting "commended the measured response" of Ukraine and "the Ukrainian Government's commitment to ensuring the representative nature and inclusiveness of governmental structures reflecting regional diversity, to ensuring the full protection of the rights of persons belonging to national minorities, to undertaking constitutional reform, to investigating all human rights violations and acts of violence and to fighting extremism", and called on Ukraine to ensure free and fair presidential elections.

The United States representative, Samantha Power, along with her unequivocal condemnation of Russia's military intervention and occupation of Crimea, called the situation "the dispute between Ukraine and Russia", and emphasized the importance of "maintaining an inclusive political dialogue that reflects every segment of Ukrainian society". Similar approaches were voiced by representatives of Liechtenstein, Cyprus, Guatemala, Nigeria, Chile, and Qatar.

(3) A significant number of States indicated the ambiguity of the events and the need to consider them in the broader context of internal Ukrainian or even geopolitical circumstances. The speech of the representative of Brazil focused on the "diversity of the Ukrainian people", the need to respect the rights of minorities, a peaceful negotiated settlement of "differences" between Ukraine and the Russian Federation, and restraint by "all stakeholders". Similar views were expressed by the representatives of Uruguay, El Salvador, Egypt, Kazakhstan, Belarus, Algeria, Libya, Botswana, and Saint Vincent and the Grenadines. Representatives of some countries indicated the need to take into account the "historical context of that particular geopolitical dispute" and questioned the legality of the "regime change in Ukraine".

The representative of China presented the vision of the "question of Ukraine" as one that "involves the interests and concerns of various parties, so there should be a balanced approach", reaching a consensus of the parties with the mediation of the United Nations. China emphasized that it consistently supported the territorial integrity of States and opposed external interference in their affairs; China declared itself ready to participate in a settlement as an impartial mediator.

(4) A group of Latin American countries spoke against the intervention of "Western Powers" in the internal affairs of States in general and in Ukraine in particular, and accordingly against the draft resolution as a proposal of a conditional "West". The representative of Cuba pointed out that "the intervention of Western Powers must stop in order to enable the Ukrainian people to exercise their right to self-determination in a legitimate way", the impossibility to accept "the violent overthrow of a constitutional

Government" and "the destruction of legitimate and legally recognized institutions and entities" in Ukraine, and "threats to citizens' integrity based on their national origin". The introduction of any sanctions against the Russian Federation and the expansion of NATO was condemned as a threat to international peace and security. Similar views were expressed in the speeches of the representatives of Nicaragua, Bolivia, Argentina, Venezuela, and Ecuador. In general, these States emphasized the principles of territorial integrity and non-interference in the internal affairs of States, but pointed to "double standards" in the use of these principles by the "West".

(5) Unequivocal public support for the actions of the Russian Federation, the declaration of the legality of the Crimean "referendum", and the "reunification" of this peninsula with the Russian Federation was contained only in the speech of the representative of the DPRK. However, this diplomat confused the facts and several times declared that this "self-determination" already applied to all of Ukraine.

3.2. Human Rights Protection in Crimea and Other Temporarily Controlled or Occupied Territories of Ukraine in Resolutions of 2016-2023

3.2.1. Resolution 71/205 (2016)

After a long break, on 19 December 2016, the General Assembly adopted the Resolution "Situation of Human Rights in the Autonomous Republic of Crimea and the city of Sevastopol (Ukraine)". The text partially repeated the 2014 Resolution, in particular the reference to the principle of non-use of force or the threat of force in international relations, and also confirmed the commitment of United Nations members to the political independence and territorial integrity of Ukraine. Fundamentally new in the Resolution was the recognition of the "temporary occupation" and non-recognition of the annexation of Crimea by the Russian Federation and condemnation of the extension of the Russian legal system to this territory. But the focus of the Resolution is different—the massive violations of human rights in the occupied territories, which are condemned both from the point of view of international human rights law and international humanitarian law. The Russian Federation as an occupying State is called upon to fulfill its obligations.[168]

During the discussion of the draft Resolution, the representative of Ukraine, Sergiy Kyslytsya, noted that the support of the document by the member States can make human rights issues in Crimea more visible; it will be a manifestation of insistence on the obligation of Russia, as the occupying power, to follow them. The representative of the Russian Federation, Olga Mozolina, reduced her speech to proclaiming the internal nature of the conflict in Ukraine and accusing the "Kyiv authorities" of massive violations of human rights, especially in the southeastern regions of the country.[169]

The draft document was previously considered by the III Committee of the General Assembly (whose competence includes social, humanitarian, and cultural issues).[170] The draft Resolution was presented by 30 countries.[171] Supported by 70 States, 26 countries voted against it (especially Armenia, Belarus, China, India, Kazakhstan, South Africa, Uzbekistan). 77 states abstained from voting (among them, Brazil, Kyrgyzstan, Nigeria, Tajikistan).[172]

Along with the "Crimean" resolution, human rights issues in various countries were considered. The resolution on North Korea was adopted by consensus (without a vote); on Syria with the result of 116/16/52; on Iran—85/35/63. The "Crimean" resolution

---

[168] Situation of human rights in the Autonomous Republic of Crimea and the city of Sevastopol (Ukraine). Resolution 71/205 adopted by the General Assembly, 19 December 2016.
[169] United Nations General Assembly. Seventy-first session. 65th plenary meeting. Official records. A/71/PV.65. 19 December 2016.
[170] United Nations General Assembly. Seventy-first session. Agenda item 68 (c). Promotion and protection of human rights: human rights situations and reports of special rapporteurs and representatives. Report of the Third Committee. A/71/484/Add.3. 7 December 2016.
[171] Situation of human rights in the Autonomous Republic of Crimea and the city of Sevastopol (Ukraine). Draft resolution A/C.3/71/L.26. 31 October 2016.
[172] United Nations General Assembly. Seventy-first session. 65th plenary meeting. Official records. A/71/PV.65. 19 December 2016.

received the fewest votes, but in all three cases of voting, the number of States that abstained was significant. The abstention from voting by such a significant number of States was explained by the representative of Kazakhstan—for some, the reason was their general position on resolutions of this type, which did not relate to supporting or not supporting the territorial integrity of Ukraine, condemning or approving the actions of the Russian Federation: "Kazakhstan does not oppose the resolution; we oppose politicizing the issue of human rights in general. Kazakhstan is against selectivity in assessing the human rights situation and against the use of human rights as an instrument to put pressure on Member States for political purposes". Similar opinions were expressed by representatives of several other States.

Another but related reason for abstaining from voting, cited by representatives of some States, was the confusion in the resolution regarding Crimea and in similar resolutions presented on the same day of human rights issues with political ones (for example, the territorial integrity of States), which is beyond the competence of III Committee of the General Assembly that recommended it. In itself, the Resolution regarding Crimea did not provoke a wide discussion during the voting in the General Assembly, except for the speech of the representative of Armenia. He pointed out that there is no hierarchy between the principles of the territorial integrity of States and the self-determination of peoples (a hint of support for the "self-determination" of Crimea).[173]

3.2.2. Resolution 72/190 (2017)

Resolutions having the same title, but with expanded content, were adopted by the General Assembly in subsequent years. Among the human rights violations outlined in the 2017 resolution: the introduction of Russian law, the judiciary and the system of governance in the occupied territories; discrimination against persons based on ethnic and religious characteristics, in particular of Ukrainians and Crimean Tatars; arbitrary detentions, torture and other cruel, inhuman and degrading treatment of detained persons; forced evictions

---

[173] Ibid.

and confiscation of private property; deportation of arrested and imprisoned persons from Crimea to the Russian Federation; failure to punish persons guilty of human rights violations; hindering the activity of independent journalists, human rights defenders and lawyers; prohibition, unjustified closure, or obstruction of the activities of cultural, religious and representative institutions (in particular, the prohibition of the Mejlis of the Crimean Tatar people), social organizations, mass media, cultural events; restrictions on teaching in the Ukrainian and Crimean Tatar languages; ban on Crimean Tatar public figures from entering Crimea; compulsion of the population to serve in the army and corresponding pressure and propaganda; forced acceptance of citizenship of the Russian Federation by the population; preventing missions of international organizations from working in Crimea to monitor human rights violations.[174]

Forty-two countries had become this time the initiators and "sponsors" of the draft Resolution.[175] The number of States that supported and opposed the Resolution did not change (70 and 26; this time Kyrgyzstan and Tajikistan voted "against"); 76 States abstained from voting. During the voting, the draft Resolution was generated little discussion, there being only the speeches of the representatives of Ukraine, Russian Federation, and Syria.[176]

3.2.3. Resolution 73/263 (2018)

The 2018 Resolution with the same name was lengthier. It contained a more expressive (although essentially the same) wording regarding the status of Crimea: "the seizure of Crimea by force is illegal and a violation of international law, ... these territories must be returned". States and international organizations were asked to officially use the following definition for Crimea: "the Autonomous

---

[174] Situation of human rights in the Autonomous Republic of Crimea and the city of Sevastopol, Ukraine. Resolution 72/190 adopted by the General Assembly on 19 December 2017.
[175] Situation of human rights in the Autonomous Republic of Crimea and the city of Sevastopol, Ukraine. Draft resolution A/C.3/72/L.42.
[176] United Nations General Assembly. Seventy-second session. 73rd plenary meeting. Official records. A/72/PV.73. 19 December 2017.

Republic of Crimea and the city of Sevastopol, Ukraine, temporarily occupied by the Russian Federation". To the enumeration of violations of human rights were added: extrajudicial executions, kidnappings, enforced disappearances; politically motivated harassment, intimidation, violence, including sexual; use of psychiatry for punitive purposes; deportations; restriction of freedom of thought and expression, association, peaceful assembly, religion, or belief; using anti-terrorism and anti-extremism laws to suppress dissent. The Russian Federation was urged to allow employees of Ukrainian consulates to visit detained citizens of Ukraine, as well as official representatives of Ukraine, including employees of the Office of the Plenipotentiary of the Verkhovna Rada of Ukraine, to prisoners and other citizens of Ukraine.[177]

The draft document was presented by 32 States.[178] Sixty-six countries voted for adoption of the Resolution, 27 — against, 71 countries abstained from voting. Another resolution on the human rights situation in Myanmar, discussed at the same meeting, was supported more convincingly (136/8/22). In addition to the representatives of Ukraine and the Russian Federation, only Syria spoke during the discussion of the "Crimean" resolution, briefly supporting the position of the Russian Federation.[179]

3.2.4. Resolution 74/168 (2019)

This Resolution contained references to a wider range of international legal documents, among them General Assembly Resolution 3314 (XXIX) of 14 December 1974 "Definition of aggression"[180] and others. With reference to the human rights violations committed by the Russian Federation on the territory of occupied Crimea, this time clearer wording was added regarding: forced sending of

---

[177] Situation of human rights in the Autonomous Republic of Crimea and the city of Sevastopol, Ukraine. Resolution 73/263 adopted by the General Assembly on 22 December 2018.

[178] Situation of human rights in the Autonomous Republic of Crimea and the city of Sevastopol, Ukraine. Draft resolution A/C.3/73/L.48. 31 October 2018.

[179] United Nations General Assembly. Seventy-third session. 65th plenary meeting. Official records. A/73/PV.65. 21 December 2018.

[180] Definition of Aggression. Resolution 3314 (XXIX) adopted by the General Assembly on 14 December 1974.

persons to psychiatric hospitals as a form of intimidation and punishment of political opponents and activists; the use of torture to obtain false confessions in politically motivated prosecutions; hindering the realization of social and economic rights of residents, in particular, children, the elderly, and persons with disabilities; pressure on religious communities, especially in the form of frequent police raids, unjustified demands during the registration of communities that affect legal status and property rights, threats and persecution of parishioners of the Eastern Orthodox Church of Ukraine (PTsU), Protestant denominations, Muslims, Ukrainian Greek Catholic Church (UGCC), Roman Catholics, Jehovah's Witnesses, unjustified persecution of dozens peaceful Muslims for their ascribed membership in certain religious organizations; mass arrests of human rights defenders on the basis of the fight against terrorism and other forms of repression against them; the targeted policy of the Russian Federation regarding the change in the demographic structure of Crimea because of, on one hand, the creation of unacceptable living conditions for the local population, which became the reason for many to leave, and on the other hand, by reason of encouraging Russians to move to this territory; various measures of the occupation authorities aimed at discrimination against ethnic and religious groups, in particular Crimean Tatars and Ukrainians; non-admission of independent doctors and representatives of international organizations to attend arrested and imprisoned persons, as well as the lack of effective investigation into the deaths of such persons.[181]

The draft document was presented by 34 countries.[182] The Resolution was supported: 66 states voted "for", 23 — "against" (including Armenia, Belarus, China, India, Kazakhstan, Kyrgyzstan), 83 abstained (among them, Brazil, Nigeria, South Africa). The results of the vote on the human rights resolutions considered on the same and the following day were: on Myanmar — 134/9/28, DPRK —

---

181 Situation of human rights in the Autonomous Republic of Crimea and the city of Sevastopol, Ukraine. Resolution 74/168 adopted by the General Assembly on 18 December 2019.
182 Situation of human rights in the Autonomous Republic of Crimea and the city of Sevastopol, Ukraine. Draft resolution A/C.3/74/L.28. 31 October 2019.

81/30/70, Syria—106/15/57. During the discussion on the "Crimean" resolution, only Ukraine and the Russian Federation spoke.[183]

3.2.5. Resolution 75/192 (2020)

In this Resolution, some traditional provisions were emphasized and detailed. It was noted that "organs and officials of the Russian Federation established in the temporarily occupied Crimea are illegitimate and should be referred to as the "occupying authorities of the Russian Federation". Among the new provisions: concern and condemnation of the unnecessary and disproportionate restrictive measures of the occupation authorities in connection with the coronavirus pandemic and the insufficiency of medical and hygienic measures to prevent this disease; inappropriate conditions in penal institutions, including overcrowded cells and lack of effective medical care; disproportionate and discriminatory searches of private residences and offices, or raids on places where Crimean Tatars gather; the negative impact of the occupation on the realization of social and economic rights of the population, especially its vulnerable groups; restrictions imposed on citizens of Ukraine in the occupied territories regarding the realization of their socio-economic rights, including the right to work, as well as the possibility of preserving their identity, culture, and education in the Ukrainian and Crimean Tatar languages; militarization and assimilation of youth and blocking their access to education in Ukraine; the construction of infrastructure facilities associated with expropriation of land, destruction of houses, depletion of natural and agricultural resources, which has a negative impact on nature and causes changes in the economic and demographic structure of the peninsula; demolishing or depriving communities of their religious buildings; consideration of civilian cases in military courts, disrespect by the occupying power for fair trial standards; criminal prosecution of Crimeans for evading conscription into the armed forces of the Russian Federation; unjustified interference in the work of mass media,

---

[183] United Nations General Assembly. Seventy-fourth session. 50th plenary meeting. Official records. A/74/PV.50. 18 December 2019.

arbitrary arrests, detention, harassment, intimidation of their employees in connection with professional activities.

The following were emphasized: the right of all internally displaced persons and refugees to return to Crimea and the demand for respect for their property rights; the requirement to disclose complete information about children deprived of parental care in Crimea since the beginning of the occupation, including those later adopted or transferred to foster families outside Crimea, in order to ensure the possibility of Ukraine taking care of them and protecting them.[184]

The draft document was presented by 27 countries.[185] The Resolution was supported by 64 States, 23 voted against (including Armenia, Belarus, China, India, Kazakhstan, Kyrgyzstan), and 86 abstained (in particular, Brazil, Nigeria, South Africa, Tajikistan). The results of the same day's voting on the resolutions on the situation of human rights in individual countries were as follows: on the DPRK—adopted by consensus, on Iran—82/30/64, on Syria—101/13/62. The draft "Crimean" resolution was mentioned during the discussion only in the speeches of the representatives of Ukraine and the Russian Federation.[186]

3.2.6. Resolution 76/179 (2021)

This Resolution added several elements to the condemnation: restrictions on the right to free movement for former convicts on political charges; prosecution of persons who refused to testify against third persons; destruction of cultural heritage, illegal archaeological works, displacement of cultural values, persecution of religious traditions, "thereby purposefully erasing Ukrainian and Crimean Tatar cultural identities from the ethnocultural landscape of Crimea"; conducting an all-Russian population census in Crimea, the

---

184 Situation of human rights in the Autonomous Republic of Crimea and the city of Sevastopol, Ukraine. Resolution 75/192 adopted by the General Assembly on 16 December 2020.
185 Situation of human rights in the Autonomous Republic of Crimea and the city of Sevastopol, Ukraine. Draft resolution A/C.3/75/L.32. 30 October 2020.
186 United Nations General Assembly. Seventy-fifth session. 46th plenary meeting. Official records. A/75/PV.46. 16 December 2020.

legality of which should not be recognized in relation to this region; deportation of Ukrainian citizens from Crimea, in particular on the basis of the application of the migration and penitentiary legislation of the Russian Federation. The Russian Federation was urged to: apply measures to limit the free migration of its citizens to Crimea; publication of detailed information on the spread of the coronavirus in Crimea and measures to combat the pandemic; ensuring proper living conditions in Crimea, including the fair and non-discriminatory distribution of water resources among the civilian population.

For the first time in the series of resolutions regarding Ukraine, the Crimean Tatars were called the indigenous people of Crimea. The Russian Federation was called upon to respect the relevant rights of the indigenous peoples of Ukraine provided in the 2007 United Nations Declaration on the Rights of Indigenous Peoples. The International Crimean Platform was mentioned among the international negotiation platforms to promote the improvement of the human rights situation on the peninsula; all member States were invited to participate in its work.[187]

The project was represented by 29 countries.[188] The Resolution was adopted by 65 votes "for", 25 states voted against (among them, Armenia, Belarus, China, India, Kazakhstan, Kyrgyzstan), and 85 abstained (Brazil, Nigeria, South Africa, Tajikistan, and others). Other resolutions on the human rights situation that day gained more support: on DPRK and Myanmar — consensus, on Iran — 78/31/69. The "Crimean" resolution was discussed only by representatives of Ukraine and the Russian Federation.[189]

---

[187] Situation of human rights in the temporarily occupied Autonomous Republic of Crimea and the city of Sevastopol, Ukraine. Resolution 76/179 adopted by the General Assembly on 16 December 2021.
[188] Situation of human rights in the temporarily occupied Autonomous Republic of Crimea and the city of Sevastopol, Ukraine. Draft resolution A/C.3/76/L.29. 28 October 2021.
[189] United Nations General Assembly. Seventy-sixth session. 53rd plenary meeting. Official records. A/76/PV.53. 16 December 2021.

3.2.7. Resolution 77/229 (2022)

This Resolution, adopted in the context of the Russian Federation's large-scale invasion of Ukraine, contained new provisions: an indication of the use of the territory of Crimea for further aggression by the Russian Federation and attempts to illegally annex the Kherson and Zaporizhzhia regions; the transfer of the experience of the occupation of Crimea to other territories of Ukraine under the "temporary military control" of the Russian Federation, the forceful holding of which is illegal, and they must be immediately returned to Ukraine; failure of the Russian Federation to comply with the 2022 interim order of the International Court of Justice (regarding the cessation of hostilities); condemnation of inciting hatred in Russia against Ukraine and Ukrainians, PTsU (Eastern Orthodox Church of Ukraine), Crimean Tatars, Muslims, Jehovah's Witnesses, public activists, spreading calls for atrocities against Ukrainians in the mass media; spread of disinformation aimed at justifying aggression against Ukraine, in particular through the education system; the adoption of new legislation of the Russian Federation aimed at the refusing residents of Crimea the right of peaceful protest; and so-called filtering procedures for displaced persons.

The Russian Federation was urged to: immediately cease its aggression and unconditionally withdraw its armed forces from the internationally recognized territory of Ukraine; stop hindering the residents of Crimea, in particular Ukrainians and Crimean Tatars, from participation in the cultural life of their communities; stop the criminal prosecution of Crimean residents for resisting conscription and mobilization into the Russian Armed Forces; repeal the decision regarding the simplified procedure for acquiring Russian citizenship for orphans and children left without parental care; stop the transfer of Ukrainian children to the territory of the Russian Federation, and take all appropriate measures for their safe return and family reunification.

A number of provisions of the previous resolutions regarding the illegal actions of the Russian Federation were extended in this document to all territories of Ukraine occupied by the Russian Federation.[190]

The draft Resolution was presented by 44 countries.[191] It was supported by 82 States, 14 voted against (Belarus, China, Kazakhstan, and others), and 80 abstained from voting (among them, Armenia, Brazil, India, Kyrgyzstan, Nigeria, South Africa, Tajikistan). Other resolutions on the human rights situation in individual countries were adopted with the following results: on the DPRK and Myanmar — consensus, Iran — 80/29/65, Syria — 92/14/71. The "Crimean" resolution was discussed only in the speeches of the representatives of Ukraine and the Russian Federation.[192]

3.2.8. Resolution 78/221 (2023)

This Resolution had a significantly expanded title: "Situation of human rights in the temporarily occupied territories of Ukraine, including the Autonomous Republic of Crimea and the city of Sevastopol". This reflects not the first, but a more consistent expansion of the provisions of this group of resolutions to all illegally controlled and annexed territories of Ukraine — Autonomous Republic of Crimea, Sevastopol, parts of Kherson, Zaporizhzhia, Donetsk, and Luhansk regions.[193] However, a significant part of the document

---

190 Situation of human rights in the temporarily occupied Autonomous Republic of Crimea and the city of Sevastopol, Ukraine. Resolution 77/229 adopted by the General Assembly on 15 December 2022.
191 Situation of human rights in the temporarily occupied Autonomous Republic of Crimea and the city of Sevastopol, Ukraine. Draft resolution A/C.3/77/L.35. 1 November 2022.
192 United Nations General Assembly. Seventy-seventh session. 54th plenary meeting. Official records. A/77/PV.54. 15 December 2022.
193 In the commentary of the Ministry of Foreign Affairs of Ukraine regarding the adoption of this resolution, it is somewhat unjustifiably stated that this document for the first time "covers the human rights situation in all the territories of Ukraine temporarily occupied by the Russian Federation". Such coverage was provided for in the 2022 Resolution from the same group. See: Коментар МЗС України щодо ухвалення Генеральною Асамблеєю ООН резолюції «Ситуація з правами людини на тимчасово окупованих територіях України, включаючи Автономну Республіку Крим та місто Севастополь» [Commentary of the Ministry of Foreign Affairs of Ukraine on the adoption by the UN General Assembly of the resolution "Situation of human rights in the temporarily occupied territories of Ukraine, including the Autonomous Republic of Crimea and the city of Sevastopol"]. 20 December 2023. (available online).

focuses on the special realities and violations of human rights on the Crimean Peninsula.

The Resolution reflects a new qualification of the Russian Federation's actions: instead of merely "temporary military control" – the formulation "temporary control or occupation" of Ukrainian territories was introduced. A single formula combined occupation as a traditional institute of international humanitarian law and the illegal exercise of effective control as an institute that consistently is being developed in decisions of international *ad hoc* tribunals and the European Court of Human Rights.[194] This may emphasize that in the vision of the authors of the draft Resolution, these two different regimes are brought together in their legal regulation and in practice are directly related to each other (for example, the second becomes the first). Therefore, the document seeks to use the norms and approaches developed for both, given the conditions of complexity, multifacetedness, and variability of the legal regime of the territories of Ukraine seized by Russia. Moreover, instead of "aggression by the Russian Federation" / "Russian aggression", the Resolution mostly uses the wording "war of aggression against Ukraine by the Russian Federation" / "Russian war of aggression against Ukraine".

The Resolution contained a number of new provisions. Reference was made to the Convention on the Rights of the Child and the Convention on the Rights of Persons with Disabilities as applicable to the subject of the Resolution; the number of references to indigenous peoples of Ukraine was increased. The following are condemned: the illegal practice of the Russian Federation regarding

---

[194] See O. V. Kresin and I. O. Kresina, "Illegal Control over Territory in International Law and the Status of Donbas Determination", *Przegląd Strategiczny*, no. 14 (2021); O. M. Stoyko, I. O. Kresina, O. V. Kresin. Відродження постконфліктних територій: світовий досвід і Україна: наукова записка / Ін-т держави і права імені В.М. Корецького НАН України [Recovery of Post-conflict Territories: Foreign Experience and Ukraine: Analytical Paper / Koretsky Institute of State and Law, National Academy of Sciences of Ukraine]. (Kyiv, 2020); O. V. Kresin. "Рішення ЄСПЛ щодо Криму 2020 р. і щодо Донбасу 2023 р.: юридична кваліфікація незаконного контролю РФ щодо території України" [Decisions of ECHR on Crimea 2020 and on Donbas 2023: Legal Qualification of the Illegal Control of Russian Federation over the Territory of Ukraine]. *Право України* [Law of Ukraine], no. 3 (2023), and others.

the arbitrary detention and capture of civilian hostages in the occupied territories; the destruction of the Kakhovka hydro power plant dam, which has and will continue to have catastrophic consequences for the entire region of Ukraine, as well as the refusal of humanitarian admission of United Nations representatives to the affected territory occupied by the Russian Federation; the violent actions of the Russian Federation at the Zaporizhzhia nuclear power plant, which may have catastrophic consequences not only for Ukraine, but also for a number of other countries; the use of occupied territories to carry out missile and unmanned aerial vehicle attacks on the rest of Ukraine (the deliberate nature of attacks on civilian objects, including hospitals and critical energy infrastructure is indicated); undermining global food security through attacks on Ukrainian civilian seaports and their infrastructure, means of navigation, grain terminals, attempts to blockade Ukrainian ports, threats to use force against civilian vessels. The condemnation of the forcible transfer of children and other civilians within the occupied territories and their deportation to the Russian Federation, the illegal change of the civil status of Ukrainian children—their adoption or transfer to foster families—are disclosed in more detail and supported by a reference to the warrants of the International Criminal Court.[195]

A few moments in text of the Resolution deserve some clarification:

(1) While expressing a grave concern about arbitral detentions, arrests and sentencing by Russian Federation of Ukrainian citizens, the Resolution names, *inter alia*, Asan and Aziz Akhmetov. Real persons are Asan and Aziz Akhtemov[196].

---

[195] Situation of human rights in the temporarily occupied territories of Ukraine, including the Autonomous Republic of Crimea and the city of Sevastopol. Resolution 78/221 adopted by the General Assembly on 19 December 2023.

[196] See, for example: "Наріман Джелялова, Асана Ахтемова та Азіза Ахтемова етапували з Криму до РФ для відбування покарання — адвокат Полозов" [Nariman Dzhelyal, Asan Akhtemov and Aziz Akhtemov Were Transferred from Crimea to Russian Federation to Execute Their Sentences — Lawyer Polozov]. *Кримська правозахисна група* [Crimean Human Rights Group]. 02. 10. 2023. (available online).

(2) The Resolution mentiones Maria Lvova-Belova as *Commissioner for Children's Rights in the Office of the President of the Russian Federation*, but correctly her office has to be named Children's Rights Commissioner for the President of the Russian Federation, or Presidential Commissioner for Children's Rights.

(3) The Resolution urges the Russian Federation (7n) "To respect freedom of opinion, association and peaceful assembly without discrimination on any grounds other than those permissible under international law". The word "discrimination" is better to replace with "restrictions".

The draft Resolution was presented by 50 countries.[197] Its adoption was supported by 78 states, 15 voted against (Belarus, Burundi, China, Cuba, DPRK, Eritrea, Honduras, Iran, Mali, Nicaragua, Niger, Russian Federation, Sudan, Syria, Zimbabwe), and 79 abstained from voting (Armenia, Brazil, South Africa, India, Indonesia, Kyrgyzstan, Mexico, Nigeria, Pakistan, Saudi Arabia, Serbia, Tajikistan, UAE, among them), 21 countries (Azerbaijan, Kazakhstan, Turkmenistan, Uzbekistan, and others) did not participate in the vote.[198]

3.3. Condemnation of Russian Aggression at Sea and Militarization of Crimea in Resolutions of 2018-2021

3.3.1. Resolution 73/194 (2018)

On 17 December 2018, the General Assembly launched a new series of resolutions—"Problem of the militarization of the Autonomous Republic of Crimea and the city of Sevastopol, Ukraine, as well as parts of the Black Sea and the Sea of Azov". The main motive for the drafting and consideration of the document was the attack by

---

[197] Situation of human rights in the temporarily occupied territories of Ukraine, including the Autonomous Republic of Crimea and the city of Sevastopol. Draft resolution A/C.3/78/L.42. 31 October 2023.
[198] Situation of human rights in the temporarily occupied territories of Ukraine, including the Autonomous Republic of Crimea and the city of Sevastopol: resolution / adopted by the General Assembly. Voting Summary. 19 December 2023.

the Russian Federation on three ships of the Ukrainian Navy in the Black Sea on 25 November 2018, shelling, damage and capture of the ships, wounding and capture of their crews—the first case of armed aggression of the Russian Federation against Ukraine carried out openly. The Resolution referred to the principle of refraining from the threat or use of force in international relations, confirmed the territorial integrity of Ukraine within internationally recognized borders, condemned Russia's "temporary occupation" of Crimea, declared non-recognition of its annexation, and called on the Russian Federation to immediately end the occupation.

But the main provisions of the Resolution are an expression of concern and protest regarding: the illegality of the presence of Russian troops in Crimea, which "undermines the security and stability of neighboring countries and the European region"; the increasing militarization of the peninsula, which is manifested, among other things, in the deployment of nuclear weapons carriers and numerous exercises, which will also have "considerable long-term negative environmental consequences in the region"; militarization of the Black Sea near Crimea and the Sea of Azov; the "dangerous increase in tensions and the unjustified use of force" by the Russian Federation in relation to Ukrainian warships and their crews in the Kerch Strait; Russia's violation of navigational rights and freedoms; the construction and operation of the Kerch bridge, which enables the further militarization of Crimea; intimidation by the Russian Federation of merchant ships and restrictions on international shipping.[199] The draft Resolution was presented by 48 States.[200]

Iran and Syria (joined by Nicaragua and Venezuela) proposed an amendment to the draft Resolution calling on Ukraine and the Russian Federation to exercise restraint and avoid "inflammatory rhetoric", such as calls for the destruction of critical infrastructure (according to the draft resolution, this could refer primarily to the

---

[199] Problem of the militarization of the Autonomous Republic of Crimea and the city of Sevastopol, Ukraine, as well as parts of the Black Sea and the Sea of Azov. Resolution 73/194 adopted by the General Assembly on 17 December 2018.

[200] Problem of the militarization of the Autonomous Republic of Crimea and the city of Sevastopol, Ukraine, as well as parts of the Black Sea and the Sea of Azov. Draft resolution A/73/L.47. 5 December 2018.

Kerch bridge); to conduct an investigation of the "incident" with the aim of bringing the perpetrators to justice (taking into account the entire text of the draft Resolution, the attack by the Russian Federation on Ukrainian ships should have been qualified as an incident, and the investigation — as part of a trial fabricated by the Russian Federation regarding the crews of these ships). The draft provided that "the incident and subsequent measures" (that is, the attack, damage and capture of ships, capture of crew members and injuries to some) do not affect the "implementation of the binding decisions adopted within the United Nations" (such as the approval of the Minsk Agreements by Resolution of the Security Council 2202 (2015) dated 17 February 2015).[201] In a speech explaining the draft amendment, the representative of Iran noted that the resolution should not have been put to a vote in general, because it could harm the process of implementation of the Minsk Agreements, and the "dispute" between Ukraine and Russian Federation should be resolved by themselves without external interference.[202]

Draft of the resolution and draft amendment were actively discussed at the session of the General Assembly. The representative of Ukraine, Sergiy Kyslytsya, proposed to consider the draft resolution as an important decision that would require a qualified majority of two-thirds of the States that will take part in the vote for its approval (apparently referring to Articles 83 and 84, Rules of Procedure of the General Assembly), and the proposal was supported by those present without objection.[203]

The draft amendment to the draft Resolution was rejected: it was supported by 25 States (including Belarus, China, Kazakhstan, Nigeria), 64 voted against, and 60 abstained from voting (including India, Kyrgyzstan, South Africa). The main Resolution was approved: supported by 66 States, 19 voted against (in particular,

---

[201] Resolution 2202 (2015). Adopted by the Security Council at its 7384th meeting, on 17 February 2015.
[202] A/73/L.68. Iran (Islamic Republic of) and Syrian Arab Republic: amendment to draft resolution A/73/L.47 Problem of the militarization of the Autonomous Republic of Crimea and the city of Sevastopol, Ukraine, as well as parts of the Black Sea and the Sea of Azov. 13 December 2018.
[203] United Nations General Assembly. Seventy-third session. 56th plenary meeting. Official records. A/73/PV.56. 17 December 2018.

Armenia, Belarus, Uzbekistan), 72 abstained (among them, Brazil, China, India, Kazakhstan, Kyrgyzstan, Nigeria, South Africa).

During the discussion, the guilt of the Russian Federation for the attack in the Kerch Strait, as well as the annexation of Crimea as the root cause of the problem, were pointed out by representatives of many members of the European Union, the latter as a whole, Turkey, Moldova, Georgia, and the United States. Several countries expressed their commitment to the territorial integrity of Ukraine and, at the same time, their doubts about the text of the resolution, which did not contribute to a peaceful solution to the problem in the Kerch Strait: Singapore, Korea, Indonesia. The speeches of the representatives of Belarus and Armenia were generally neutral in nature. The position of the Russian Federation regarding the legality of the Crimean "referendum", but without considering the attack in the strait, was supported only by Syria.[204]

3.3.2. Resolution 74/17 (2019)

This Resolution was significantly longer, the following being added: a reference to the 1974 General Assembly Resolution "Definition of aggression"; concern and condemnation regarding the Russian Federation establishment of control over nuclear facilities and materials in Crimea; the use of school education in Crimea to prepare pupils for service in the armed forces of the Russian Federation; destabilization of the economy and social services, particularly in the coastal regions of Ukraine, due to fears about security and the deployment of troops in the Black Sea-Azov region; the Russian Federation use of captured Ukrainian military plants in Crimea; restriction of shipping in the Kerch Strait due to the construction of the Kerch bridge, as well as through intimidation and illegal regulation, which worsens the economic and social situation in the neighboring regions of Ukraine; visits to occupied Crimea by representatives of the Russian authorities. Calls were made to the Russian Federation: to return equipment and weapons from captured and subsequently returned Ukrainian ships; to return all illegally detained citizens of Ukraine. Member States and international

---

204 Ibid.

organizations were urged to cooperate with the United Nations to "encourage and support efforts to put an end to the Russian occupation of Crimea as rapidly as possible and to refrain from any dealings with the Russian Federation regarding Crimea that are inconsistent with this aim", as well as to refrain from visits to occupied Crimea not agreed with Ukraine.[205]

The draft Resolution was presented by 39 states.[206] It was supported by 62 States, 19 voted "against" (among them, Armenia, Belarus, China, Kyrgyzstan) and 67 abstained (in particular, Brazil, India, Kazakhstan, Nigeria, South Africa). In addition to the Ukrainian and Russian positions, the following were declared: the European Union together with the candidate countries and Singapore, which supported Ukraine; Belarus, Iran, Indonesia, who insisted on a diplomatic settlement of the conflict in the Kerch Strait; and Syria, which supported the Russian Federation.[207]

3.3.3. Resolution 75/29 (2020)

Minor clarifications were made and new provisions added in this Resolution. The following were condemned: Russia's conscription of Crimean residents who retain Ukrainian citizenship; establishment of military educational institutions of the Russian Federation and pre-conscription military training courses in schools on the peninsula; construction of warships in Crimea; dangerous increase in tension and unjustified use of force by the Russian Federation against Ukraine at sea, including obstruction of international shipping.[208]

---

205 Problem of the militarization of the Autonomous Republic of Crimea and the city of Sevastopol, Ukraine, as well as parts of the Black Sea and the Sea of Azov. Resolution 74/17 adopted by the General Assembly, 9 December 2019.
206 Problem of the militarization of the Autonomous Republic of Crimea and the city of Sevastopol, Ukraine, as well as parts of the Black Sea and the Sea of Azov. Revised draft resolution: addendum A/74/L.12/Rev.1/Add.1. 9 December 2019.
207 United Nations General Assembly. Seventy-fourth session. 41st plenary meeting. Official records. A/74/PV.41. 9 December 2019.
208 Problem of the militarization of the Autonomous Republic of Crimea and the city of Sevastopol, Ukraine, as well as parts of the Black Sea and the Sea of Azov. Resolution 75/29 adopted by the General Assembly on 7 December 2020.

The draft Resolution was put forward by 42 States[209] and supported by 63 countries; 17 voted against (among them, Armenia, Belarus, China, Kyrgyzstan), and 62 abstained (Brazil, India, Kazakhstan, Nigeria, South Africa, and others). Consideration of the draft was accompanied by justifications of the voting position by representatives of many States. The European Union (also on behalf of Turkey, North Macedonia, Albania, Liechtenstein, Moldova, and Georgia), eight Scandinavian and Baltic states, United Kingdom, United States, Azerbaijan, and Singapore (with undisclosed reservations) supported the resolution and emphasized their commitment to the territorial integrity of Ukraine. Indonesia generally confirmed the recognition of the territorial integrity of Ukraine and the non-recognition of any annexation or illegal occupation of territories, but advocated a peaceful settlement of the "problem" and therefore voted against the Resolution. Belarus, Iran, and Algeria pointed to the "imbalance" of the draft resolution, insisted on a peaceful settlement of the "situation", however, directly mentioning only "south-eastern Ukraine", and the need to adhere to the Minsk Agreements. Only Syria has traditionally supported the position of the Russian Federation ("the fact is that the results of the Crimean referendum have translated into stability"; "the draft resolution reflects political polarization. It only fuels conflict and dissent and is certainly not an attempt to calm the situation").[210]

3.3.4. Resolution 76/70 (2021)

This Resolution contained new provisions: a condemnation of the destabilization of international arms control regimes as a result of the occupation of Crimea and the mass transfer of Russian weapons and troops there; blocking commercial and other shipping to and from Ukrainian ports (and the adoption of new legislation that creates grounds for this); expansion of Russian naval bases in Crimea;

---

[209] Problem of the militarization of the Autonomous Republic of Crimea and the city of Sevastopol, Ukraine, as well as parts of the Black Sea and the Sea of Azov. Revised draft resolution: addendum A/75/L.38/Rev.1/Add.1. 7 December 2020.

[210] United Nations General Assembly. Seventy-fifth session. 36th plenary meeting. Official records. A/75/PV.36. 7 December 2020.

deploying units of the Russian Armed Forces and security agencies to control captured marine oil and gas platforms belonging to Ukraine, and thus also the exploitation of Ukrainian natural resources and the restriction of Ukraine's access to its maritime spaces. The Resolution contained an expression of support for the activities of the International Crimean Platform aimed at the peaceful de-occupation of the peninsula.[211]

The draft Resolution was presented by 44 States.[212] It was supported by 62 votes against 22 (Armenia, Belarus, China, Kyrgyzstan, and others), and 57 countries abstained (Brazil, India, Kazakhstan, Nigeria, and others). The adoption of the Resolution was accompanied by numerous declarations of States explaining the reasons for their vote. Along with the expression of the traditional positions of Iran, Singapore, Indonesia, the Scandinavian and Baltic states, United States, European Union and the candidate countries, and United Kingdom, worthy of mention are the speeches of the representatives of Mexico and the Republic of Korea, who emphasized the commitment to the territorial integrity of Ukraine, but indicated the need for a peaceful resolution of disputes. The representative of Mexico also noted that the member States did not have the opportunity to make proposals for changes in the draft Resolution. The representative of Belarus defined his position more precisely ("crisis within Ukraine", "conflict in Ukraine", "to put the peace process in Ukraine on a sustained positive trajectory"). Only Syria has traditionally supported the position of the Russian Federation.[213]

---

[211] Problem of the militarization of the Autonomous Republic of Crimea and the city of Sevastopol, Ukraine, as well as parts of the Black Sea and the Sea of Azov. Resolution 76/70 adopted by the General Assembly on 9 December 2021.

[212] Problem of the militarization of the Autonomous Republic of Crimea and the city of Sevastopol, Ukraine, as well as parts of the Black Sea and the Sea of Azov. Draft resolution: addendum A/76/L.22/Add.1. 9 December 2021.

[213] United Nations General Assembly. Seventy-sixth session. 48th plenary meeting. Official records. A/76/PV.48*. 9 December 2021.

3.4. Complex of Resolutions of the 2022-2023 Emergency Special Session

3.4.1. Eleventh Emergency Special Session of General Assembly

The new stage of the Russian Federation aggression against Ukraine, which began on 24 February 2022, generated the discussion and adoption of new resolutions at the 11th emergency special session of the General Assembly. It was convened in accordance with Security Council Resolution 2623 (2022) of 27 February 2022 – in connection with "the lack of unanimity of its permanent members at the 8979th meeting has prevented it from exercising its primary responsibility for the maintenance of international peace and security"[214] (here are elements of citations of the United Nations Charter and General Assembly "Uniting for Peace" Resolution). The Security Council submitted to the General Assembly for examination the issue of the decision regarding the letter from the Permanent Representative of Ukraine in the United Nations dated 28 February 2014, which demanded consideration of the security situation in Ukraine.[215] The Resolution was supported by eleven out of fifteen members of the Security Council (permanent members – France, United Kingdom, United States, as well as Albania, Brazil, Gabon, Ghana, Ireland, Kenya, Mexico, Norway), only the Russian Federation voted against, three countries abstained (permanent member – China, as well as India and the United Arab Emirates).[216]

It should be noted that the Security Council transfer of an issue of maintaining international peace and security to the General Assembly for consideration occurred only for the eighth time in the

---

214 Resolution 2623 (2022) adopted by the Security Council at its 8980th meeting, 27 February 2022.
215 Letter dated 28 February 2014 from the Permanent Representative of Ukraine Yuriy Sergeyev to the United Nations addressed to the President of the Security Council (S/2014/136).
216 Security Council. 8980th meeting. Sunday, 27 February 2022. S/PV.8980.

history of the United Nations and the first time in forty years (since 1982).[217]

All issues during this session were considered according to the special procedure provided for in Article 18(2) and (3) of the United Nations Charter, — that is, in this case, as decisions on important issues — "recommendations on the maintenance of international peace and security". This accordingly provides for the adoption by a qualified majority (at least two-thirds of the votes of the representatives of the States present at the meeting and participating in the vote). During each vote, this special procedure was proposed by the President of the General Assembly and unanimously approved by the representatives of the member States. The eleventh emergency session of the General Assembly was not completed within a certain period, only breaks were announced, meetings were resumed at the request of groups of States and took place in 2022 and 2023.

3.4.2. Resolution "Aggression against Ukraine"

On 2 March 2022, the Resolution "Aggression against Ukraine" was adopted. The document referred to the 1950 General Assembly "Uniting for Peace" Resolution, which was also adopted when it was impossible to achieve unanimity of the permanent members of the Security Council,[218] the 1974 Resolution on the "Definition of aggression", and others.

The Resolution condemned the "special military operation" of the Russian Federation in Ukraine as the use of force by one country against another, which is contrary to the United Nations Charter, and is recognized as aggression; it pointed to the military offensive, which is unprecedented during recent decades in Europe in terms of its scale, and declared "that urgent action is needed to save this generation from the scourge of war"; the involvement of Belarus in committing aggression is condemned. The General Assembly

---

[217] L. Blanchfield and M. C. Weed, "United Nations Security Council and General Assembly Responses to the Russian Invasion of Ukraine", *Congressional Research Service Insight*, 7 March 2022, p. 2. (available online).
[218] Uniting for peace. Resolution 377 (V) adopted by the General Assembly on 3 November 1950.

confirmed the commitment of the member States to the sovereignty, independence, unity, and territorial integrity of Ukraine in its internationally recognized borders, including territorial waters.

The Russian Federation was urged to: immediately cease the use of force against Ukraine and refrain from further illegal threats or use of force against any member State; immediately, completely, and unconditionally withdraw its armed forces from the territory of Ukraine; and reverse the decision to recognize the "independence" of certain districts of Donetsk and Luhansk regions.

The Russian Federation and Ukraine are called upon to: observe the Minsk Agreements, return to work in the Normandy Format and the Trilateral Contact Group for the implementation of these agreements; comply with the norms of international humanitarian law, and ensure the population's access to humanitarian aid and protection of the civilian population and medical personnel; and pursue "the immediate peaceful resolution of the conflict between the Russian Federation and Ukraine through political dialogue, negotiations, mediation and other peaceful means".

Concern and condemnation were expressed regarding: attacks by Russian troops on civilian objects and civilians; bringing Russian Federation strategic nuclear forces into heightened combat readiness; deterioration of the humanitarian situation in and around Ukraine with an increase in the number of internally displaced persons and refugees in need of humanitarian assistance; the potential negative impact of the conflict on global food security, taking into account the importance of Ukrainian agricultural exports, as well as global energy security.[219]

The draft resolution was presented by 96 States.[220] The resolution was supported by 141 States (including Brazil, Mexico, Nigeria, Serbia), 5 voted against (Belarus, DPRK, Eritrea, Russian Federation, Syria), 35 abstained (in particular, Armenia, China, India, Kazakhstan, Kyrgyzstan, South Africa, Tajikistan, and others), twelve

---

219 Aggression against Ukraine. Resolution ES-11/1 adopted by the General Assembly on 2 March 2022.
220 Aggression against Ukraine. Draft resolution A/ES-11/L.1. 1 March 2022.

States did not participate in the vote (Azerbaijan, Turkmenistan, Uzbekistan, and others).[221]

Representatives of 52 member States, the European Union, two observer States, and one international organization took part in the discussion. The positions expressed,[222] which are more diverse than "for", "against" and "abstained", can generally be combined into the following groups:

(1) Some representatives of the member States and the European Union as an observer unconditionally supported the territorial integrity of Ukraine and condemned Russian aggression (some as intervention, invasion) and war crimes, but called for a negotiated solution to the conflict. One of the most clearly articulated such speeches was made by the representative of Turkey.

(2) The majority of representatives and an observer from the Vatican during the discussion supported the territorial integrity of Ukraine, but advocated a negotiated solution to the conflict, avoiding its qualification and mention of the Russian Federation (Laos and Eritrea also opposed the introduction of any sanctions); they gave attention to humanitarian issues, especially to the problem of evacuating their citizens from Ukraine.

(3) A significant number of States perceived the draft resolution as ambiguous. The representatives of India and Iraq reduced their speeches to a call for negotiations and ensuring the security and rights of citizens of third countries. Pakistan and Jordan pointed to the aggregate principles of international law, including the right of peoples to self-determination and unified and indivisible security, and avoided qualifying the conflict and condemning the actions of the Russian Federation. A similar position was expressed by the representatives of Algeria and Tanzania. The representative of China noted that the resolution did not take into account the "history and complexity of the current crisis" and the principle of indivisible security (against the expansion of regional military alliances), avoided qualifying the conflict, insisted on a

---

[221] United Nations General Assembly. Eleventh Emergency Special session. 5th plenary meeting. Official records. A/ES-11/PV.5. 2 March 2022.
[222] Ibid.

negotiated solution of the "issue of Ukraine" by the "relevant parties", and pointed out that not all member States had the opportunity to participate in preparing the draft resolution. Similar views were expressed by representatives of Egypt, South Africa, Lebanon, and Iran. The latter also accused the United States and NATO of constantly destabilizing the political situation in Eastern Europe, and suggested that only the Security Council, and not the General Assembly, has the authority to determine the presence of an act of aggression. The representatives of Brazil and the United Arab Emirates, supporting the resolution but avoiding the qualification of the situation, indicated the need to "to address the security concerns of the parties". They expressed reservations about using this resolution to introduce indiscriminate sanctions or the deployment of troops (having in view the troops of third countries) and stressed the need for negotiations between the parties.

(4) The representative of Belarus took a moderately negative position regarding the content of the draft resolution. He pointed out that the conflict is a consequence of the long civil war in Ukraine and its failure to implement the Minsk Agreements, as well as the inability of the international community to force the "Kyiv authorities" to implement them and conduct negotiations with the "Donetsk People's Republic" and "Luhansk People's Republic", "to consider their legitimate interests", and cease attacking them. He categorically denied any participation of his country in the conflict, called for abandoning the introduction of sanctions against Belarus, and urged that the conflict between Ukraine and the Russian Federation be resolved through negotiations because "in any war, each side has its own truth".

(5) Only Syria supported the intervention of the Russian Federation: "the legitimate positions that Russia has taken based on its security concerns and its right to protect its territory and people from genuine threats to national security".

There is a somewhat exaggerated opinion in Ukrainian scholarly literature about the extraordinary nature of the Resolution "Aggression against Ukraine" given the practice of the General Assembly ("Hardly in the long history of the activities of the United Nations, had its General Assembly adopted a resolution in whose title was the word 'aggression' used"); or, another example: the Resolution is a "unique fundamental contribution to the restoration of international legal justice, international security, and also, by the way, to the development of international law in general".[223]

In fact, a number of General Assembly resolutions have condemned acts of aggression, emphasizing this in their titles: resolutions condemning the aggression of the DPRK against the Republic of Korea in 1951 (A/Res/500(V)), the United States against Cuba in 1961 (A/Res/1616 (XV)), Israel against Iraq in 1981 and later (A/Res/36/27 et al.), Portugal against Guinea-Bissau in 1974 (A/Res/3061 (XXVIII)), not to mention general resolutions.

3.4.3. Resolution "Humanitarian Consequences of Aggression against Ukraine"

On 24 March 2022, the Resolution "Humanitarian consequences of the aggression against Ukraine" was adopted. In addition to the provisions contained in previous General Assembly resolutions, this document stated that the Russian military invasion of Ukraine has humanitarian consequences unprecedented in Europe in recent decades. It referred to: siege and shelling from the air of densely populated cities of Ukraine; shelling of civilians, including journalists, civilian objects, such as schools and other educational institutions, water supply and sewage systems, medical facilities and medical transport, and evacuation convoys; kidnapping of local officials; attacks against diplomatic missions and cultural objects; the large number of civilian casualties; and the growing number of internally displaced persons and refugees in need of humanitarian assistance. The indiscriminate and disproportionate nature of the attacks, including shelling and the use of explosive weapons, was condemned. The parties to the conflict were urged to fully comply

---

[223] R. Topolevskyi, T. Dudash, V. Honcharov, A. Nakonechna, ed. by P. Rabinovych, "Науковий коментар [до резолюції Генеральної Асамблеї ООН, ухваленої 2 березня 2022 року, ES-11/1 "Агресія проти України"]" [Scholarly commentary [to the UN General Assembly resolution *Aggression against Ukraine*]. *Право України* [Law of Ukraine], no. 8 (2022), pp. 118, 120.

with international humanitarian law.[224] The draft resolution was presented by 90 States.[225]

An alternative draft resolution was presented by South Africa. Its representative recognized the emergence of a humanitarian crisis in Ukraine, and pointed out that we should not ignore the (unnamed) "context that gave rise to this crisis or any violations of the Charter of the United Nations and international law"; the territorial integrity and sovereignty of Ukraine should be respected, but he stated that for the authors of the first draft the answer to this crisis is secondary. In the view of South Africa, the main goals are geopolitical, and the draft is engaged and politicized. The aim of the Resolution regarding the "conflict in Ukraine" should be the end of the war through a call to end hostilities and the good offices of the United Nations.[226]

This alternative draft partially repeated the General Assembly Resolution of 2 March 2022 analyzed above and the first draft of the resolution on the humanitarian consequences of the aggression against Ukraine, but was entitled "Humanitarian situation emanating from the conflict in Ukraine" and in substance was abstract, filled with general calls for compliance by the unnamed "all parties to the conflict" with the norms and principles of humanitarian law and for the immediate cessation of hostilities followed by a diplomatic resolution of the conflict, as well as for the conclusion of the emergency special session of the General Assembly.[227]

As the representative of Ukraine, Kyslytsya, pointed out during the debate, this alternative draft mostly repeated the draft resolution presented by the Russian Federation in the Security Council,[228] which during the vote was supported only by the Russian

---

224 Humanitarian consequences of the aggression against Ukraine. Resolution ES-11/2 adopted by the General Assembly, 24 March 2022.
225 Humanitarian consequences of the aggression against Ukraine. Draft resolution A/ES-11/L.2. 21 March 2022.
226 United Nations General Assembly. Eleventh Emergency Special session. 9th plenary meeting. Official records. A/ES-11/PV.9. 24 March 2022.
227 Humanitarian situation emanating out of the conflict in Ukraine. Draft resolution A/ES-11/L.3. 22 March 2022.
228 Belarus, Democratic People's Republic of Korea, Russian Federation and Syrian Arab Republic: draft resolution. S/2022/231. 23 March 2022.

Federation itself and one other member State of the Security Council.[229]

This draft was not coordinated with Ukraine, and the representatives of Austria and eight Scandinavian and Baltic States drew attention to the unacceptability of such an approach in the case of a humanitarian resolution. As the representative of Denmark noted on behalf of the latter group, "our problem with the text was less about what was in it and more about what was not in it. It mentioned only Ukraine. Yet Russia alone bears the responsibility for the humanitarian catastrophe we are discussing today, and Russia alone can end it".[230]

The main/first draft was supported by 140 States (including Brazil and Nigeria), 5 voted against (Belarus, DPRK, Eritrea, Russian Federation, Syria), and 38 abstained (Armenia, China, India, Kazakhstan, Kyrgyzstan, South Africa, Tajikistan, Uzbekistan, and others). Ten States (Azerbaijan, Turkmenistan, and others) did not participate in the vote. After that, on the proposal of the representative of Ukraine, not the alternative draft itself was put to the vote, but the question regarding the expediency of its consideration. The General Assembly decided not to consider it (67 States against, 50 in favor, 36 abstained).[231]

Active discussion continued during three sessions of the General Assembly on 23 and 24 March 2022. More than ninety speeches individually or collectively presented the positions of 108 States and three observers (European Union, Vatican, Order of Malta).[232] The discussion showed a spectrum of opinions and motives, much wider and not fully corresponding to the results of the vote. They can be conditionally combined into the following groups:

---

229 Security Council. 9002nd meeting. 23 March 2022. S/PV.9002.
230 United Nations General Assembly. Eleventh Emergency Special session. 9th plenary meeting. Official records. A/ES-11/PV.9. 24 March 2022.
231 Ibid.
232 United Nations General Assembly. Eleventh Emergency Special session. 7th plenary meeting. Official records. A/ES-11/PV.7. 23 March 2022; United Nations General Assembly. Eleventh Emergency Special session. 8th plenary meeting. Official records. A/ES-11/PV.8. 23 March 2022; United Nations General Assembly. Eleventh Emergency Special session. 9th plenary meeting. Official records. A/ES-11/PV.9. 24 March 2022.

(1) Full support for the resolution, condemnation of Russian aggression, and the demand to withdraw Russian troops from the territory of Ukraine were expressed in speeches on behalf of 67 States. These were almost all European countries (except Hungary, Cyprus, Greece, Andorra, San Marino, Vatican, Belarus, Russian Federation, Azerbaijan, Armenia), Oceania (including Australia and New Zealand), United States, Canada, some Asian countries (Republic of Korea, Japan, Turkey, Singapore) and Latin America (Uruguay, Colombia, Argentina, Jamaica, Chile, Costa Rica). Among them, representatives of 19 States (mostly European, as well as the United States and New Zealand) emphasized the need to bring to justice the military leadership of the Russian Federation and its citizens who committed war crimes.

(2) Representatives of seven States mentioned that the Russian-Ukrainian conflict should be qualified as a war started by Russia (Hungary, Mexico, Peru, Cyprus, Andorra, San Marino, Myanmar).

(3) Concerns about the humanitarian crisis without naming the causes of its occurrence or mentioning the "dispute" between the Russian Federation and Ukraine, a call to the parties to the conflict to cease hostilities, to ensure the free departure of foreign citizens from Ukraine, and to solve problems through negotiations were contained in the speeches of representatives of 34 States, as well as observers from the Vatican and the Order of Malta. These are mostly the States of Asia (China, India, Indonesia, Pakistan, Israel, Iraq, Iran, and others), Africa (South Africa, Egypt, and others), Latin America (Brazil, and others), but also Europe (Greece, Azerbaijan).

The overall position of these States was emphasized in the speech of the representative of Lesotho: "The fundamental focus of Lesotho's vote was therefore on humanitarian action rather than the causes of the conflict or any other factors that could escalate, fuel or lead to further suffering". Fourteen speeches qualified the Resolution as politicized, as going beyond its declared humanitarian character; representatives of ten States expressed regret that the alternative draft resolution proposed by South Africa was not put to a vote; representatives of China, Egypt, and Brazil opposed the introduction of sanctions against Russian Federation and Belarus due to the harm such sanctions would cause to the world economy.

The representative of China emphasized the recognition of Ukraine's territorial integrity, but pointed out that "the legitimate security concerns of all countries [should be] taken seriously". He said that "geopolitical conflicts and major power struggles" were the cause of the humanitarian crisis, in which not everything was as clear as it might seem. The representative of Egypt pointed out the need to "address the concerns and interests of all the parties involved as well as the root causes of the crisis itself" (similar opinions were expressed in the speech of the representative of Iran), Eritrea emphasized the "current campaign or drive to return to a unipolar world order by tightening the noose on Russia", and Jordan proposed to investigate violations of humanitarian law by both sides of the conflict.

(4) The position of the Russian Federation was to emphasize the "compelled" character of the "special military operation in Ukraine" as a response to "root causes" (the need to stop the "Kyiv regime's eight-year war against the civilian population of Donbas", to "de-Nazify and demilitarize" Ukraine so that it "no longer to pose a threat to us", a threat to the "vital interests" of the Russian Federation due to Ukraine's desire to join NATO and renounce its nuclear-free status), and the role of Western countries in fueling the conflict. The representative of the Russian Federation accused Ukraine itself of a humanitarian crisis due to the actions of its military, and called the resolution politicized and "allegedly humanitarian", adopted *ultra vires* of the powers of the General Assembly in the field of maintaining international peace and security, and therefore null and void. The position of the Russian Federation was directly supported only by Syria.

3.4.4. Resolution on Suspension of Membership of Russian Federation in the United Nations Human Rights Council

On 7 April 2022, the General Assembly adopted a Resolution suspending the membership of the Russian Federation in the United

Nations Human Rights Council. The reason indicated by the document was the flagrant and systematic violation of human rights (provided for in General Assembly Resolution 60/251 of 15 March 2006)[233] during the aggression of the Russian Federation against Ukraine.[234] The draft Resolution was presented by 58 States.[235] States declared positions with regard to the draft before and after the vote. The Resolution was supported by 93 States, 24 voted against (Belarus, China, Kazakhstan, Kyrgyzstan, Tajikistan, and Uzbekistan, among them), 58 abstained (Brazil, India, Nigeria, South Africa, and others), and 18 States did not participate in the vote (among them, Armenia, Azerbaijan, Turkmenistan). After the vote at the same meeting of the General Assembly, the representative of the Russian Federation announced the decision of this country to completely terminate its membership in the United Nations Human Rights Council (this meant the early termination of membership of the Russian Federation as an elected member State for a specified period, but not a refusal to be elected to the Council in the future).[236]

In order to understand the results of the vote, it is important that the day before, the Russian mission to the United Nations sent a non-public diplomatic note to the offices of representatives of the member States that it would perceive a positive vote by each specific country and even abstention or non-participation therein as an unfriendly step that would have immediate consequences for bilateral relations, as well as the need to publicly oppose the draft resolution.[237]

---

[233] Human Rights Council. Resolution 60/251 adopted by the General Assembly on 15 March 2006.

[234] Suspension of the rights of membership of the Russian Federation in the Human Rights Council. Resolution ES-11/3 adopted by the General Assembly on 7 April 2022.

[235] Suspension of the rights of membership of the Russian Federation in the Human Rights Council. Draft resolution A/ES-11/L.4. 6 April 2022.

[236] United Nations General Assembly. Eleventh Emergency Special session. 9th plenary meeting. Official records. A/ES-11/PV.10. 7 April 2022.

[237] Russia threatens states with consequences over UN vote on Human Rights Council // Euractiv. 7 April 2022 (available online).

There have previously been cases of States voluntarily withdrawing from membership in this Council, as, for example, the United States did in 2018 (until 2021) due to disagreement with the Council's anti-Israel policy and the lack of reforms. But the exclusion from the Council by the decision of the General Assembly happened only for the second time: such expulsion occurred for the first time in 2011 in relation to Libya in connection with mass violence against the political opposition during the time of Muammar Gaddafi.[238]

3.4.5. Resolution "Territorial Integrity of Ukraine: Defending the Principles of the Charter of the United Nations"

On 12 October 2022, the Resolution "Territorial integrity of Ukraine: defending the principles of the Charter of the United Nations" was adopted. By name and partially by content, this document was based on General Assembly Resolution 68/262 "Territorial integrity of Ukraine", dated 27 March 2014, but contains important innovations, emphasizing that parts of the Donetsk, Kherson, Luhansk and Zaporizhzhia regions are "under the temporary military control of the Russian Federation, as a result of aggression, in violation of the sovereignty, political independence and territorial integrity of Ukraine", and an attempt to annex these territories had been made. The recognition by the Russian Federation of the independence of so-called "Donetsk People's Republic" and "Luhansk People's Republic" on 21 February 2022 and the admission of four regions of Ukraine into the Russian Federation on 29

---

238 M. Nichols, "U.N. suspends Russia from human rights body, Moscow then quits", *Reuters*. 7 April 2022. (available online). The statement of Ukrainian observers that the Russian Federation was the first State to be excluded from the United Nations Human Rights Council is exaggerated. See.: R. Topolevskyi, T. Dudash, V. Honcharov, A. Nakonechna, ed. by P. Rabinovych, "Науковий коментар [до резолюції Генеральної Асамблеї ООН, ухваленої 7 квітня 2022 року, ES-11/3 "Зупинення прав, пов'язаних з членством Російської Федерації в Раді з прав людини ООН"]" [Scholarly Commentary [to the UN General Assembly Resolution *Suspension of the rights of membership of the Russian Federation in the Human Rights Council*]]. *Право України* [Law of Ukraine], no. 4. (2023), p. 32.

September 2022, as well as "referendums" on 23 to 27 September 2022, were declared illegal and incompatible with the United Nations Charter. These actions and decisions "have no validity under international law and do not form the basis for any alteration of the status of these regions of Ukraine".

Member States are called not to recognize such attempts by the Russian Federation. The Russian Federation is urged to immediately and unconditionally repeal its decisions of 21 February and 29 September 2022 and withdraw its military units from the territory of Ukraine within its internationally recognized borders. Support for the efforts of the United Nations Secretary General, member States, and international organizations aimed at de-escalating the situation and a peaceful resolution of the conflict, which would involve respect for the sovereignty and territorial integrity of Ukraine and correspond to the principles of the United Nations Charter, was announced.[239]

The draft Resolution was presented by 76 States.[240] It was supported by 143 States (including Brazil, Nigeria), 5 voted against (Belarus, North Korea, Nicaragua, Russian Federation, Syria), 35 abstained (Armenia, China, India, Kazakhstan, Kyrgyzstan, South Africa, Tajikistan, Uzbekistan, and others). Ten States did not participate in the vote (in particular, Azerbaijan, Turkmenistan, Iran).[241]

During the discussion, the Russian Federation proposed to make the vote on the draft Resolution secret due to the alleged reluctance of many States to publicly express their position on the document under pressure from the West. This proposal was rejected: 107 States supported the open vote on the draft resolution, 13 were against, 39 abstained, and several countries refused to

---

[239] Territorial integrity of Ukraine: defending the principles of the Charter of the United Nations. Resolution ES-11/4 adopted by the General Assembly on 12 October 2022.

[240] Territorial integrity of Ukraine: defending the principles of the Charter of the United Nations. Draft resolution A/ES-11/L.5. 7 October 2022.

[241] United Nations General Assembly. Eleventh Emergency Special session. 14th plenary meeting. Official records. A/ES-11/PV.14. 12 October 2022.

express their position (including the Russian Federation itself and China).[242]

The discussion of the draft resolution continued during two meetings of the General Assembly on 12 October 2022. Sixty-six speeches were made representing 81 member States and three observers. The expressed positions,[243] not all of which corresponded to the votes of the States, can be conditionally combined into the following groups:

(1) European countries (European Union members, Montenegro, Moldova, Georgia, Azerbaijan), Canada, United States, some Latin American countries (Guatemala, Ecuador, Chile, Argentina, Uruguay), Africa (Congo, Ghana, Liberia), Asia (Japan, Republic of Korea, Cambodia), Oceania (members of the Pacific Islands Forum) and the Caribbean region (St. Vincent and the Grenadines) condemned the aggression of the Russian Federation and recognized the "referendums" in the occupied regions of Ukraine and their annexation as null and void. Some representatives of these countries pointed to the commission on war crimes by the Russian Federation and criticized the Security Council as an insufficiently effective United Nations organ.

(2) General confirmation of the territorial integrity of Ukraine was contained in the speeches of the representatives of Greece, South Africa, Nepal, Angola, Algeria, and Timor-Leste. However, the representative of Greece called for an investigation of all committed war crimes (hinting at the possible guilt of both the Russian Federation and Ukraine), and the representative of Timor-Leste blamed the Russian Federation, Ukraine, and NATO for the emergence of the conflict.

(3) Speeches by representatives of some States of Asia (China, India, Saudi Arabia, Bangladesh, Vietnam, Thailand), Latin America and the Caribbean region (Brazil, Colombia, Venezuela, Bolivia, Cuba), Africa (Egypt and Mauritius), as well as observers (Vatican

---

[242] M. Nichols, "U.N. publicly rejects Russia's call for secret vote on Ukraine", *Reuters*, 11 October 2022. (available online).
[243] With 143 Votes in Favour, 5 Against, General Assembly Adopts Resolution Condemning Russian Federation's Annexation of Four Eastern Ukraine Regions. Press-release GA/12458. 12 October 2022. (available online).

and the Order of Malta) were reduced to calls for the de-escalation of the conflict. Some representatives of these States criticized the Resolution for politicization, and the representative of China also stated that it reflects a "Cold War mentality".

(4) The actions of the Russian Federation were supported with reservations by Pakistan (the right to self-determination is important, although referendums are dubious), and to the full extent by the DPRK (the self-determination of the people of several regions of Ukraine is a fact and must be respected) and Syria (the text of the resolution is based on falsified facts).

3.4.6. Resolution "Furtherance of Remedy and Reparation for Aggression against Ukraine"

This Resolution of 14 November 2022 was completely new in terms of its subject. The document referred to the Resolution of the General Assembly "Basic principles and guidelines on the right to a remedy and reparation for victims of gross violations of international human rights law and serious violations of international humanitarian law", dated 16 December 2005.[244] The new Resolution indicated that the consequences of aggression of the Russian Federation against Ukraine became human casualties, displacement of civilians, destruction of infrastructure and natural resources, loss of State and private property, and economic disaster.

Therefore, the Russian Federation should be held accountable for all violations of international law in or regarding Ukraine. The Russian Federation must be held accountable for all its internationally illegal actions, including aggression itself, and this must include reparations for losses and damage of any nature caused by these actions ("the injury, including any damage", "damage, loss or injury").

It was recognized that the member States, in cooperation with Ukraine, need to establish an international mechanism for ensuring

---

[244] Basic Principles and Guidelines on the Right to a Remedy and Reparation for Victims of Gross Violations of International Human Rights Law and Serious Violations of International Humanitarian Law. Resolution 60/147 adopted by the General Assembly on 16 December 2005.

reparations for losses, damages, and injury caused by the Russian Federation. Member States were recommended, in cooperation with Ukraine, to create an international register of the damage caused, which should record in documentary form the evidence and claims of individuals, legal entities, and Ukraine as a State, facilitate the collection of evidence, and coordinate it.[245] Justifying the necessity of adopting the Resolution, the representative of Ukraine, Kyslytsya, referred to the experience of reparations after the Second World War and Iraq's aggression against Kuwait.[246]

The draft Resolution was presented by 57 States[247] and adopted by 94 votes to 14 (Bahamas, Belarus, Central African Republic, China, Cuba, DPRK, Eritrea, Ethiopia, Iran, Mali, Nicaragua, Russian Federation, Syria). Seventy-three States abstained (among them, Armenia, Brazil, India, Kazakhstan, Kyrgyzstan, Nigeria, South Africa, Tajikistan, Uzbekistan). Twelve countries (Azerbaijan, Turkmenistan, and others) did not participate in the vote.[248] Later, the Minister of Foreign Affairs of the Bahamas stated that their vote against the resolution was mistakenly counted, and in fact the representative of his country abstained from voting.[249]

The draft document was discussed in 35 speeches individually and collectively representing 85 member States, as well as two observers. The presented positions[250] can be conditionally combined into the following groups:

---

[245] Furtherance of remedy and reparation for aggression against Ukraine. Resolution ES-11/5 adopted by the General Assembly on 14 November 2022. See also: Ch. Giorgetti, M. Kliuchkovsky, P. Pearsall, J. K. Sharpe, "Historic UNGA Resolution Calls for Ukraine Reparations", *Just Security*, 16 November 2022. (available online).

[246] United Nations General Assembly. Eleventh Emergency Special session. 15th plenary meeting. Official records. A/ES-11/PV.15. 14 November 2022.

[247] Furtherance of remedy and reparation for aggression against Ukraine. Draft resolution A/ES-11/L.6. 7 November 2022.

[248] United Nations General Assembly. Eleventh Emergency Special session. 15th plenary meeting. Official records. A/ES-11/PV.15. 14 November 2022.

[249] C. Dames, "UN record showing 'no' vote from Bahamas on Russia reparations an 'error', Mitchell said", *The Nassau Guardian*, 17 November 2022. (available online).

[250] United Nations General Assembly. Eleventh Emergency Special session. 15th plenary meeting. Official records. A/ES-11/PV.15. 14 November 2022.

(1) The comprehensive civil liability of the Russian Federation for the damage caused and the need to ensure the payment of appropriate reparations were declared in speeches on behalf of 45 States — Ukraine, members of and candidates for joining the European Union, United Kingdom, United States, Canada, Australia, New Zealand, Japan, Mexico, and Guatemala. The Scandinavian and Baltic States demanded that Belarus be brought to justice as an accomplice in Russian crimes, while they, together with France and Japan, stated the need to bring to criminal responsibility the top leadership of the Russian Federation and the perpetrators of war crimes. The representative of Mexico stated that his country would support the Resolution with a reservation — without the question of creating an international mechanism to ensure reparations for the damage caused by the Russian Federation.

(2) In a speech on behalf of the fourteen member States of the Caribbean Community, the need for the withdrawal of Russian troops from the territory of Ukraine and the holding of negotiations between the parties was emphasized, the responsibility of the Russian Federation for the damage caused to Ukraine was declared, but it was indicated that the proposal to create a compensation mechanism was beyond the powers of the General Assembly, the principles for the creation of the mechanism are unclear, there is no corresponding jurisdictional base, and it was also proposed to create similar mechanisms for reparations to States for climate change, historical slavery, and genocides, regardless of the time that has elapsed since these events.

(3) In the speeches on behalf of the six States of the Persian Gulf, the general principles of the Resolution were supported, but it was declared that the compensation mechanism should be created with the consent of the United Nations and be under the control of this organization.

(4) General theses regarding the need to establish peace between the Russian Federation and Ukraine through negotiations were contained in the speech of the representative of Vietnam.

(5) The speeches of representatives of the Russian Federation and eighteen States that supported Russia (Eritrea, Angola, Belarus, Bolivia, Cambodia, China, Cuba, North Korea, Equatorial Guinea,

Iran, Laos, Nicaragua, Saint Vincent and the Grenadines, Syria, Venezuela, Zimbabwe, Sri Lanka, South Africa), as well as the State of Palestine, declared the nullity of the Resolution and emphasized a set of these:

(a) exceeding the powers of the General Assembly, which is a political, not a judicial body and cannot form legally significant qualifications regarding aggression and the responsibility of States;

(b) the uncertainty of the legal basis of the mechanism of responsibility and the illegality of its possible creation outside the framework of the United Nations at the will of a group of States;

(c) the inviolability of the sovereign immunity of States regarding their property — as a customary norm of international law — and the inadmissibility of "theft of other people's assets";

(d) the need to avoid double standards and instead form a unified approach to compensation for all historical and modern cases of aggression, genocide, colonialism, slave trade, climate change, and others;

(e) the need to establish peace through negotiations and the impossibility of resolving the issue of reparations in the absence of defeat of one of the parties;

(f) the need to avoid sanctions against States from which other States suffer;

(g) the need to stop supporting the parties to the conflict by third States;

(h) lack of clarity about the nature and causes of the conflict, manipulation of information about it, inadmissibility of ignoring the concerns of the Russian Federation regarding its security caused by the expansion of NATO;

(i) lack of consultations with all member States in the process of preparing the draft resolution;

(j) the harmfulness of the Resolution, which divides the General Assembly and hinders efforts to establish peace.

Most of these speeches did not mention the Russian Federation; the conflict was characterized as the "Ukrainian crisis" or "war in Ukraine". The degree of realism of some of these disagreements was demonstrated by the speech of the representative of Cuba, who demanded from the former metropolitan States compensation for all former colonies for 500 years of colonialism. The representative of China also stated that: previous resolutions adopted at this emergency session did not contain grounds for the responsibility of the Russian Federation and reparations; the Resolution is based on the "Articles on Responsibility of States for Internationally Wrongful Acts" (references to this document are not actually in the Resolution, but they were in the speeches of representatives of several States), which have no legal significance, "are only a research product of the International Law Commission, an expert body".

Modern Ukrainian international lawyers believe "a huge number of states that abstained during the voting of this resolution were motivated, mainly, by historical resentments of African, Asian and South American countries".[251] However, the assessment of another author regarding the "greater sensitivity of human rights issues for many states, in contrast to the condemnation of aggression or annexation,"[252] is less convincing, because the speeches of representatives of many "Third World" States were dominated by anti-colonial discourse, disagreement with the supposedly higher attention to the European conflict compared to acts of aggression in Africa, Asia, Latin America, and elsewhere—skillfully strengthened by the Russian Federation with the help of various levers of persuasion.

3.4.7. Resolution "Principles of the Charter of the United Nations Underlying a Comprehensive, Just and Lasting Peace in Ukraine"

This Resolution, adopted 23 February 2023, is the most recent in the series of acts of the eleventh emergency special session of the

---

[251] I. Todorov. "Російська інвазія в Україну та ООН" [Russian Invasion to Ukraine and UN], in: M. M. Palinchak, M. M. Korol, V. V. Khiminets (eds.), *Міжнародне співтовариство та Україна в сучасних глобальних цивілізаційних процесах: актуальні економічні, політико-правові, безпекові та соціально-гуманітарні аспекти*: матер. доп. міжнар. наук.-практ. конф. (Ужгород, 18-19 квітня 2023 р.) [The International Community and Ukraine in Modern Global Civilization Processes: Current Economic, Political and Legal, Security, Social and Humanitarian Aspects: Conference Collection]. Uzhgorod, 2023, p. 475; Todorov, Todorova, note 3 above, p. 37.

[252] Tymchuk, note 3 above, p. 31.

General Assembly. Compared to previous resolutions, it contained several important new provisions, and first and foremost, the definition of the parameters of peace, laid down in the title itself and repeated several times in the text with the clarification "including the principles of sovereign equality and territorial integrity of States", as well as an emphasis on "ensure accountability for the most serious crimes under international law committed on the territory of Ukraine through appropriate, fair and independent investigations and prosecutions at the national or international level, and ensure justice for all victims and the prevention of future crimes". It was emphasized that activities aimed at achieving peace in Ukraine must take into account the global impact of the war on food security, energy, finance, environmental and nuclear security.

The document contained calls for: cessation of hostilities; detention of prisoners of war in accordance with the norms of international humanitarian law, comprehensive exchange of them; the release of all illegally detained, interned, displaced, and deported persons, including children; cessation of attacks on critical infrastructure and civilian objects of Ukraine.[253]

The draft resolution was presented by 75 States.[254] 141 countries voted for its adoption, 7 against (Belarus, North Korea, Eritrea, Mali, Nicaragua, Russian Federation, Syria), and 32 abstained (Armenia, China, India, Kazakhstan, Kyrgyzstan, South Africa, Tajikistan, Uzbekistan, and others). Thirteen did not participate (Azerbaijan, Turkmenistan, among them).[255]

Before considering the draft resolution, Belarus (with the later support of Nicaragua) presented proposals for changes. The first proposal was to remove from the text the references to the "one year into the full-scale invasion of Ukraine", "the aggression by the Russian Federation against Ukraine", as well as the demand for the

---

[253] Principles of the Charter of the United Nations underlying a comprehensive, just and lasting peace in Ukraine. Resolution ES-11/6 adopted by the General Assembly on 23 February 2023.
[254] Principles of the Charter of the United Nations underlying a comprehensive, just and lasting peace in Ukraine. Draft resolution A/ES-11/L.7. 16 February 2023.
[255] United Nations General Assembly. Eleventh Emergency Special session. 19th plenary meeting. Official records. A/ES-11/PV.19. 23 February 2023.

withdrawal of Russian troops from Ukraine. Instead, it was proposed to define the essence of the events simply as "hostilities in Ukraine". It was further proposed to condemn the "statements made by certain leaders of the Normandy Contact Group regarding their true intentions when devising the Package of Measures for the Implementation of the Minsk Agreements which were inconsistent with the aim of peaceful resolution of the conflict in certain areas of the Donetsk and Lugansk regions of Ukraine".[256] The proposal was rejected: eleven States (Belarus, Cuba, North Korea, Eritrea, Ethiopia, Mali, Nicaragua, Russian Federation, Sudan, Syria, Zimbabwe) voted in favor, 94 against, 56 abstained.

The second proposal consisted of: expressing concern about the supply of weapons by third parties to the "zone of conflict", which hinders the prospects for lasting peace, and calling on member States to refrain from such supplies; call for the start of peace negotiations; calling on member States to "address the root causes of the conflict in and around Ukraine, including legitimate security concerns of Member States".[257] This proposal was likewise rejected: fifteen States (Angola, Belarus, China, Cuba, North Korea, Egypt, Eritrea, Ethiopia, Honduras, Iran, Mali, Nicaragua, Russian Federation, Syria, Zimbabwe) voted for it, 91 against, 52 abstained.

The position of the opponents of the Belarus proposals was presented in the most detailed manner in the speech of the representative of the United Kingdom:

> The draft amendments attempt to create a false equivalence between Russia, which the General Assembly and the Secretary-General have made clear is engaged in a full-scale invasion, and Ukraine, which is exercising its right of self-defense against that aggression. Put simply, these draft amendments are an attempt to undermine the Charter. They are not aimed at peace, but at defending the aggressor. They are not proposed in good faith.[258]

---

[256] Principles of the Charter of the United Nations underlying a comprehensive, just and lasting peace in Ukraine. Draft amendment to draft resolution A/ES-11/L.7. A/ES-11/L.8. 21 February 2023.

[257] Principles of the Charter of the United Nations underlying a comprehensive, just and lasting peace in Ukraine. Draft amendment to draft resolution A/ES-11/L.7. A/ES-11/L.9. 21 February 2023.

[258] United Nations General Assembly. Eleventh Emergency Special session. 19th plenary meeting. Official records. A/ES-11/PV.19. 23 February 2023

The draft Resolution and proposals for changes were considered during three sessions of the General Assembly on 22 and 23 February 2023.[259] After the speeches of the United Nations Secretary General and the President of the General Assembly, the draft was presented by the Minister of Foreign Affairs of Ukraine, Dmytro Kuleba, and the proposals for changes were presented by the representative of Belarus. In total, seventy-two speeches individually or collectively represented the positions of 97 States and three observers.

The expressed positions of the States can be conditionally combined into groups that only partially coincide with the voting results and represent a wider range of expressed opinions.

(1) Most widely represented was the position that Russian aggression is a war against the international rule-based order, and the future peace should include the territorial integrity of Ukraine and the responsibility of the Russian Federation. These principles were reflected in 33 speeches representing 45 countries: European Union members together with candidate States and members of the European Free Trade Association, as well as the United States, Canada, United Kingdom, Australia, New Zealand, Liberia, Republic of Korea, Guatemala, Singapore, Turkey, Chile, Ecuador, Marshall Islands, Micronesia, Argentina, Palau.

(2) Support for the preservation of the territorial integrity of Ukraine during the conclusion of the future peace, but without mentioning the responsibility of the Russian Federation, was expressed in the speeches of the representatives of Israel and Mexico.

(3) Representatives of Djibouti, Nepal, Fiji, Tonga, and Nigeria pointed to the same thing, but without mentioning responsibility for war crimes and ensuring justice for their victims. The latter representative directly expressed a reservation regarding clause 9 of the draft Resolution, dedicated to ensuring criminal responsibility

---

[259] 'We Don't Have a Moment to Lose', Secretary-General Tells General Assembly's Emergency Special Session on Ukraine as Speakers Debate Draft Resolution. Eleventh Emergency Special Session, 17th Meeting (PM). 22 February 2023 (available online); United Nations General Assembly. Eleventh Emergency Special session. 19th plenary meeting. Official records. A/ES-11/PV.19. 23 February 2023

for war crimes, announcing that this issue is not the most urgent, it can complicate the positions of the parties, the mechanisms of investigation and punishment of such crimes in this case are not sufficiently understandable, and if they are created, then they will have to be applied to other cases of aggression. In addition, the representative of Fiji presented the war in Ukraine as a manifestation of the rivalry of military blocs.

(4) Representatives of Belarus, Azerbaijan, South Africa, Brazil, India, Pakistan, Indonesia, Oman (on behalf of the six States of the Cooperation Council for the Arab States of the Persian Gulf), Costa Rica, Vietnam, Peru, Sri Lanka, Tunisia, Angola, South Sudan, as well as observers — the Vatican and the Order of Malta — pointed out the need to achieve peace, but without revealing its parameters. These speeches are characterized by definitions of events as "Ukrainian conflict", "Ukrainian crisis", "war in Ukraine" or abstractly as a "war", as well as by various doubts about the objectivity of the available information. In addition, the representative of Angola expressed reservations about paragraph 9 of the project on the punishment of war criminals due to "we do not think that this is the right time" and the presence of crimes on both sides of the conflict.

(5) The presence of objective geopolitical "root" causes of the war and, because of this, the legitimacy of the Russian invasion, the impossibility of victory for one of the parties and the restoration of the pre-war situation, and instead the need to find a compromise peace with a change in the international security architecture, the cessation of the supply of weapons to the parties, and the waiver of sanctions were declared in the speeches of the Russian Federation, Venezuela (on behalf of an unspecified "group of like-minded countries"), Syria, Thailand, Malaysia, Cuba, Egypt, DPRK, and Lesotho. The representative of the Russian Federation declared that the real causes of the conflict are ignored, the desire of Western countries to achieve a strategic defeat of the Russian Federation, as well as about Russia's protection of Donbas, against which Ukraine started a war. The speech contained a hidden threat ("the futile illusion that they could defeat a nuclear Power"). The representative

of the DPRK stated that this country does not supply and does not intend to supply weapons to the Russian Federation.

There is a widely shared opinion that the General Assembly Resolution "Principles of the Charter of the United Nations underlying a comprehensive, just and lasting peace in Ukraine" reproduced the principles for achieving peace announced by the President of Ukraine, Volodymyr Zelenskyy.[260] As generally known, the "peace formula" was proposed in an online speech by Zelenskyy on 15 November 2022 at the G20 Leaders' Summit.[261] A comparison of the two documents shows that the text of the General Assembly resolution more or less fully corresponds, but with different wording, to only three principles of the "peace formula": the release of war prisoners and deported persons (paragraph 4), confirmation of the territorial integrity of Ukraine (paragraph 5), and withdrawal of Russian troops and cessation of hostilities (paragraph 6). Some other, but not all, ideas similar to the "peace formula" are mentioned in fairly general terms.

---

260 See for example: N. Sobenko. "Генасамблея ООН ухвалила резолюцію з українською 'формулою миру'" [UN General Assembly Adopted the Resolution with Ukrainian 'Peace Formula']. *Суспільне. Новини* [Society TV. News]. 23 February 2023 (available online); "ООН переважною більшістю голосів схвалила українську 'формулу миру', шкідливі поправки 'збили'" [UN with Overwhelming Majority Adopted the Ukrainian 'Peace Formula', Harmful Amendments Were Refuted". *Європейська правда* [European Pravda]. 23 February 2023 (available online).
261 V. O. Zelenskyy. "Україна завжди була лідером миротворчих зусиль; якщо Росія хоче закінчити цю війну, хай доведе це діями — виступ Президента України на саміті 'Групи двадцяти'" [Ukraine has always been a leader of peacekeeping efforts; if Russia wants to end this war, it should prove it with actions — President of Ukraine's speech at the G20 summit]. *Сайт «Президент України Володимир Зеленський. Офіційне інтернет-представництво»* [Site "President of Ukraine Volodymyr Zelenskyy. Official Internet Office]. (available online).

IV Perspectives

Beyond the endless discussions about the actuality or uselessness of the United Nations or its imaginary alternatives, as well as about the legal or purely political nature of the resolutions of the United Nations General Assembly, it is obvious that the latter require the consistent attention of international lawyers, scholars, and experts in order to evaluate their real significance in general and in conditions of counteracting Russian aggression, as well as for the purpose of forming an adequate, effective, consistent position of Ukraine in the United Nations General Assembly to solve its urgent problems.

(1) This study gives grounds for asserting that the provisions of the United Nations Charter regarding the powers of the main organs of this organization are imprecise. This was realized when drafting this constitutive treaty. It was expected that these norms and their interpretation will continue to develop, and that complex issues would become the subject of adjustment between United Nations organs.

Although the General Assembly is a United Nations organ with vaguely defined powers, it is the only organ representing the will of all members. The Security Council is also an organ with a defined competence, but, given that its permanent members have the right of veto, it acts as *le Directoire*, whose legitimacy and powers are largely based on the vision of international security immediately after the Second World War, with enemies defined directly in the United Nations Charter and responsibility for colonies and mandated territories that no longer exist.[262]

The legitimacy of the United Nations Security Council is significantly reduced by the uncontrolled use of the right of veto by its

---

[262] As Andrew J. Carswell pointed out, "compromise that took place between the great Allied victors of the Second World War and the remainder of the UN membership. The result was a division of powers between the Security Council and the General Assembly that has never found a satisfactory equilibrium". Therefore, the scholar calls the Security Council hegemonistic, and the United Nations Charter is not aimed at achieving sovereign equality between member states. Carswell, note 157 above, pp. 453, 456, 478-479.

permanent members, which makes the decisions relating to important international issues dependent on the will of a single country. This has no logical explanation, and even more so, it cannot be considered as a norm that corresponds to the collective will of the so-called international community.[263]

It can be argued that the democratic political legitimacy of the General Assembly has grown immeasurably over the last nearly eighty years, at least in proportion to the radical increase in the number of members and observers and taking into account the impact of developments in the form of conventions and declarations; instead, the political legitimacy of the Security Council has significantly decreased, because all the previously listed factors of this legitimacy have disappeared, and the political and economic realities of the world have changed. In these conditions, the interpretation of the United Nations Charter cannot fail to evolve, which is reflected and recognized in General Assembly resolutions, the judgements and advisory opinions of the International Court of Justice, and in the practice of United Nations members.

According to the United Nations Charter, the Security Council is an independent organ of the United Nations, but to some extent accountable to the General Assembly. The competence of the General Assembly is universal, and the competence of the Security Council is specialized. In addition, this competence of the Security Council — in the field of maintaining international peace and security — is not exclusive, but shared with the General Assembly. The use of coercive measures within the scope of this competence is a means at the disposal of the Security Council, but preventive measures can be applied both by the Security Council and the General Assembly.

The nature of the decisions of these two organs in maintaining international peace and security also differs: the decisions of the Security Council are binding on the member States, and the decisions of the General Assembly are recommendatory. But according to the

---

263 About this see also: M. Petsa. "Сергій Кислиця: 'Вся російська місія в ООН — це серпентарій, розвідники і шпигуни'" [Sergiy Kyslytsya: 'The entire Russian mission to the UN is a serpentarium, spies and intelligence officers']. *BBC News Ukraine*. 10 November 2023.

United Nations Charter, member States are obliged to provide assistance to the United Nations (and not to one of its organs) in actions of a preventive and coercive nature, and the General Assembly has the right to recommend preventive measures. And according to the interpretation of the International Court of Justice, the recommendations of the main United Nations organs are not just material for reflection, but a tool that initiates or authorizes individual and collective actions of States—legitimate, desirable, but not binding. Only the limits of the use of armed forces during preventive measures, which should be based on the invitation or consent of the host State and therefore not turn into coercive actions, are debatable.

The same applies to the powers of the General Assembly to interpret the norms of the United Nations Charter and to provide legal conclusions in its resolutions. Indeed, the decisions of the Security Council on certain issues are binding, but according to the intention of the States—creators of the Charter, all main organs of the United Nations have the right to interpret the provisions of this treaty on an equal basis. The General Assembly declared the right to legal qualification (in particular, of aggression) back in 1950 and used it many times—and this right was not denied by the International Court of Justice.

For a correct understanding of the powers of the General Assembly, it is necessary to take into account that the United Nations Charter is an international treaty and is subject to the rules and principles of interpretation of such acts. Therefore, an out-of-context textual analysis of the United Nations Charter is unpromising. Instead, its meaning is revealed in the context of the preparatory documents adopted at the San Francisco Conference in 1945, the interpretation by the International Court of Justice, and the development of the practice of the United Nations organs. This also applies to the provisions on the scope of powers and the nature of decisions of the General Assembly.

For almost eighty years, the activities of the General Assembly revealed and developed its charter powers in the domain of maintaining international peace and security, including those powers that "are conferred upon it by necessary implication as being essential to the performance of its duties" (formulation of the International Court of Justice in 1949). This is how, despite the endless and unfruitful theoretical discussions, the limits of the General Assembly activities in this area should be considered. This is based on the democratic legitimacy and growing potential of the General Assembly as the sole organ that reflects the positions and will of almost all the States of the world — unlike the Security Council, all the original assumptions concerning which are obsolete.

Among the arsenal of measures initiated and implemented by the General Assembly in the field of maintaining international peace and security, there were: an appeal to the International Court of Justice for an advisory opinion; removal of a State from participation in the work of the United Nations due to termination (non-recognition) of the credentials of its representatives; trade and transport embargo; investigation of violations of international law and preparation of materials for court proceedings; conducting peacekeeping operations, including military and police operations; creation of a hybrid tribunal based on a contract with the State.

This wide range of tools and measures is quite effective. It has its limitations and peculiarities. Most important among the latter, in our opinion, is the hybrid nature of actions: the General Assembly carries out a significant part of its activities in the field of maintaining international peace and security together with other United Nations organs or member States, and also authorizes the latter to carry out collective actions.

The 1950 "Uniting for Peace" Resolution became a concentrated expression of the understanding by the member States of the broad competence of the General Assembly. Without violating the charter recommendatory powers of this organ, it created new mechanisms for their implementation. First, this applies to the algorithm of actions in cases of the inability of the Security Council to realize its primary responsibility in the field of maintaining international peace and security, the efficiency of convening sessions and the simplified procedure for preparing issues for consideration by the General Assembly, as well as not only the authorization, but also the direct coordination by the General Assembly of the collective actions of member States in this field.

The procedural innovations of this Resolution, in particular regarding the holding of emergency special sessions, were incorporated into the Rules of Procedure of the General Assembly. In addition, the "Uniting for Peace" mechanism has been repeatedly initiated by the Security Council and essentially recognized as legitimate by the International Court of Justice. Therefore, the presence or absence of an indication of this mechanism in resolutions of the General Assembly has no legal significance. The emphasis in the resolutions on the use of this mechanism when convening emergency special sessions of the General Assembly is to a greater extent political, to stress the special importance of the issue under consideration.

Therefore, the most important material, not procedural, element of the "Uniting for Peace" mechanism, which still retains its independent significance, is the creation and long-standing existence of a system of coordination of collective coercive measures against States that violate international peace and security. This element significantly complements the arsenal of means for carrying out the activities of the General Assembly in this area.

It is difficult to determine the place of General Assembly resolutions among the sources of international law. Such a place was not provided for in the Statute of the International Court of Justice, and the United Nations Charter indicates the recommendatory nature of the resolutions of the General Assembly except for matters that ensure the functioning of the organization. The latter, however, can acquire a significantly broader significance (for example, the admission or exclusion of members). But the understanding of the nature of General Assembly resolutions has evolved significantly. The General Assembly itself—that is, the member States represented therein—insists on the right to set normative standards (political or legal?) in resolutions.

However, first, the development of the practice of the General Assembly, certain (not summarized by the present study) elements of the practice of States and the judgements of the International Court of Justice, at least since 1986, indicate that a State's unconditional support of General Assembly resolutions is considered as recognition of their binding nature for this State. Second, the creation of norms of international law by any of the United Nations organs was not foreseen from the beginning of the existence of this organization. Even the decisions of the International Court of Justice were considered as binding only for the parties to the case and as not creating a general norm or precedent.

But at least since 1986, the International Court of Justice has been consistently developing the vision of General Assembly resolutions as a material source of norms of customary international law, which also become a legal source if they have normative content, gain mass and representative support while member States have unequivocal intentions, and States' practice conforms with these intentions. The same vision is consistently developed by the International Law Commission, while paying attention to the importance of assessing the mass and representativeness of support for General Assembly resolutions, the presence and nature of reservations, the repetition of these resolutions or their norms.

At least since 1949, the International Court of Justice has been developing the doctrine of implicit powers of the United Nations organs, which are generated not only by the specific norms of its Charter, but also by its general spirit (in particular, the purposes of the organization) and the principles of international law. The resolutions of the main United Nations organs should be considered not only as obliging or recommending other United Nations organs and member States to take or not to take certain actions, but also exclude the legitimacy of the opposite actions; that is, they outline the framework of the legitimacy of their activities. The International Court of Justice pointed out that General Assembly resolutions within the framework of the charter purposes of the United Nations should be considered as decisions of the entire organization, impose obligations on member States, and cannot be perceived as purely recommendations for voluntary implementation.

All this together creates a presumption of the legal nature of the norms of General Assembly resolutions, which gained convincing support upon adoption. In other words, the norms of these resolutions, which, by the way, always refer to resolutions or other acts of the United Nations, OSCE and other organizations, and customary international law, do not need proof. On the contrary, the assumptions of the representatives of some State regarding the not legal, but purely political nature of certain norms of the General Assembly resolutions, require detailed justification.

Resolutions and initiatives of the General Assembly in 2022-2023 regarding the supervision of the use of the right of veto in the Security Council[264] are of great importance for understanding both the powers of the General Assembly in correlation with the powers of the Security Council and the nature of the resolutions of the General Assembly. The member States actually declared that: (a) their interests are represented by the General Assembly; (b) they partially delegate the protection of their interests in the field of maintaining international peace and security to the Security Council; (c) they do not lose their initial rights in connection with this and, through the General Assembly, have the authority to supervise the decisions of the Security Council and, in particular, to evaluate the application of the right of veto.

It is evident that the right to one way or another overcome the consequences of the application of the veto in the event that it turns out to be unreasonable follows from this. That is, the powers and resolutions of the General Assembly, in particular in the field of maintaining international peace and security, are indirectly placed above the corresponding powers and resolutions of the Security Council. This, as well as the idea of accountability of the Security Council to the General Assembly, fully corresponds to the holistic understanding of the United Nations Charter in modern conditions.

All this is based on the long-term development of the practice of the General Assembly, including its establishment of various auxiliary organs in the field of maintaining international peace and security, as well as on the real significance of its recommendations to member States regarding the application of collective measures of a preventive and coercive nature in this area, and on the

---

[264] Conventional and already rooted name for situations that, according to the United Nations Charter, can be qualified as a lack of unanimity among the permanent members of the Security Council.

perception by States of General Assembly resolutions as legally binding and similar in nature to international treaties.

(2) It is impossible to summarize all doctrinal positions regarding the nature of United Nations General Assembly resolutions within the framework of this study. The most important monographs, a number of articles, and the views of well-known international lawyers reflected in instructional literature have been consulted. This, and the rather extensive geography of the opinions presented, allow some conclusions to be drawn, which, of course, do not pretend to be exhaustive.

Based on the generalization of doctrinal works, a classification is proposed of the views of international lawyers regarding the nature of General Assembly resolutions as: (a) purely recommendatory acts that have moral and political significance; (b) acts of a political nature, which, due to the reflection of the positions of a large number of States and adoption by an authoritative United Nations organ, are perceived as a standard of conduct and affect the individual and group policy of States; (c) acts of soft law, which are considered as customary or treaty law in the process of formation or formalization and which cause the readiness of a certain number of States to voluntarily implement them; (d) unilateral acts of States (adopted together with other States) or unilateral acts of an international organization. In addition, the discussion of international lawyers regarding the nature of the qualifications contained in the resolutions makes it possible to assume the understanding of the latter as another category — (e) interpretative legal acts.

The understanding of General Assembly resolutions not related to resolving of issues of the organizational development of the United Nations as purely recommendatory and do not have direct legal consequences follows from the United Nations Charter, and therefore allegedly does not need additional argumentation. But this is not quite the case, as evidenced by both the practice of the General Assembly and international legal doctrine. In any case, this does not contradict the general recognition that General Assembly resolutions acquire a significant degree of political normativity, regulate certain spheres of international relations, influence the conduct of States due to their authority, and form criteria for lawful and unlawful conduct. Without being legally binding, these resolutions create a presumption of legitimacy or illegitimacy of certain individual and collective actions of States.

Understanding General Assembly resolutions as a form of soft law (or norms *de lege ferenda*) does not encounter objections in international legal doctrine. This is evident in their role in the creation of international customary and treaty law. But the opinions of international lawyers differ on the extent to which and whether General Assembly resolutions directly reflect *opinio iuris* (recognition of certain norms as legal) and are the evidence of States' practice; that is, the two main elements necessary for the formation of international legal custom. International lawyers more or less concur that norms of these resolutions are not yet customary law by themselves, but can become so if they have the appropriate legal content, convincing support, and are embodied in States' practice. The role of the resolutions General Assembly resolutions in the process of, so to speak, the "maturing" of international treaty law is not in doubt, but international lawyers one way or another admit that it is difficult to generalize the nature and degree of influence of the resolutions in this context. In general, the question of whether General Assembly resolutions can be considered, as *de lege ferenda*, to be an auxiliary source of international law remains ambiguous.

Even less clear is the opinion that the State support for a resolution during the voting in the General Assembly makes this act binding for it and a unilateral act. International lawyers point to possible additional manifestations of the external recognition by a State of the resolution as binding. Without changing the recommendatory nature of the resolution as such, a State can, of course, make this resolution a *de facto* part of its legislation. The proposal made by international lawyers to consider General Assembly resolutions as unilateral acts of an international organization does not affect the definition of their nature.

All the authors of the works analyzed herein acknowledge that the empirical (factual) and legal qualifications contained in General Assembly resolutions are based on the interpretation of international treaty and customary law. There is no doubt that such qualifications have normative significance and have an essential impact on both the behavior of States and the development of international law. International lawyers, however, taking into account the unsettled nature of the issue in the United Nations Charter, are not ready to give this normativity a legal character, to recognize General Assembly resolutions as interpretative legal acts. The recognition of the normativity of General Assembly resolutions is also reflected in the views of international lawyers on the meaning of their individual types (declarations and resolutions regarding specific situations) and the circumstances of adoption (indicators of support, the presence of reservations by States, repetition of resolutions).

With regard to the assessment in doctrinal writings of the specific features of the resolutions adopted by the General Assembly within the framework of the "Uniting for Peace" mechanism, the view expressed in political debates and in the positions of individual States, regarding the general inconsistency of this mechanism with the United Nations Charter is not perceived by Western international lawyers. The reservations of some authors regarding the use of this mechanism without the initiative of the Security Council, though still expressed, are mostly based on general out-of-context normativist or political considerations.

This cannot call into question either the real long-term practice of the General Assembly, or the meaning of judgements of the International Court of Justice, but instead should be perceived primarily as useful wishes. Optimists, critics, and skeptics in this matter agree that the essence of the General Assembly resolutions adopted within the framework of the "Uniting for Peace" mechanism is the authorization of the collective actions of the member States to implement their collective self-defense, and recently in addition the individual or collective implementation of the principle "responsibility to protect". There is essentially no difference between the skeptical (the "Uniting for Peace" mechanism does not have any added value) and optimistic (the expediency of this mechanism) positions, because, as already mentioned, the norms of the relevant resolution are integrated into the Rules of Procedure of the General Assembly. Opinions regarding the gradual replacement of the decisions of the Security Council with General Assembly resolutions are still analytical or prognostic, largely evaluative in nature, based on the development of the practice of United Nations organs, but do not affect the Charter of this organization.

Summarizing the consideration of international legal doctrine, there is a consensus among international lawyers regarding the political normative significance of General Assembly resolutions, their recognition as soft law, and their authorizing function based on the presumption (justified or not) of the legality or illegality of State conduct. The possibility of qualifying these resolutions as actual legal acts with binding effect is not provided for by the United Nations Charter. However, general studies of the impact of General Assembly resolutions on the development of international law, the evolution of the practice of their authorizing effect, the entry of reservations regarding them, and unilateral accession to them may lead to the formulation of the concept of customary institutional law of an international organization — by analogy, for example, with customary constitutional law of some modern States.

Regardless of the endless formal dispute regarding the legal or purely political significance of General Assembly resolutions, no one essentially denies that their provisions are a part of the, so to speak, international normative system and can generate significant consequences: they create a presumption of legality or illegality of certain actions of States; create an authoritative (albeit not formally normative), and sometimes consensual interpretation of acts of international law, provide qualifications for specific situations; authorize States individually and jointly to take or refrain from taking certain actions, create grounds for coordinating their actions; enable and legitimize actions of States that violate their other obligations in bilateral relations and within international organizations; and create grounds for decision-making by other intergovernmental and non-governmental international organizations. It is these consequences, and not the formal status of General Assembly resolutions, that played and continue to play an important role in countering Russian aggression, the processes of restoring Ukraine's territorial integrity, and holding the Russian Federation and its leadership accountable.

(3) When considering the significance of United Nations General Assembly resolutions dedicated to countering Russian aggression, we must take into account both the specific substance of their content and the circumstances of their adoption. However, both their legal content and political background and consequences are important.

Some of these issues are beyond the scope of this study, especially the potential impact of these resolutions on the development of international law. For example, all the provisions devoted to an aggressor's responsibility for crimes and damage caused require a detailed comparative study. Some formulations of types of crimes or types of harm caused may turn out to be innovative, which may later develop into norms of a general nature and require separate analysis.

First, the resolutions on countering Russian aggression are aimed at resolving a specific problem and are not directly aimed at creating general norms. The conclusions herein regarding the evolution of the understanding of the United Nations Charter regarding the regulation of the activities of the General Assembly and the development of the doctrinal interpretation of its powers give grounds for asserting that General Assembly resolutions on specific problems enjoy significant authority. The latter also informally depends on the results of the voting—the number of States that took part, the number of votes in support of the resolution, the positions of the most economically developed and the most populated States, individual regions of the world, and other factors.

By content, the "Ukrainian" General Assembly resolutions adopted between 2014 and 2023, can be divided into three groups: (1) the resolution "Territorial integrity of Ukraine" of 2014; (2) resolutions of regular sessions held between 2016 and 2023; (3) resolutions of the emergency session held in 2022-2023.

The short General Assembly Resolution "Territorial Integrity of Ukraine" was presented for consideration on 24 March 2014—at a time when the prospects for the expansion of Russian aggression were not yet clear, and Russian propaganda had a significant impact on the information field. This document did not clearly qualify the "situation" in Crimea as an international or internal conflict.

The parties to the conflict were not named, Ukraine is actually urged to properly protect the rights of national minorities and organize a political (not international) dialogue, States are urged to refrain from interfering in the conflict, and the Russian Federation is not directly mentioned.[265]

However, both in the title and in the content of the resolution, the principle of territorial integrity of Ukraine is emphasized, the "referendum" in Crimea is condemned and its results are not recognized (that is, both the "independence" of Autonomous Republic of Crimea and the city of Sevastopol, and their annexation by the Russian Federation—but without direct indications of this). There was a reference to the principles of non-recognition of territorial acquisitions resulting from the threat or use of force and to the peaceful settlement of international disputes. This middle-of-the-road and not fully defined nature enabled the Resolution to obtain substantial convincing support from United Nations members. But even under such conditions, the legalization of the "referendum" as an alleged realization of the right of the "people of Crimea" to self-determination, which Russia needed, did not take place. The territorial integrity of Ukraine was confirmed, but the resolution did not become a normative basis for the introduction of any measures against the Russian Federation at the global level.

From 2016 to 2023, the General Assembly adopted annual resolutions on the human rights situation in Crimea (in 2023—in all territories of Ukraine, occupied by Russian Federation), and from

---

[265] A linkage of the internal political situation in Ukraine, with its real and imagined problems, and the visible external invasion, despite all the obvious illogicality, was perceived as quite possible in 2014. Quite characteristically, the well-known Kazakh scholar Sergey Sayapin, when analyzing this resolution, noted: "The success of the political settlement will certainly affect the future of Ukraine both in the short-term and in the medium-term perspective, and will lay the foundation for its further development in the family of European nations"; "It is in the interests of Ukraine ... to implement all measures to ensure the equality of civil, social and cultural rights of all persons under its jurisdiction ...". See: S. Sayapin. "Территориальная целостность Украины в свете Резолюции 68/262 Генеральной Ассамблеи ООН" [Territorial Integrity of Ukraine in the light of the UN General Assembly Resolution 68/262]. Журнал конституционализма и прав человека [The Journal of Constitutionalism and Human Rights], nos. 1-2(5) (2014), pp. 75, 77.

2018 to 2021, also on the militarization of Crimea, the Black Sea, and the Sea of Azov. Despite the differences in the subject-matter of the resolutions, their content is similar in many respects and certain provisions were transferred from one group of documents to another. Each year they became more detailed, covering an increasing range of violations of international human rights law and international humanitarian law by the Russian Federation, as well as expressing concerns about Russian violations of arms control regimes.

All these resolutions contain an unequivocal condemnation of the temporary occupation regime and annexation of the Autonomous Republic of Crimea and the city of Sevastopol, the demand for the immediate withdrawal of Russian troops from the territory of Ukraine and the Russian navy from the territorial waters of Ukraine, and the qualification of the actions of the Russian Federation as continuing aggression.

All resolutions were supported by a sufficient number of member States, but the number of "yes" votes even in 2023 was lower than the number of abstentions, and in general, support for these acts before 2022 gradually declined year by year. A significant number of States (such as Azerbaijan) consistently avoided not only voting, but also being present in the hall during it. On one occasion (militarization issue in 2018), Ukraine even insisted on the adoption of a resolution by a qualified majority as a "decision on important question" (according to Article 18, United Nations Charter).

The formal adoption of all resolutions made it possible to apply several measures in support of Ukraine and against the Russian Federation by individual regional organizations. But the support of these resolutions was not convincing enough to perceive these acts as the will of the majority of States of the world, a truly "decision on important question" and a basis for some significant measures at the global level. The result of voting for the resolution on human rights in Crimea in 2022, although positive and formally the most favorable, was not convincing enough, and the draft resolution on militarization was not proposed during that or the next year.

The complex of resolutions of 2022-2023 regarding countering Russian aggression against Ukraine, the consequences of this aggression, and ensuring responsibility for it fundamentally differed from the previous group in terms of its nature, content, and level of support. All of them, except for the serial resolutions on the human rights situation on occupied territories, were adopted at the eleventh emergency special session of the General Assembly, the work of which has not yet been completed.

The reason for holding this session was the decision of the Security Council to refer to the General Assembly the issue of the security situation in Ukraine raised back in 2014. In itself, such a referral is uncommon because it involves the recognition by the Security Council of its inability to perform the charter duty assigned to it to maintain international peace and security. In contrast to substantive decisions, the decision to refer the matter to the General Assembly cannot be vetoed by permanent members of the Security Council.

Formal transfer of consideration of the issue does not mean a transfer by the Security Council of its powers to adopt binding decisions in the sphere of maintenance of international peace and security. And yet—this means that resolving a certain issue on behalf of the United Nations becomes the prerogative of another organ of this organization, namely the General Assembly. This presupposes a broad understanding of the General Assembly powers to recommend and the nature of the measures it recommends. The aspects of the problem that can be considered by the General Assembly are fundamentally expanded. When the issue was being discussed in the Security Council, the General Assembly did not have the authority to consider it in essence as a threat to or breach of international peace and security; the General Assembly had to confine itself to some ancillary aspects (such as, for example, human rights violations or the militarization of the territory).

The resolutions of this emergency session of the General Assembly directly refer to the 1950 "Uniting for Peace" Resolution, and there is no conflict with the powers of the Security Council, as in 1950. The General Assembly legitimately assumed the resolving of issues related to the aggression of the Russian Federation in Ukraine, albeit with the help of more limited means than those available to the Security Council. Although the 1950 resolution was severely criticized, it was never repealed or contested, and pursuant thereto the General Assembly may: establish the facts and provide their legal qualification, identify the aggressor, recommend to member states urgent collective measures, including the creation, authorization, and use of collective armed forces on behalf of the United Nations.

The special importance of the set of resolutions adopted at the 2022-2023 emergency session is emphasized by their adoption by a qualified majority (two-thirds) of State representatives present and vote. Besides the Resolution dedicated to the suspension of the Russian Federation membership on the United Nations Human Rights Council, the reasons for which are defined rather vaguely and generally, the other five resolutions were directly related to the Russian Federation aggression against Ukraine and its consequences.

These five resolutions qualify the actions of the Russian Federation as ongoing aggression and attempted annexation, and the actions of Belarus as complicity in aggression. Illegal entities on the territory of Ukraine, later incorporated into the Russian Federation, are recognized as being under the temporary military control of the Russian Federation. "Referendums" regarding their independence and decisions regarding their inclusion into the Russian Federation are recognized as null and void. The call in the first of these resolutions (dated 2 March 2022) to return to the Minsk Agreements in subsequent acts is no longer repeated.

Instead, it is declared that a comprehensive, just, and lasting peace can be established only on the basis of the territorial integrity of Ukraine, and this should also include punishment for the most serious crimes under international law. All these provisions won the support of no less than 140 States when voting with a minimum number (5 to 7) of votes against. The Resolution dedicated to remedy and reparation for aggression against Ukraine gained less support, although it was sufficient for adoption. It provided for the responsibility of the Russian Federation for any damage caused by its aggression against Ukraine, the creation of an international register of this damage, and for the formation of an unspecified international mechanism for reparation for damage, loss or injury, arising from the internationally wrongful acts of the Russian Federation in or against Ukraine.

The alternative proposals of South Africa, Belarus, and Nicaragua were convincingly rejected: to absolve the Russian Federation of responsibility, justify its actions with reference to the alleged escalation of the conflict in Ukraine from internal to a conflict involving a third State, as well as stating the impelled character of Russian Federation actions caused by its security concerns; call for the cessation of the supply of weapons to Ukraine and the cessation of hostilities based on the current front line.

The consideration of draft General Assembly resolutions reflected the features of the current political situation in the world and the trends of development, which is important for clarifying the foreign policy priorities of Ukraine. Therefore, it was entirely appropriate to indicate the voting results of States that did not support the adoption of these resolutions—especially, certain post-Soviet countries (members of the Collective Security Treaty Organization and Uzbekistan), as well as heavily populated and economically significant States of the "Global South"—China, India, Nigeria, Brazil, South Africa, Mexico. Some trends can be traced to the change in their voting—the further gradual stratification of these groups of States and a significant decrease in the official support of the Russian Federation by most after the full-scale invasion into Ukraine.

Support for preserving the territorial integrity of Ukraine by the Western countries and other States in the General Assembly between 2014 and 2021 was not sufficiently consistent and evident. The blurring of formulations and qualifications on the cusp of the distinction between internal and international conflicts, the reference to the Minsk Agreements, and the weak and gradually lessening support for the resolutions left a theoretical or even actual opportunity for a retreat from the principles and norms of international law and the abandonment of vital Ukrainian interests.

The arguments of the Russian Federation, being in essence absurd and null, had a chance to gradually gain greater support and recognition in substance within the context of the positions of anti-Western, post-colonial, and authoritarian States. Formal references to the people's right to self-determination, abuse of minority rights, and the like always can be recalled, whether or not sincerely, on the basis of objective information or manipulation.

But starting from 2022, the General Assembly resolutions demonstrate that the West can no longer refuse to support Ukraine. The aggression is perceived as a direct challenge to own security, own values, and the existing system of international law. This significantly affects also the positions of a large number of non-Western States.

Moreover, the analysis of the process of consideration of the "Ukrainian" resolutions of 2014 to 2023 makes it possible to reach the following general conclusions of a political nature. First, it is important to take into account not only normatively significant votes "for" and "against", and not only the recorded position of certain States on abstention from voting. The list of States whose representatives are present, but do not participate in all or practically all votes on resolutions fundamentally important for Ukraine, is of significant importance. Perhaps the position of the latter is due to pressure on them (it is known that the Russian Federation directly blackmails member states), their difficult political situation, or the hope of receiving benefits for any solution to this or that issue. In any case, it would be an exaggeration to assume, based on the convincing voting results for some of the "Ukrainian" resolutions in 2022-2023, that a reliable, long-term, conscious majority of States has been formed in support of preserving the independence and territorial integrity of Ukraine and ending the aggression of the Russian Federation.

Second, the results of the discussion of the resolutions have both legal and political significance. One should take into account not only alternative draft resolutions, draft amendments, and the voting outcomes, or the direct textual reservations entered by States, but also their expressed vision of the essence of the adopted resolutions. The expressed positions reflected a wider range of opinions, ideas, and doubts than the general support or rejection of an individual resolution.

Other indicators are important — for example, a negative indicator from 2014 to 2021 was a gradual decrease in the number of

States that submitted "Ukrainian" draft resolutions for consideration, as well as the lack of discussion when considering "serial", but dynamic, relevant drafts. This may testify to the insignificant interest on the part of many member States and/or to a gradual loss of support—especially against the background of the simultaneous more significant support of other resolutions in this same area.

Third, the determining motive of a significant, if not overwhelming, number of States when voting for the "Ukrainian" resolutions was the restoration of peace as an end to the war—regardless of considering the causes or assessing the consequences for preserving the territorial integrity of Ukraine or stopping Russian aggression. Whereas for Ukrainians the matter is about the preservation of their State, country and the lives of their citizens, along with moral values and international law, then for a significant number of States it is only about the restoration of peace and the functioning of their economies. Therefore, many United Nations members and influential observers preferred in one way or another to block or "smooth down" resolutions regarding Russian aggression, allegedly in order to enable a bilateral negotiated solution to the problem between Ukraine and the Russian Federation without prejudicing their own political and economic interests from the introduction of anti-Russian sanctions.

The large-scale war crimes of the Russian Federation in Ukraine in 2022-2023 and the impossibility of substantiating the expediency or accidental character of their commission, as well as the unequivocal and tough position of the West, significantly influenced the orientation of many States. They became inclined to see peace as the need to improve the humanitarian situation and restore the pre-war state of affairs. This may also involve the restoration of the territorial integrity of Ukraine. But a consensus or convincing support for ensuring the responsibility of the Russian Federation and punishing its political and military leadership, the perpetrators of war crimes, has not yet been reached. Even the existing agreement cannot be perceived as stable or enduring, especially considering the calls of representatives of a number of States not to mix humanitarian issues with the "root causes of the conflict".

Fourth, in the process of consideration and voting on these resolutions, other political factors were revealed, which are generally not new, but were applied to the subject of these acts. Of importance is the existence of a strong anti-colonial position on the part of the countries of Latin America, Africa, Asia, Oceania, and the Caribbean region. There is a deep distrust of any actions of the West, unwillingness to deal with matters related to relations between Western States, dissatisfaction with the overly meticulous (in their opinion) attention of the General Assembly to problems with democracy and human rights in these States and seeing double standards in this, and efforts to benefit (economic benefit or satisfaction due for a history of oppression) from the contradictions between them.

Such positions are embodied in the activities of the intergovernmental organization "Group of 77", which currently includes 133 United Nations members and Palestine, adopts decisions in a joint format with China, and encompasses almost all States of the "Global South", and constantly promotes within and outside the United Nations system an increase of international assistance to its member States and the idea of redistributing economic wealth in their favor from the always guilty and unjust West, while strongly opposes any potential interference of United Nations in internal processes within these States.[266] This affects the support or non-support of Ukraine, which is considered as an ally or a part of the West, and the position towards the Russian Federation, which is considered as the rival of the West.

Fifth, many authoritarian and totalitarian States, primarily from the "Global South", negatively perceive any consideration of issues related to mass violations of human rights and the application of certain measures against States and their governments in this regard as a practice potentially threatening them. This conditional Authoritarian International acts under the slogans of non-admittance of the politicization of the human rights situation, the

---

[266] See for example: Statement on Behalf of the Group of 77 and China by the Delegation of the Republic of Cuba at the Informal Consultation on the Chapter 3 for the Zero Draft of the Pact for the Future (New York, 11 December 2023). *The Group of 77 at the United Nations*. (available online).

ambiguity and vague character of any problems, and their generation by geopolitical rivalry. These States easily unite against any relevant resolutions (except, as practice shows, resolutions condemning Israel's actions against the Palestinian people).

Worthy of mention in this regard was the creation in 2021 of the "Group of Friends in Defense of the Charter of the United Nations", which consists of eighteen States (Algeria, Belarus, Bolivia, Cambodia, China, Cuba, DPRK, Equatorial Guinea, Eritrea, Iran, Laos, Mali, Nicaragua, Russian Federation, Saint Vincent and the Grenadines, Syria, Venezuela, Zimbabwe), as well as the partially recognized State of Palestine (formerly Angola was also a member of the group).[267] As stated in the "Concept Note" of this Association, the threat of unilateral policy, currently growing in the world, manifests itself in "isolationist and arbitrary actions, including the imposition of unilateral coercive measures", "disowning the diversity of our world", harming countries that are developing through an engaged assessment of their fulfillment of international obligations, and so on. Among the priorities of this group is protection of the principle of non-interference in the internal affairs of States and opposition to forceful measures (it is not specified who is imposing them, but the group is fully represented only in the United Nations General Assembly). The main form of achieving the group's goals is the coordination of its members' activities in the United Nations General Assembly.[268] The group website added the rejection of the international "so-called 'rules-based order' with norms that remain unknown and have not been necessarily agreed upon by States".[269] The permanent representative of Ukraine at the United Nations,

---

267 About Us. *Group of Friends in Defense of the Charter of the United Nations* (available online).
268 Concept Note of the Group of Friends in Defense of the Charter of the United Nations, including background, objectives and format. New York, 6 July 2021. *Group of Friends in Defense of the Charter of the United Nations.* See also: Political Declaration adopted during the first ministerial meeting of the Group of Friends in Defense of the Charter of the United Nations, New York, 23 September 2021. *The Ministry of Foreign Affairs of the Russian Federation.* (available online).
269 About Us, note 266 above.

Sergiy Kyslytsya, has drawn attention to the activities of this group.[270]

One of the major objectives of the group is to prevent General Assembly resolutions from being understood as binding—especially regarding the assessment of the human rights situation in members of this association, as well as the possibility of applying collective measures against individual States. The members of the group (mostly States that retain socialist features of development in the economy and politics, as well as those that are under significant financial, political, and military control of the Russian Federation), except for Saint Vincent and the Grenadines, have never condemned the aggressive war of the Russian Federation against Ukraine and jointly took a clear anti-Ukrainian position when relevant draft resolutions were considered.[271]

Sixth, a significant factor is the position of China and several other States, which consider Russian aggression against Ukraine in the context of geopolitical confrontation and geopolitical interests of their own countries. This presupposes the situational nature of their voting and causes them to express doubts about the legal nature of United Nations General Assembly resolutions in the field of maintaining international peace and security.

Seventh, the evolution of consideration of "Ukrainian" resolutions in the General Assembly in the context of the Russian challenge to neighboring States (together with the qualification of the USSR as a virtually unitary State with purely administrative internal divisions) indicates the erosion of the concept of "post-Soviet space". The Russian Federation gradually lost the support of the members of the Commonwealth of Independent States and the Collective Security Treaty Organization, which avoid direct support of

---

[270] S. Kyslytsya. "Група з підриву Статуту ООН: як Росія та її друзі планують 'захищати' організацію" [Group to Undermine the UN Charter: How Russia and its Friends Plan to 'Protect' the Organization]. *Європейська правда* [European Pravda]. 17 February 2022. (available online).
[271] See for example: Promotion and protection of human rights: human rights situations and reports of special rapporteurs and representatives. Report of the Third Committee. 30 November 2023. A/78/481/Add.3.

Russia, supporting Ukraine, preferring to abstain from voting or not participate in it.

Some recommendations regarding the realization of the legal potential of the General Assembly resolutions have to be further emphasized.

(1) First, given the difficulty of creating an *ad hoc* international tribunal to bring the Russian Federation and its political and military leadership to responsibility and the impossibility of adjudicating the crime of aggression by the Russian Federation at the International Criminal Court, the provisions of Resolution ES-11/5 should be further elaborated and implemented (by concluding an agreement between the United Nations or group of member States and Ukraine) regarding the creation of an international or hybrid mechanism for reparation of damage, loss, or injury caused by the Russian Federation, as well as an international register of damage. In this regard, the personnel, financial, and technical capabilities of the Independent International Commission of Inquiry on Ukraine, established in 2022, should also be expanded as much as possible.

(2) It is possible and important to apply for an advisory opinion to the International Court of Justice regarding the legality of the continuation or succession of the Russian Federation to the Union of Soviet Socialist Republics — both as a member of the United Nations and as a member of the United Nations Security Council. In addition, having committed the crime of aggression against a sovereign State, flagrant and systematic violations of human rights, as well as a well-founded suspicion of a serious and systematic violation of international humanitarian law, which together points to the criminality of the ruling regime, the recognition of credentials of the Russian Federation representatives to the United Nations may be terminated, which will suspend their participation in the work of all organs of this organization. An additional important reason for this may be the results of the presidential elections in the Russian Federation in the March 2024 — the legitimacy of the elected President (and, accordingly, the Government of the Russian Federation appointed by him) is undermined with the holding of elections at the occupied territories of Ukraine, not even to mention the problems of constitutional and legal basis and features of these elections.

But this would require the adoption of a relevant resolution of the General Assembly.

(3) It is appropriate to consider the issue of initiating peacekeeping operations of a military and police character on the territory of Ukraine by a General Assembly resolution, in particular on the borders with Belarus and Moldova (its temporarily occupied Transnistrian region), as well as for the protection of all nuclear power plants and storages of spent nuclear fuel, including those located in temporarily occupied territories.

(4) It is likely that member States will support a potential General Assembly resolution regarding the establishment of a trade and transport embargo against the Russian Federation, in particular regarding weapons, components thereof, military equipment, dual-use materials, industrial and high-tech equipment, microcircuits, oil, petroleum products, liquefied gas, gold and diamonds, grain and fertilizers, and others.

In conclusion, it is worth recalling the words of Italian President Sergio Mattarella: The "fragmented world war" that is going on today can "create false perspectives, deceiving our ability to analyze and understand". It may appear that this is "the end of a system based on common rules" and the beginning of an "era of chaos" in the world, when everything is allowed, where "an act of aggression is no longer prohibited as a violation, but on the contrary, even justified by alleged national interests". Before us is the same wave of destabilization of international law that once led to the creation of the United Nations. And yes, shortcomings and limitations of this organization are known, they are determined by the "political will of the states that are part of it". But "we must realize that in order to survive, our planet definitely needs a multilateral system capable of developing forms of cooperation and integration".[272]

Criticism of the significance of the activities of the General Assembly and skepticism regarding the normativity or effectiveness of its resolutions should be scholarly and balanced. The dialectic of

---

[272] Intervento del Presidente della Repubblica Sergio Mattarella in occasione della Cerimonia per lo scambio degli auguri di fine anno con il Corpo Diplomatico. 15 December 2023. (available online).

optimism and pessimism here is irrational and unproductive. The General Assembly is composed of representatives of almost all States gathered in one organ, with all the diversity and contradictions of the world that they reflect. And despite the significant charter restrictions on the activity of this organ, there is no other real, rather than imagined, alternative—only to argue and prove one's position, study in detail and use correctly the available arsenal of resolutions and means of the United Nations General Assembly.

Sources and Literature

I Resolutions, other acts, and documents of the United Nations and other international organizations, judgments of international courts, international treaties, national legislation

2005 World Summit Outcome. Resolution 60/1 adopted by the General Assembly on 16 September 2005.

A/73/L.68. Iran (Islamic Republic of) and Syrian Arab Republic: amendment to draft resolution A/73/L.47 Problem of the militarization of the Autonomous Republic of Crimea and the city of Sevastopol, Ukraine, as well as parts of the Black Sea and the Sea of Azov. 13 December 2018.

Additional measures to be employed to meet the aggression in Korea. Resolution 500 (5) adopted by the General Assembly. 18 May 1951.

Aggression against Ukraine. Draft resolution A/ES-11/L.1. 1 March 2022.

Aggression against Ukraine. Resolution ES-11/1 adopted by the General Assembly on 2 March 2022.

Agreement Between the United Nations and the Royal Government of Cambodia Concerning the Prosecution Under Cambodian Law of Crimes Committed During the Period of Democratic Kampuchea. *United Nations Treaty Series. Treaties and international agreements registered or filed and recorded with the Secretariat of the United Nations.* 2005. Vol. 2329.

Announcement of U.S. Support for the United Nations Declaration on the Rights of Indigenous Peoples. U.S. Department of State (December 16, 2010). URL: https://2009-2017.state.gov/documents/organization/184099.pdf

Basic Principles and Guidelines on the Right to a Remedy and Reparation for Victims of Gross Violations of International Human Rights Law and Serious Violations of International Humanitarian Law. Resolution 60/147 adopted by the General Assembly on 16 December 2005.

Belarus, Democratic People's Republic of Korea, Russian Federation and Syrian Arab Republic: draft resolution. Security Council. S/2022/231. 23 March 2022.

Case concerning military and paramilitary activities in and against Nicaragua (Nicaragua vs. United States of America. Merits. Judgement of 27 June 1986. *International Court of Justice. Reports of judgements, advisory opinions and orders.* 1986.

Certain Expenses of the United Nations. Advisory opinion of 20 July 1962. *International Court of Justice. Reports of judgements, advisory opinions and orders.* 1962.

Competence of the General Assembly for the Admission of a State to the United Nations. Advisory opinion of March 3rd, 1950. *International Court of Justice. Reports of judgements, advisory opinions and orders.* 1950.

Concept Note of the Group of Friends in Defense of the Charter of the United Nations, including background, objectives and format. New York, 06 July 2021. *Group of Friends in Defense of the Charter of the United Nations.* URL: https://www.gof-uncharter.org/portfolio-collections/my-portfolio/project-6-1-e1c79e-1-1-1-1-5f67f7

Definition of Aggression. Resolution 3314 (XXIX) adopted by the General Assembly on 14 December 1974

Establishment of the United Nations Register of Damage Caused by the Construction of the Wall in the Occupied Palestinian Territory. Resolution ES-10/17 adopted by the General Assembly 15 December 2006.

Formation and evidence of customary international law. Elements in the previous work of the International Law Commission that could be particularly relevant to the topic. Memorandum by the Secretariat. 14 March 2013. A/CN.4/659.

Furtherance of remedy and reparation for aggression against Ukraine. Resolution ES-11/5 adopted by the General Assembly on 14 November 2022.

Furtherance of remedy and reparation for aggression against Ukraine. Draft resolution A/ES-11/L.6. 7 November 2022.

General Assembly Holds First-Ever Debate on Historic Veto Resolution, Adopts Texts on Infrastructure, National Reviews, Council of Europe Cooperation. Press-release of the seventy-seventh UN General Assembly session, 68th and 69th meetings. GA/12500. 26 April 2023. URL: https://reliefweb.int/report/world/general-assembly-holds-first-ever-debate-historic-veto-resolution-adopts-texts-infrastructure-national-reviews-council-europe-cooperation

Human Rights Council. Resolution 60/251 adopted by the General Assembly on 15 March 2006.

Humanitarian consequences of the aggression against Ukraine. Draft resolution A/ES-11/L.2. 21 March 2022.

Humanitarian consequences of the aggression against Ukraine. Resolution ES-11/2 adopted by the General Assembly on 24 March 2022.

Humanitarian situation emanating out of the conflict in Ukraine. Draft resolution A/ES-11/L.3. 22 March 2022.

Identification of Customary International Law [Agenda item 9]. Document A/CN.4/672. Second report on identification of customary international law, by Sir Michael Wood, Special Rapporteur. 22 May 2014.

International Criminal Tribunal for the Former Yugoslavia. Prosecutor v. Tadic. Case No. IT-94-1-I. Decision on Defense Motion for Interlocutory Appeal on Jurisdiction. October 2, 1995. URL: https://www.icty.org/x/cases/tadic/acdec/en/51002.htm

International, Impartial and Independent Mechanism to Assist in the Investigation and Prosecution of Persons Responsible for the Most Serious Crimes under International Law Committed in the Syrian Arab Republic since March 2011. Resolution 71/248 adopted by the General Assembly on 21 December 2016.

Interpretation of the Charter. Doc. 887. IV/2/39. June 9, 1945. *Documents of the United Nations Conference on the International Organization*. San Francisco, 1945. Vol. XIII: Commission IV Judicial Organization. London, New York: United Nations Information Organizations, 1945.

Intervention of the Central People's Government of the People's Republic of China in Korea. Resolution 498 (5) adopted by the General Assembly. 1 February 1951.

Khmer Rouge trials. Resolution 57/228 adopted by the General Assembly. 18 December 2002.

Legal Consequences of the Construction of a Wall in the Occupied Palestinian Territory. Advisory opinion of 9 July 2004. *International Court of Justice. Reports of judgements, advisory opinions and orders*. 2004.

Legality of the Threat or Use of Nuclear Weapons. Advisory opinion of 8 July 1996. *International Court of Justice. Reports of judgements, advisory opinions and orders*. 1996.

Letter dated 28 February 2014 from the Permanent Representative of Ukraine Yuriy Sergeyev to the United Nations addressed to the President of the Security Council (S/2014/136).

Observations of the United States with respect to the Declaration on the Rights of Indigenous Peoples. URL: https://archive.vn/20070612010029/http://www.un.int/usa/press_releases/20070913_204.html#selection-309.0-311.44

Political Declaration adopted during the first ministerial meeting of the Group of Friends in Defense of the Charter of the United Nations, New York, September 23, 2021. *The Ministry of Foreign Affairs of the Russian Federation*. URL: https://archive.mid.ru/en/foreign_policy/news/-/asset_publisher/cKNonkJE02Bw/content/id/4865844

Principles of the Charter of the United Nations underlying a comprehensive, just and lasting peace in Ukraine. Resolution ES-11/6 adopted by the General Assembly on 23 February 2023.

Principles of the Charter of the United Nations underlying a comprehensive, just and lasting peace in Ukraine. Draft resolution A/ES-11/L.7. 16 February 2023.

Principles of the Charter of the United Nations underlying a comprehensive, just and lasting peace in Ukraine. Draft amendment to draft resolution A/ES-11/L.7. A/ES-11/L.8. 21 February 2023.

Principles of the Charter of the United Nations underlying a comprehensive, just and lasting peace in Ukraine. Draft amendment to draft resolution A/ES-11/L.7. A/ES-11/L.9. 21 February 2023.

Problem of the militarization of the Autonomous Republic of Crimea and the city of Sevastopol, Ukraine, as well as parts of the Black Sea and the Sea of Azov. Resolution 73/194 adopted by the General Assembly on 17 December 2018.

Problem of the militarization of the Autonomous Republic of Crimea and the city of Sevastopol, Ukraine, as well as parts of the Black Sea and the Sea of Azov. Draft resolution A/73/L.47. 5 December 2018.

Problem of the militarization of the Autonomous Republic of Crimea and the city of Sevastopol, Ukraine, as well as parts of the Black Sea and the Sea of Azov. Resolution 74/17 adopted by the General Assembly on 9 December 2019.

Problem of the militarization of the Autonomous Republic of Crimea and the city of Sevastopol, Ukraine, as well as parts of the Black Sea and the Sea of Azov. Revised draft resolution: addendum A/74/L.12/Rev.1/Add.1. 9 December 2019.

Problem of the militarization of the Autonomous Republic of Crimea and the city of Sevastopol, Ukraine, as well as parts of the Black Sea and the Sea of Azov. Resolution 75/29 adopted by the General Assembly on 7 December 2020.

Problem of the militarization of the Autonomous Republic of Crimea and the city of Sevastopol, Ukraine, as well as parts of the Black Sea and the Sea of Azov. Revised draft resolution: addendum A/75/L.38/Rev.1/Add.1. 7 December 2020.

Problem of the militarization of the Autonomous Republic of Crimea and the city of Sevastopol, Ukraine, as well as parts of the Black Sea and the Sea of Azov. Resolution 76/70 adopted by the General Assembly on 9 December 2021.

Problem of the militarization of the Autonomous Republic of Crimea and the city of Sevastopol, Ukraine, as well as parts of the Black Sea and the Sea of Azov. Draft resolution: addendum A/76/L.22/Add.1. 9 December 2021.

Sources and Literature   159

Promotion and protection of human rights: human rights situations and reports of special rapporteurs and representatives. Report of the Third Committee. 30 November 2023. A/78/481/Add.3.

Provisional Rules of Procedure for the General Assembly (As amended during the first and second parts of the first session). Lake Success, New York: United Nations, 1947.

Question of equitable representation on and increase in the membership of the Security Council and related matters. Decision A/DEC/62/557 adopted by UN Security Council adopted at 122nd plenary meeting. 15 September 2008.

Reparation for Injuries Suffered in the Service of the United Nations. Advisory opinion of 11 April 1949. *International Court of Justice. Reports of judgements, advisory opinions and orders*. 1949. Leiden: A.W. Sijthoff's Publishing Company, 1949.

Report of the detailed findings of the commission of inquiry on human rights in the Democratic People's Republic of Korea. Human Rights Council. A/HRC/25/CRP.1. 7 February 2014.

Report of the Rapporteur of Committee IV/2, as Approved by the Committee. Doc. 933. IV/2/42 (2). June 12, 1945. *Documents of the United Nations Conference on the International Organization*. San Francisco, 1945. Vol. XIII: Commission IV Judicial Organization. London, New York: United Nations Information Organizations, 1945.

Resolution 2202 (2015). Adopted by the Security Council at its 7384th meeting, on 17 February 2015.

Resolution 2623 (2022) adopted by the Security Council at its 8980th meeting, on 27 February 2022.

Revised Summary Report of Fourteen Meeting of Committee IV/2. Doc. 873. IV/2/37. June 9, 1945. *Documents of the United Nations Conference on the International Organization*. San Francisco, 1945. Vol. XIII: Commission IV Judicial Organization. London, New York: United Nations Information Organizations, 1945.

Revitalization of the General Assembly. Resolution adopted by the General Assembly on 8 September 2006. A/RES/60/286.

Rules of Procedure of the General Assembly (embodying amendments and additions adopted by the General Assembly up to and including its seventy-fifth session). A/520/Rev*. New York: United Nations, 2022.

Security Council Deadlocks and Uniting for Peace: An Abridged History / Security Council Report. October 2013. URL: https://www.security councilreport.org/atf/cf/%7B65BFCF9B-6D27-4E9C-8CD3-CF6E4F F96FF9%7D/Security_Council_Deadlocks_and_Uniting_for_Peace. pdf

Security Council. 8980th meeting. Sunday, 27 February 2022. S/PV.8980.

Security Council. 9002nd meeting. 23 March 2022. S/PV.9002.

Situation of human rights in the Autonomous Republic of Crimea and the city of Sevastopol (Ukraine). Resolution 71/205 adopted by the General Assembly on 19 December 2016.

Situation of human rights in the Autonomous Republic of Crimea and the city of Sevastopol (Ukraine). Draft resolution A/C.3/71/L.26. 31 October 2016.

Situation of human rights in the Autonomous Republic of Crimea and the city of Sevastopol, Ukraine. Resolution 72/190 adopted by the General Assembly on 19 December 2017.

Situation of human rights in the Autonomous Republic of Crimea and the city of Sevastopol, Ukraine. Draft resolution A/C.3/72/L.42

Situation of human rights in the Autonomous Republic of Crimea and the city of Sevastopol, Ukraine. Resolution 73/263 adopted by the General Assembly on 22 December 2018.

Situation of human rights in the Autonomous Republic of Crimea and the city of Sevastopol, Ukraine. Draft resolution A/C.3/73/L.48. 31 October 2018.

Situation of human rights in the Autonomous Republic of Crimea and the city of Sevastopol, Ukraine. Resolution 74/168 adopted by the General Assembly on 18 December 2019.

Situation of human rights in the Autonomous Republic of Crimea and the city of Sevastopol, Ukraine. Draft resolution A/C.3/74/L.28. 31 October 2019.

Situation of human rights in the Autonomous Republic of Crimea and the city of Sevastopol, Ukraine. Resolution 75/192 adopted by the General Assembly on 16 December 2020.

Situation of human rights in the Autonomous Republic of Crimea and the city of Sevastopol, Ukraine. Draft resolution A/C.3/75/L.32. 30 October 2020.

Situation of human rights in the Democratic People's Republic of Korea. Resolution 22/13 adopted by the Human Rights Council. 21 March 2013.

Situation of human rights in the temporarily occupied Autonomous Republic of Crimea and the city of Sevastopol, Ukraine. Resolution 76/179 adopted by the General Assembly on 16 December 2021.

Situation of human rights in the temporarily occupied Autonomous Republic of Crimea and the city of Sevastopol, Ukraine. Draft resolution A/C.3/76/L.29. 28 October 2021.

Situation of human rights in the temporarily occupied Autonomous Republic of Crimea and the city of Sevastopol, Ukraine. Resolution 77/229 adopted by the General Assembly on 15 December 2022.

Situation of human rights in the temporarily occupied Autonomous Republic of Crimea and the city of Sevastopol, Ukraine. Draft resolution A/C.3/77/L.35. 1 November 2022.

Situation of human rights in the temporarily occupied territories of Ukraine, including the Autonomous Republic of Crimea and the city of Sevastopol. Resolution 78/221 adopted by the General Assembly on 19 December 2023.

Situation of human rights in the temporarily occupied territories of Ukraine, including the Autonomous Republic of Crimea and the city of Sevastopol. Draft resolution A/C.3/78/L.42. 31 October 2023.

Situation of human rights in the temporarily occupied territories of Ukraine, including the Autonomous Republic of Crimea and the city of Sevastopol: resolution / adopted by the General Assembly. Voting Summary. 19.12.2023. URL: https://digitallibrary.un.org/record/4030715?ln=en

Situation of human rights in Ukraine stemming from the Russian aggression. Resolution 49/1 adopted by the Human Rights Council on 4 March 2022.

Situation of human rights of Rohingya Muslims and other minorities in Myanmar. Resolution 39/2 adopted by the Human Rights Council on 27 September 2018.

South West Africa Cases (Ethiopia v. South Africa; Liberia v. South Africa). Second phase. Judgement of 18 July 1966. *International Court of Justice. Reports of judgements, advisory opinions and orders*. 1966.

Standing mandate for a General Assembly debate when a veto is cast in the Security Council. Resolution A/RES/76/262 adopted by the General Assembly on 26 April 2022.

Statement on Behalf of the Group of 77 and China by the Delegation of the Republic of Cuba at the Informal Consultation on the Chapter 3 for the Zero Draft of the Pact for the Future (New York, 11 December 2023). *The Group of 77 at the United Nations*. URL: https://www.g77.org/statement/getstatement.php?id=231211b

Summary Report of Fourteenth Meeting of Committee IV/2. Doc. 843. IV/2/37. June 7, 1945. *Documents of the United Nations Conference on the International Organization*. San Francisco, 1945. Vol. XIII: Commission IV Judicial Organization. London, New York: United Nations Information Organizations, 1945.

Summary Report of Twelfth Meeting of Committee IV/2. Doc. 664. IV/2/33. May 29, 1945. *Documents of the United Nations Conference on the International Organization.* San Francisco, 1945. Vol. XIII: Commission IV Judicial Organization. London, New York: United Nations Information Organizations, 1945.

Suspension of the rights of membership of the Russian Federation in the Human Rights Council. Resolution ES-11/3 adopted by the General Assembly on 7 April 2022.

Suspension of the rights of membership of the Russian Federation in the Human Rights Council. Draft resolution A/ES-11/L.4. 6 April 2022.

Territorial integrity of Ukraine. Draft resolution A/68/L.39. 24 March 2014.

Territorial integrity of Ukraine. Resolution 68/262, adopted by the General Assembly on 27 March 2014.

Territorial integrity of Ukraine: defending the principles of the Charter of the United Nations. Resolution ES-11/4 adopted by the General Assembly on 12 October 2022.

Territorial integrity of Ukraine: defending the principles of the Charter of the United Nations. Draft resolution A/ES-11/L.5. 7 October 2022.

United Nations Charter. URL: https://www.un.org/en/about-us/un-charter/full-text

United Nations General Assembly. Eleventh Emergency Special session. 5th plenary meeting. Official records. A/ES-11/PV.5. 2 March 2022.

United Nations General Assembly. Eleventh Emergency Special session. 9th plenary meeting. Official records. A/ES-11/PV.9. 24 March 2022.

United Nations General Assembly. Eleventh Emergency Special session. 7th plenary meeting. Official records. A/ES-11/PV.7. 23 March 2022.

United Nations General Assembly. Eleventh Emergency Special session. 8th plenary meeting. Official records. A/ES-11/PV.8. 23 March 2022.

United Nations General Assembly. Eleventh Emergency Special session. 9th plenary meeting. Official records. A/ES-11/PV.10. 7 April 2022.

United Nations General Assembly. Eleventh Emergency Special session. 14th plenary meeting. Official records. A/ES-11/PV.14. 12 October 2022.

United Nations General Assembly. Eleventh Emergency Special session. 15th plenary meeting. Official records. A/ES-11/PV.15. 14 November 2022.

United Nations General Assembly. Eleventh Emergency Special session. 19th plenary meeting. Official records. A/ES-11/PV.19. 23 February 2023.

SOURCES AND LITERATURE 163

United Nations General Assembly. Seventy-fifth session. 36th plenary meeting. Official records. A/75/PV.36. 7 December 2020.

United Nations General Assembly. Seventy-fifth session. 46th plenary meeting. Official records. A/75/PV.46. 16 December 2020.

United Nations General Assembly. Seventy-first session. 65th plenary meeting. Official records. A/71/PV.65. 19 December 2016.

United Nations General Assembly. Seventy-first session. Agenda item 68 (c). Promotion and protection of human rights: human rights situations and reports of special rapporteurs and representatives. Report of the Third Committee. A/71/484/Add.3. 7 December 2016.

United Nations General Assembly. Seventy-fourth session. 41st plenary meeting. Official records. A/74/PV.41. 9 December 2019.

United Nations General Assembly. Seventy-fourth session. 50th plenary meeting. Official records. A/74/PV.50. 18 December 2019.

United Nations General Assembly. Seventy-second session. 73rd plenary meeting. Official records. A/72/PV.73. 19 December 2017.

United Nations General Assembly. Seventy-seventh session. 54th plenary meeting. Official records. A/77/PV.54. 15 December 2022.

United Nations General Assembly. Seventy-sixth session. 48th plenary meeting. Official records. A/76/PV.48*. 9 December 2021.

United Nations General Assembly. Seventy-sixth session. 53rd plenary meeting. Official records. A/76/PV.53. 16 December 2021.

United Nations General Assembly. Seventy-third session. 56th plenary meeting. Official records. A/73/PV.56. 17 December 2018.

United Nations General Assembly. Seventy-third session. 65th plenary meeting. Official records. A/73/PV.65. 21 December 2018.

United Nations General Assembly. Sixty-eight session. 80th plenary meeting. Official records. A/68/PV.80. 27 March 2014.

Uniting for peace. Resolution 377 (V) adopted by the General Assembly on 3 November 1950.

Use of the terms "declaration" and "recommendation". Memorandum by the Office of Legal Affairs. UN doc. E/CN.4/L.610. 2 April 1962. URL: https://undocs.org/Home/Mobile?FinalSymbol=E%2FCN.4%2FL.610&Language=E&DeviceType=Desktop&LangRequested=False

Vienna Convention on the Law of Treaties of 1969. URL: https://legal.un.org/ilc/texts/instruments/english/conventions/1_1_1969.pdf

'We Don't Have a Moment to Lose', Secretary-General Tells General Assembly's Emergency Special Session on Ukraine as Speakers Debate Draft Resolution. Eleventh Emergency Special Session, 17th Meeting (PM). 22 February 2023. URL: https://press.un.org/en/2023/ga12491.doc.htm?_gl=1*1l34zav*_ga*MzYyOTc3NzYzLjE2OTMxMjk1Nzc.*_ga_TK9BQL5X7Z*MTY5OTQ1ODg1NC4zNC4xLjE2OTk0NjAzMDkuMC4wLjA

With 143 Votes in Favour, 5 Against, General Assembly Adopts Resolution Condemning Russian Federation's Annexation of Four Eastern Ukraine Regions. Press-release GA/12458. 12 October 2022. URL: https://press.un.org/en/2022/ga12458.doc.htm?_gl=1*6s6cbp*_ga*MzYyOTc3NzYzLjE2OTMxMjk1Nzc.*_ga_TK9BQL5X7Z*MTY5OTIxMTg2NS4zMS4xLjE2OTkyMTE4NzcuMC4wLjA

II. Scholarly publications

Ahmad N. The Erosion of the Prohibition on the Use of Force in the Face of United Nations Security Council Inaction: How Can the United Nations General Assembly Maintain International Peace? *Chicago Journal of International Law Online*. 2002. Vol. 1. No. 2.

Arangio-Ruiz G. The concept of international law and the theory of international organization / Arangio-Ruiz G. The United Nations Declaration on Friendly Relations and the system of the sources of international law. Alphen aan den Rijn; Germantown, Maryland: Sijthoff & Noordhoff, 1979.

Arangio-Ruiz G. The United Nations Declaration on Friendly Relations and the system of the sources of international law. Alphen aan den Rijn; Germantown, Maryland: Sijthoff & Noordhoff, 1979.

Barber R. An exploration of the General Assembly's troubled relationship with unilateral sanctions. *International and Comparative Law Quarterly*. 2021. Vol. 70.

Barber R. The Powers of the UN General Assembly to Prevent and Respond to Atrocity Crimes: A Guidance Document. St Lucia, Brisbane: Asia Pacific Centre for the Responsibility to Protect, The University of Queensland, 2021.

Barber R. The Role of the General Assembly in Determining the Legitimacy of Governments. *International and Comparative Law Quarterly*. 2022. Vol. 71. Iss. 3.

Blanchfield L., Weed M.C. United Nations Security Council and General Assembly Responses to the Russian Invasion of Ukraine. *Congressional Research Service Insight*. March 7, 2022. URL: https://crsreports.congress.gov/product/pdf/IN/IN11876

Carswell A.J. Unblocking the UN Security Council: The Uniting for Peace Resolution. *Journal of Conflict & Security Law*. 2013. Vol. 18. No. 3.

De-Occupation of Ukraine. Legal expertise [Electronic publication] / State University of Trade and Economics, Ukrainian Association of Comparative Jurisprudence, Ukrainian Association of International Law, Association of Reintegration of Crimea; ed. by O.V. Kresin. Kyiv: State University of Trade and Economics, 2022.

Distefano G. International Judicial Review of the Legality of Acts Adopted by United Nations Organs. *Journal Sharia and Law*. 2018. Year 32. Iss. 73.

Falk R.A. On the quasi-legislative competence of the General Assembly. *The American Journal of International Law*. 1966. Vol. 60.

Giorgetti Ch., Kliuchkovsky M., Pearsall P., Sharpe J.K. Historic UNGA Resolution Calls for Ukraine Reparations. *Just Security*. November 16, 2022. URL: https://www.justsecurity.org/84146/historic-unga-resolution-calls-for-ukraine-reparations/

Higgins R. The Development of International Law by the Political Organs of the United Nations. *Proceedings of the American Society of International Law at Its Annual Meeting*, April 22-24, 1965. 1965. Vol. 59.

Higgins R. The United Nations and Lawmaking: the Political Organs. *The American Journal of International Law*. 1970. Vol. 64, No. 4.

Jessup Ph.C. International Parliamentary Law. *The American Journal of International Law*. 1957. Vol. 51, No. 2.

Jessup Ph.C. The U. N. General Assembly as a Parliamentary Body. *Pakistan Horizon*. 1961. Vol. 14, No. 1.

Johnson L.D. "Uniting for Peace": Does It Still Serve Any Useful Purpose? *American Journal of International Law*. 2014. Vol. 108.

Kerwin G.J. The Role of United Nations General Assembly Resolutions in Determining Principles of International Law in United States Courts. *Duke Law Journal*. 1983. Vol. 32. Iss. 4.

Kirgis F.L. He Got It Almost Right. *American Journal of International Law Unbound*. 2014. Vol. 108.

Krasno J., Das M. The Uniting for Peace resolution and other ways of circumventing the authority of the Security Council. *The UN Security Council and the Politics of International Authority* / ed. by B. Cronin, I. Hurd. New York: Routledge, 2008.

Malanczuk P. Akehurst's modern introduction to international law. 7th revised ed. London, New York: Routledge, 1997.

Mamlyuk B.N. Uniting for "Peace" in the Second Cold War: A Response to Larry Johnson. *American Journal of International Law Unbound*. 2014. Vol. 108.

Nanda V.P. The Security Council Veto in the Context of Atrocity Crimes, Uniting for Peace and the Responsbility to Protect. *Case Western Reserve Journal of International Law.* 2020. Vol. 52. Iss. 1.

Nichols M. U.N. publicly rejects Russia's call for secret vote on Ukraine. *Reuters.* October 11, 2022. URL: https://www.reuters.com/world/un-publicly-rejects-russias-call-secret-vote-ukraine-2022-10-10/

Nichols M. U.N. suspends Russia from human rights body, Moscow then quits. *Reuters.* April 7, 2022. URL: https://www.reuters.com/world/un-vote-suspending-russia-human-rights-council-over-ukraine-2022-04-07/

Öberg M.D. The Legal Effects of Resolutions of the UN Security Council and General Assembly in the Jurisprudence of the ICJ. *The European Journal of International Law.* 2006. Vol. 16. No 5.

Peacekeeping Operations in Ukraine / ed. by O.V. Kresin; transl. and ed. by W.E. Butler. London: Wildy, Simmonds & Hill, 2019.

Peters A. The War in Ukraine and the Curtailment of the Veto in the Security Council. *La Revue Européenne du Droit.* 2023. Vol. 5. Iss. 1.

Ramsden M. Collective Legalization as a Strategic Function of the UN General Assembly in Responding to Human Rights Violations. URL: https://papers.ssrn.com/sol3/papers.cfm?abstract_id=4048484

Ramsden M. Uniting for MH17. *Asian Journal of International Law.* 2017. Vol. 7. Iss. 2.

Ramsden M. Uniting for Peace: The Emergency Special Session on Ukraine. *Harvard International Law Journal Online.* April 1, 2022. URL: https://journals.law.harvard.edu/ilj/2022/04/uniting-for-peace-the-emergency-special-session-on-ukraine/

Richardson H. Comment on Larry Johnson, "Uniting for Peace". *American Journal of International Law Unbound.* 2014. Vol. 108.

Scharf M.P. Power Shift: The Return of the Uniting for Peace Resolution. *Case Western Reserve Journal of International Law.* 2023. Vol. 55.

Schwebel S.M. The Effect of Resolutions of the U.N. General Assembly on Customary International Law. *Proceedings of the ASIL Annual Meeting.* 1979. Vol. 73.

Shaw M.N. International Law. 8th ed. Cambridge: Cambridge University Press, 2017.

Skubiszewski Kr. The Elaboration of General Multilateral Conventions and of Non-contractual Instruments Having a Normative Function or Objective. Resolutions of the General Assembly of the United Nations. *Annuaire. Institut de Droit International.* 1985. Vol. 61. T. I. Session d'Helsinki 1985.

Skubiszewski Kr. The elaboration of general multilateral conventions and of non-contractual instruments having a normative function or objective. Resolutions of the General Assembly of the United Nations. Definitive Report and Draft Resolution. *Annuaire. Institut de Droit International.* 1985. Vol. 61. T. I. Session d'Helsinki 1985.

Talmon S. The Legalizing and Legitimizing Function of UN General Assembly Resolutions. *Bonn research papers on public International Law.* Paper No 8/2011, 14 October 2014.

The Elaboration of General Multilateral Conventions and of Non-contractual Instruments Having a Normative Function or Objective. Thirteenth Commission. Session of Cairo — 1987. Rapporteur K. Skubiszewski. *Institute of International Law. Compilation Resolutions 1873 – 2017.* URL: https://www.idi-iil.org/app/uploads/2019/06/Annexe-1bis-Compilation-Resolutions-EN.pdf

The philosophy of international law / ed. by S. Besson, J. Tasioulas. New York: Oxford University Press, 2010.

Tomuschat C. Uniting for Peace. Assembly resolution. URL: https://legal.un.org/avl/ha/ufp/ufp.html

Ušiak J., Saktorová L. The International Court of Justice and the Legality of UN Security Council Resolutions. *DANUBE: Law and Economics Review.* 2014. Vol. 5. Iss. 3.

Бабін Б.В., Гріненко О.О., Приходько А.В. Питання розвитку та реалізації міжнародних стандартів прав корінних народів: монографія. Одеса: Фенікс, 2018.

Батлер У.Э. Сравнительное международное право. *Ідея порівняльного міжнародного права: pro et contra:* зб. наук. праць на честь іноземного члена НАН України та НАПрН України Уїльяма Елліотта Батлера / за ред. Ю.С. Шемшученка, О.В. Кресіна; упор. О.В. Кресін, І.М. Ситар. Київ; Львів: Ліга-прес, 2015.

Бруз В.С. ООН і врегулювання міжнародних конфліктів. Київ: Либідь, 1995.

Вибрана бібліографія з міжнародного права за 2022 рік / Васільєва Н., Гула І., Данік Д., Іванкович М., Курочка С. *Український часопис міжнародного права.* 2022. № 4.

Денисов В.Н. Міжнародне співтовариство як правова реальність функціонування міжнародних відносин. *Правова держава.* 2017. Вип. 28.

Денисов В.Н. Організація Об'єднаних Націй. *Енциклопедія міжнародного права.* У 3 т. Т. 3. Київ: Академперіодика, 2019.

Денисов В.Н. Резолюції Генеральної Асамблеї ООН. *Енциклопедія міжнародного права.* У 3 т. Т. 3. Київ: Академперіодика, 2019.

Деокупація. Юридичний фронт [Електронне видання]: матеріали Міжнародного експертного круглого столу (Київ, 18 березня 2022 р.) / Державний торговельно-економічний університет, Українська асоціація порівняльного правознавства, Українська асоціація міжнародного права, Асоціація реінтеграції Криму; упор і наук. ред. О. В. Кресін. Київ: Держ. торг.-екон. ун-т, 2022.

Задорожній О.В., Буткевич В.Г., Мицик В.В. Основи теорії міжнародного права: Конспект лекцій. Київ: Ін-т міжнародних відносин Київського національного університету ім. Т. Шевченка, 2001.

Краевский А.А. Отражение международного права в советской теории государства и права конца 1930-х — 1980-х годов. *Право и политика*. 2015. № 12(192).

Кресін О.В. Доктрина міжнародного права про характер резолюцій Генеральної Асамблеї ООН. *Війна в Україні: зроблені висновки та незасвоєні уроки*: зб. тез Міжнар. круглого столу (23 лютого 2023 р.) / упор. Л.В. Павлик, У.О. Цмоць. Львів: Львівський держ. ун-т внутрішніх справ, 2023.

Кресін О.В. Зміст, характер, правове і політичне значення резолюцій Генеральної Асамблеї ООН щодо протидії агресії РФ проти України у 2014—2023 рр. *Право України*. 2023. № 11.

Кресін О.В. Корінні народи: міжнародне право та законодавство України: монографія / Ін-т держави і права імені В.М. Корецького НАН України. Київ: Норма права, 2021.

Кресін О.В. Новітні виклики і загрози у війні Росії проти України: правові оцінки й рекомендації (за матеріалами Міжнародного експертного круглого столу «Деокупація. Юридичний фронт»). *Національна стійкість України: стратегія відповіді на виклики та випередження гібридних загроз*: національна доповідь / ред. кол. С. І. Пирожков, О. М. Майборода, Н. В. Хамітов, Є. І. Головаха, С. С. Дембіцький, В. А. Смолій, О. В. Скрипнюк, С. В. Стоєцький / Ін-т політичних і етнонаціональних досліджень ім. І. Ф. Кураса НАН України. Київ, 2022.

Кресін О.В. Питання щодо характеру резолюцій Генеральної Асамблеї ООН у доктрині міжнародного права. *Право України*. 2022. № 11.

Кресін О.В. Повноваження та акти Генеральної Асамблеї: еволюція тлумачення Статуту ООН у діяльності ГА ООН. *Захищаючи державу – захищаємо право*: зб. матер. конфер. в пам'ять про О. Поліводського. Київ, 2023. (у друці)

Кресін О.В. Правовий і політичний характер резолюцій Генеральної Асамблеї ООН та їх значення для деокупації України й притягнення РФ до відповідальності. *Принцип незастосування сили в сучасних умовах функціонування колективної безпеки*: монографія. Київ, 2023. (у друці)

Кресін О.В. Правові аспекти протидії російській агресії та відновлення територіальної цілісності України (за матер. доповіді на засіданні Президії НАН України 13 квітня 2022 року). *Вісник НАН України*. 2022. № 6.

Кресін О.В. Правові засади механізму «Єднання заради миру» та його використання в умовах війни рф проти України. *Право України*. 2024. № 1. (у друці)

Кресін О.В. Рішення ЄСПЛ щодо Криму 2020 р. і щодо Донбасу 2023 р.: юридична кваліфікація незаконного контролю РФ щодо території України. *Право України*. 2023. № 3.

Кресін О.В. Тлумачення характеру повноважень та актів Генеральної Асамблеї ООН Міжнародним Судом ООН. *Актуальні проблеми міжнародного права*: Всеукраїнська наук.-практ. конф. (Харків, 10 березня 2023 р.): зб. матер. / за ред. Т. Л. Сироїд, О. А. Гавриленка, В. М. Шамраєвої. Харків: ХНУ імені В. Н. Каразіна, 2023.

Кресін О.В. Характер і особливості резолюцій Генеральної Асамблеї ООН, їх значення для протидії агресії РФ проти України. *Науковий вісник Національної академії СБУ*. 2024. № 1.

Кресін О.В. Характер повноважень та актів Генеральної Асамблеї ООН: статутні положення та еволюція їх тлумачення. *Право України*. 2022. № 7.

Куок Динь Н., Дайє П., Пелле А. Международное публичное право: В 2 т. Т. 1. Киев: Сфера, 2000.

Лангстрём Т. Россия в переходный период: эволюция международно-правовых доктрин. Сравнительный анализ учебников "Международное право" под ред. Г.И. Тункина (Москва, 1982) и под ред. Ю.М. Колосова и В.И. Кузнецова (Москва, 1995). *Московский журнал международного права*. 1999. № 1.

Международное право: учебник / отв. ред. Г. В. Игнатенко, О. И. Тиунов. 6-е изд., перераб. и доп. Москва: Норма: ИНФРА М, 2013.

Международное право: учеб. / отв. ред. Р.М. Валеев, Г.И. Курдюков. Москва: Статут, 2017.

Науковий коментар / Тополевський Р., Дудаш Т., Гончаров В., Наконечна А.; під кер. П. Рабіновича. *Право України*. 2022. № 12.

Науковий коментар [до резолюції Генеральної Асамблеї ООН, ухваленої 2 березня 2022 року, ES-11/1 "Агресія проти України"] / Тополевський Р., Дудаш Т., Гончаров В., Наконечна А.; під кер. П. Рабіновича. *Право України*. 2022. № 8.

Науковий коментар [до резолюції Генеральної Асамблеї ООН, ухваленої 24 березня 2022 року, ES-11/2 "Гуманітарні наслідки агресії проти України"] / Тополевський Р., Дудаш Т., Гончаров В., Наконечна А.; під кер. П. Рабіновича. *Право України*. 2023. № 2.

Науковий коментар [до резолюції Генеральної Асамблеї ООН, ухваленої 7 квітня 2022 року, ES-11/3 "Зупинення прав, пов'язаних з членством Російської Федерації в Раді з прав людини ООН"] / Тополевський Р., Дудаш Т., Гончаров В., Наконечна А.; під кер. П. Рабіновича. *Право України*. 2023. № 4.

Приходько А.В. Стандарти ООН стосовно прав корінних народів: автореф. … канд. юрид. н. Одеса, 2017.

Рабінович П.М. Діяльність Організації Об'єднаних Націй у протидії військовій агресії Російської Федерації проти України. *Конституційні права і свободи людини та громадянина в умовах воєнного стану*: матер. наук. семінару (23 червня 2022 р.) / упор. М. В. Ковалів, М. Т. Гаврильців, Н. Я. Лепіш. Львів: ЛьвДУВС, 2022.

Реньов Є.В. Щодо деяких аспектів діяльності ООН в контексті підтримки суверенітету та територіальної цілісності України. *Juris Europensis Scientia*. 2022. Вип. 5.

Саяпин С. Территориальная целостность Украины в свете Резолюции 68/262 Генеральной Ассамблеи ООН. *Журнал конституционализма и прав человека*. 2014. № 1-2(5).

Стойко О.М., Кресіна І.О., Кресін О.В. Відродження постконфліктних територій: світовий досвід і Україна: наукова записка / Ін-т держави і права імені В.М. Корецького НАН України. Київ: Норма права, 2020.

Тимчук О.Л. Реакція Генеральної Асамблеї ООН на російське вторгнення в Україну. *Актуальні проблеми та перспективи розвитку юридичної науки, освіти та технологій у XXI столітті в дослідженнях молодих учених*: зб. матер. доп. учасників всеукраїнської наук.-практ. конф. (Харків, 3 березня 2023 р.). Харків, 2023.

Тодоров І. Російська інвазія в Україну та ООН. *Міжнародне співтовариство та Україна в сучасних глобальних цивілізаційних процесах: актуальні економічні, політико-правові, безпекові та соціально-гуманітарні аспекти: матер.* доп. міжнар. наук.-практ. конф. (Ужгород, 18-19 квітня 2023 р.) / за заг. ред.: М.М. Палінчак, М.М. Король, В.В. Химинець. Ужгород: Вид-во УжНУ «Говерла», 2023.

Тодоров І., Тодорова Н. ООН у протидії російській агресії в Україні. *Геополітика України: історія і сучасність.* 2023. № 1 (30).

Толстых В. Курс международного права: учеб. Москва: Волтерс Клувер, 2010.

Шварцева М. Реформирование Парламентской Ассамблеи Совета Европы. *Legea si Viata.* 2015. Август.

III. Information releases, publications in mass media

About Us. Group of Friends in Defense of the Charter of the United Nations. URL: https://www.gof-uncharter.org/about-us

Dames C. UN record showing 'no' vote from Bahamas on Russia reparations an 'error', Mitchell said. *The Nassau Guardian.* November, 17, 2022. URL: https://www.thenassauguardian.com/home/un-record-showing-no-vote-from-bahamas-on-russia-reparations-an-error-mitchell-said/article_0a64879d-ad89-5d15-9b24-50c742d22b2a.html

Intervento del Presidente della Repubblica Sergio Mattarella in occasione della Cerimonia per lo scambio degli auguri di fine anno con il Corpo Diplomatico. 15.12.2023. URL: https://www.quirinale.it/elementi/103730?fbclid=IwAR0d70clRpblEzIJuJf6oWofBBVoYtnSTgLm5utZmG61bBCinkeE7fCoZUY

Le national enterre une initiative sur les réexportations d'armes / L'Assemblée fédérale. 27 septembre 2023. URL: https://www.parlament.ch/fr/services/news/Pages/2023/20230927122336125194158159038_bsf087.aspx

Russia threatens states with consequences over UN vote on Human Rights Council. *Euractiv.* April 7, 2022. URL: https://www.euractiv.com/section/global-europe/news/russia-threatens-states-with-consequences-over-un-vote-on-human-rights-council/

Wintour P. EU foreign policy chief fears rightwing surge in June elections. *The Guardian.* 24 December 2023. URL: https://www.theguardian.com/world/2023/dec/24/eu-foreign-policy-chief-fears-rightwing-surge-in-june-elections

Ерман Г. Росія стає головою Ради безпеки ООН. Як це може нашкодити Україні і як можна виключити РФ звідти? *BBC News Україна*. URL: https://www.bbc.com/ukrainian/articles/cv2440434zdo

Зеленський В.О. Україна завжди була лідером миротворчих зусиль; якщо Росія хоче закінчити цю війну, хай доведе це діями — виступ Президента України на саміті «Групи двадцяти». *Президент України Володимир Зеленський. Офіційне інтернет-представництво*. URL: https://www.president.gov.ua/news/ukrayina-zavzhdi-bula-liderom-mirotvorchih-zusil-yaksho-rosi-79141

Кислиця С. Група з підриву Статуту ООН: як Росія та її друзі планують "захищати" організацію. *Європейська правда*. 17 лютого 2022. URL: https://www.eurointegration.com.ua/experts/2022/02/17/7134117/

Коментар МЗС України щодо ухвалення Генеральною Асамблеєю ООН резолюції «Ситуація з правами людини на тимчасово окупованих територіях України, включаючи Автономну Республіку Крим та місто Севастополь». *Веб-сайт Міністерства закордонних справ України*. 20 грудня 2023 р. URL: https://mfa.gov.ua/news/komentar-mzs-ua-shchodo-uhvalennya-generalnoyu-asambleyeyu-oon-rezolyuciyi-situaciya-z-pravami-lyudini-na-timchasovo-okupovanih-teritoriyah-ukrayini-vklyuchayuchi-ar-krim-ta-misto-sevastopol

Нарімана Джелялова, Асана Ахтемова та Азіза Ахтемова етапували з Криму до РФ для відбування покарання — адвокат Полозов. *Кримська правозахисна група*. 02. 10. 2023. URL: https://crimeahrg.org/uk/narimana-dzhelyala-asana-ahtemova-ta-aziza-ahtemova-etapuvali-z-krimu-do-rf-dlya-vidbuvannya-pokarannya-advokat-polozov/

ООН переважною більшістю голосів схвалила українську "формулу миру", шкідливі поправки "збили". *Європейська правда*. 23 лютого 2023 р. URL: https://www.eurointegration.com.ua/news/2023/02/23/7156819/

Пеца М. Сергій Кислиця: «Вся російська місія в ООН — це серпентарій, розвідники і шпигуни». *BBC News Україна*. 10 листопада 2023 р. URL: https://www.bbc.com/ukrainian/articles/c0d2zx8gkwgo

Собенко Н. Генасамблея ООН ухвалила резолюцію з українською "формулою миру". *Суспільне. Новини*. 23 лютого 2023 р. URL: https://suspilne.media/395432-genasamblea-oon-uhvalila-rezoluciu-z-formulou-miru/

Appendices

1. Territorial integrity of Ukraine. Resolution 68/262, adopted by the General Assembly on 27 March 2014

United Nations
A/RES/68/262
General Assembly
Sixty-eighth session
Agenda item 33 (b)

Resolution adopted by the General Assembly on 27 March 2014

[without reference to a Main Committee (A/68/L.39 and Add.1)]

68/262. Territorial integrity of Ukraine

The General Assembly,

Reaffirming the paramount importance of the Charter of the United Nations in the promotion of the rule of law among nations,

Recalling the obligations of all States under Article 2 of the Charter to refrain in their international relations from the threat or use of force against the territorial integrity or political independence of any State, and to settle their international disputes by peaceful means,

Recalling also its resolution 2625 (XXV) of 24 October 1970, in which it approved the Declaration on Principles of International Law concerning Friendly Relations and Cooperation among States in accordance with the Charter of the United Nations, and reaffirming the principles contained therein that the territory of a State shall not be the object of acquisition by another State resulting from the threat or use of force, and that any attempt aimed at the partial or total disruption of the national unity and territorial integrity of a State or country or at its political independence is incompatible with the purposes and principles of the Charter,

Recalling further the Final Act of the Conference on Security and Cooperation in Europe, signed in Helsinki on 1 August 1975, the Memorandum on Security Assurances in Connection with Ukraine's Accession to the Treaty on the Non-Proliferation of Nuclear Weapons (Budapest Memorandum) of 5 December 1994,[1] the Treaty on Friendship, Cooperation and Partnership between Ukraine and the Russian Federation of 31 May 1997[2] and the Alma-Ata Declaration of 21 December 1991,

Stressing the importance of maintaining the inclusive political dialogue in Ukraine that reflects the diversity of its society and includes representation from all parts of Ukraine,

Welcoming the continued efforts by the Secretary-General and the Organization for Security and Cooperation in Europe and other international and regional organizations to support de-escalation of the situation with respect to Ukraine,

Noting that the referendum held in the Autonomous Republic of Crimea and the city of Sevastopol on 16 March 2014 was not authorized by Ukraine,

1. *Affirms* its commitment to the sovereignty, political independence, unity and territorial integrity of Ukraine within its internationally recognized borders;

2. *Calls upon* all States to desist and refrain from actions aimed at the partial or total disruption of the national unity and territorial integrity of Ukraine, including any attempts to modify Ukraine's borders through the threat or use of force or other unlawful means;

3. *Urges* all parties to pursue immediately the peaceful resolution of the situation with respect to Ukraine through direct political dialogue, to exercise restraint, to refrain from unilateral actions and inflammatory rhetoric that may increase tensions and to engage fully with international mediation efforts;

4. *Welcomes* the efforts of the United Nations, the Organization for Security and Cooperation in Europe and other international and regional organizations to assist Ukraine in protecting the rights of

---

1 A/49/765, annex I.
2 A/52/174, annex I.

all persons in Ukraine, including the rights of persons belonging to minorities;

5. *Underscores* that the referendum held in the Autonomous Republic of Crimea and the city of Sevastopol on 16 March 2014, having no validity, cannot form the basis for any alteration of the status of the Autonomous Republic of Crimea or of the city of Sevastopol;

6. *Calls upon* all States, international organizations and specialized agencies not to recognize any alteration of the status of the Autonomous Republic of Crimea and the city of Sevastopol on the basis of the above-mentioned referendum and to refrain from any action or dealing that might be interpreted as recognizing any such altered status.

80th plenary meeting
27 March 2014

2. Problem of the militarization of the Autonomous Republic of Crimea and the city of Sevastopol, Ukraine, as well as parts of the Black Sea and the Sea of Azov. Resolution 76/70 adopted by the General Assembly on 9 December 2021

United Nations
A/RES/76/70
General Assembly
Seventy-sixth session
Agenda item 35 (a)
Prevention of armed conflict: prevention of armed conflict

Resolution adopted by the General Assembly on 9 December 2021

[without reference to a Main Committee (A/76/L.22 and A/76/L.22/Add.1)]

76/70. Problem of the militarization of the Autonomous Republic of Crimea and the city of Sevastopol, Ukraine, as well as parts of the Black Sea and the Sea of Azov

The General Assembly,

Recalling the Charter of the United Nations, in which it was stated, inter alia, that all Members of the United Nations shall refrain in their international relations from the threat or use of force against the territorial integrity or political independence of any State, or in any other manner inconsistent with the purposes of the United Nations,

Recalling also its resolution 2625 (XXV) of 24 October 1970, in which it approved the Declaration on Principles of International Law concerning Friendly Relations and Cooperation among States in accordance with the Charter of the United Nations, and the principles contained therein,

Mindful of the 1975 Helsinki Final Act of the Conference on Security and Cooperation in Europe and the Declaration on Principles Guiding Relations between Participating States contained therein,

Recalling its resolution 68/262 of 27 March 2014 on the territorial integrity of Ukraine, in which it affirmed its commitment to the sovereignty, political independence, unity and territorial integrity of Ukraine within its internationally recognized borders,

Recalling also its resolutions 73/194 of 17 December 2018, 74/17 of 9 December 2019 and 75/29 of 7 December 2020 on the problem of the militarization of the Autonomous Republic of Crimea and the city of Sevastopol, Ukraine, as well as parts of the Black Sea and the Sea of Azov,

Recalling further its resolutions 71/205 of 19 December 2016, 72/190 of 19 December 2017, 73/263 of 22 December 2018, 74/168 of 18 December 2019 and 75/192 of 16 December 2020 on the situation of human rights in the Autonomous Republic of Crimea and the city of Sevastopol, Ukraine,

Gravely concerned that the provisions of those resolutions and relevant decisions of international organizations, specialized agencies and bodies within the United Nations system have not been implemented by the Russian Federation,

Recalling its resolution 3314 (XXIX) of 14 December 1974, in the annex to which it was stated, inter alia, that no territorial acquisition or special advantage resulting from aggression is or shall be recognized as lawful,

Condemning the ongoing temporary occupation of part of the territory of Ukraine, namely, the Autonomous Republic of Crimea and the city of Sevastopol (hereinafter referred to as "Crimea"), by the Russian Federation, and reaffirming the non-recognition of its annexation,

Recalling that the temporary occupation of Crimea and the threat or use of force against the territorial integrity or political independence of Ukraine by the Russian Federation is in contravention of commitments made in the Memorandum on Security Assurances in Connection with Ukraine's Accession to the Treaty on the Non- Proliferation of Nuclear Weapons (Budapest Memorandum) of 5 December 1994,[1] in which, inter alia, the obligations to refrain from the threat or use of force against the territorial integrity or political independence of Ukraine and the commitment to respect the independence and sovereignty and the existing borders of Ukraine were reaffirmed,

Deeply concerned by the illegal seizure and establishment of control by the Russian Federation over the former nuclear weapons storage sites in Crimea, which may pose a threat to regional and global security,

Expressing concern over the efforts of the Russian Federation to extend its jurisdiction over the nuclear facilities and material in Crimea, in respect of which the Agreement between Ukraine and the International Atomic Energy Agency for the Application of Safeguards in connection with the Treaty on the Non-Proliferation of Nuclear Weapons and the Additional Protocol thereto continue to apply,

Expressing concern also about the ongoing deterioration of the international security and arms control architecture, including as a result of the temporary occupation by the Russian Federation of the territories of the Autonomous Republic of Crimea and the city of Sevastopol, which has had a destabilizing impact on the international arms control regimes and confidence- and security-building measures, including those established by the Treaty on Open Skies, the Treaty on Conventional Armed Forces in Europe[2] and the Vienna Document 2011 on Confidence- and Security-Building Measures, and rejecting the attempts by the Russian Federation to advance its narrative about its actions in the temporarily occupied Crimea through the implementation of international arms control regimes,

Affirming that the seizure of Crimea by force is illegal and a violation of international law, and affirming also that those territories must be immediately returned,

Recalling the prohibition, under international humanitarian law, for the occupying Power to compel protected persons to serve

---

[1] A/49/765-S/1994/1399, annex I.
[2] See CD/1064.

in its armed or auxiliary forces, including through pressure or propaganda that is aimed at securing voluntary enlistment, and condemning the ongoing recruitment and conscription campaigns in Crimea and criminal prosecutions, which include fines, correctional labour and imprisonment of Crimean residents for draft evasion,

Concerned by efforts to use the education of children in Crimea in order to indoctrinate them to join the Russian military forces,

Recalling the order of the International Tribunal for the Law of the Sea of 25 May 2019 on provisional measures in the *Case concerning the detention of three Ukrainian naval vessels (Ukraine v. Russian Federation)* and Procedural Order No. 1 of the Arbitral Tribunal Constituted under Annex VII to the 1982 United Nations Convention on the Law of the Sea between Ukraine and the Russian Federation in respect of a Dispute concerning the Detention of Ukrainian Naval Vessels and Servicemen of 22 November 2019,

Noting the fact that security concerns, the unprovoked build-up of forces in and around Ukraine and the holding of Russian military exercises in the Black Sea and the Sea of Azov regions, accompanied by closures and restrictions of the lawful exercise of navigational rights and freedoms, further destabilize the economy and social services, particularly in the coastal regions of Ukraine,

Supporting the commitment by Ukraine to adhere to international law in its efforts to put an end to the temporary Russian occupation of Crimea,

Noting the establishment of the International Crimea Platform and the adoption of the Joint Declaration of the International Crimea Platform Participants,[3]

1. *Urges* the Russian Federation, as the occupying Power, immediately, completely and unconditionally to withdraw its military forces from Crimea and end its temporary occupation of the territory of Ukraine without delay;

2. *Calls upon* all Member States and relevant international organizations to cooperate with the United Nations to encourage and support efforts to put an end to the Russian occupation of Crimea as rapidly as possible and to refrain from any a ction or dealing with

---

[3] A/76/503-S/2021/908, annex.

the Russian Federation regarding Crimea that is inconsistent with this aim;

3. *Supports* commitments and concerted efforts by the international community, including within international frameworks and the International Crimea Platform, to address existing and emerging challenges resulting from the progressive militarization of Crimea and parts of the Black Sea and the Sea of Azov, which undermines security and stability in the region and beyond, and supports the peaceful de-occupation of Crimea;

4. *Stresses* that the presence of Russian troops in Crimea is contrary to the national sovereignty, political independence and territorial integrity of Ukraine and undermines the security and stability of neighbouring countries and the European region;

5. *Reiterates its grave concern* over the progressive militarization of Crimea by the Russian Federation, as the occupying Power, namely the continuing destabilization of Crimea owing to transfers by the Russian Federation of conventional weapons, including advanced weapon systems, battle tanks, armoured combat vehicles, nuclear-capable aircraft, helicopters and missiles, as well as small arms and light weapons, ammunition and military personnel, to the territory of Ukraine, and urges the Russian Federation to stop such activity without delay;

6. *Calls upon* the Russian Federation to engage constructively with confidence- and security-building and risk reduction mechanisms to build transparency over its regular military activity in Crimea, which undermines stability, military predictability and trust in the broader region;

7. *Condemns* the use of seized Ukrainian military industry enterprises in the occupied Crimea by the Russian Federation, including for further development and build-up of forces;

8. *Calls upon* the Russian Federation to refrain from efforts to extend its jurisdiction over the nuclear facilities and material in Crimea;

9. *Expresses its deep concern* over the continued conscription by the Russian Federation of the residents of Crimea, including those holding Ukrainian citizenship, into its armed forces, including assignment to military bases in the Russian Federation, and urges the

Russian Federation to stop such activity, which contradicts international humanitarian law, without delay;

10. *Calls upon* the Russian Federation to refrain from establishing educational institutions that provide combat training to Crimean children with the stated aim of training for military service in the Russian armed forces, to refrain from establishing combat training courses at Crimean schools and to cease efforts to formally incorporate Crimean educational institutions into the "military-patriotic" education system of the Russian Federation;

11. *Reiterates its concern* regarding multiple military exercises of Russian armed forces held in Crimea and parts of the Black Sea and the Sea of Azov, which undermine regional security and entail considerable long-term negative environmental consequences in the region;

12. *Calls upon* the Russian Federation to refrain from unlawful activities in Crimea and parts of the Black Sea and the Sea of Azov, including but not limited to interfering and blocking navigation both for commercial vessels going to and from ports of Ukraine and for government ships sailing under various flags, which further exacerbate tensions in the region and beyond;

13. *Condemns* the construction by the Russian Federation of navy vessels at the seized shipyards in the temporarily occupied Crimea, which further contributes to the build-up of forces and poses a threat to regional security and stability;

14. *Expresses its concern* over the extension of naval bases for the Black Sea fleet of the Russian Federation in Crimea;

15. *Also expresses its concern* about the adoption by the Russian Federation of legislation that grants its National Guard the right to block areas adjacent to certain infrastructure facilities in Crimea and parts of the Black Sea, the Sea of Azov and the Kerch Strait, and which therefore may be used to interfere with navigational rights in violation of international law;

16. *Further expresses its concern* over the deployment by the Russian Federation of military and security forces for the protection of the offshore oil platforms located in the Black Sea, which are the property of Ukraine and which have been seized by the Russian Federation, thus excluding Ukraine from its maritime areas, the

exploitation by the Russian Federation of the underlying natural resources in those areas and its usurpation of the jurisdiction of Ukraine the re;

17. *Expresses its utmost concern* about the dangerous increase in tensions and the unjustified use of force by the Russian Federation against Ukraine, in the Black Sea, the Sea of Azov and the Kerch Strait, including the intentional obstruction of traffic;

18. *Calls upon* the Russian Federation to return to Ukraine unconditionally and without delay all equipment and weapons seized from the vessels *Berdyansk, Nikopol* and the tugboat *Yani Kapu* during the unjustified use of force by the Russian Federation on 25 November 2018;

19. *Encourages* further negotiations to ensure the release by the Russian Federation of all illegally detained Ukrainian citizens and their safe return to Ukraine;

20. *Calls upon* the Russian Federation to refrain from impeding the lawful exercise of navigational rights and freedoms, exercised in accordance with applicable international law, including provisions of the 1982 United Nations Convention on the Law of the Sea,[4] including but not limited to closure of sea areas under the pre text of military exercises, in the Black Sea, the Sea of Azov and the Kerch Strait;

21. *Condemns* the construction and opening by the Russian Federation of the Kerch Strait bridge and the railway bridge, which form a part of the Tavrida highway project, between the Russian Federation and the temporarily occupied Crimea, which facilitates the further militarization of Crimea and restricts the size of vessels that can reach the Ukrainian ports on the Azov coast;

22. *Also condemns* the increasing military presence of the Russian Federation in parts of the Black Sea and the Sea of Azov, including the Kerch Strait, and the harassment by the Russian Federation of commercial vessels and its restriction of international shipping there, which further aggravates the economic and social situation in the broader Donetsk region already affected by the

---

4   United Nations, Treaty Series, vol. 1833, No. 31363.

temporary occupation of Crimea and subsequent ongoing destabilizing acts by the Russian Federation;

23. *Further condemns* visits of Russian officials to the temporarily occupied Crimea, including those in connection with conducting military exercises, military parades and other activities;

24. *Calls upon* all Member States, as well as international organizations and specialized agencies, to refrain from any visits to Crimea that are not agreed with Ukraine;

25. *Decides* to continue its consideration of the matter at its seventy-seventh session.

48th plenary meeting
9 December 2021

3. **Situation of human rights in the temporarily occupied territories of Ukraine, including the Autonomous Republic of Crimea and the city of Sevastopol. Resolution 78/221 adopted by the General Assembly on 19 December 2023**

United Nations
A/RES/78/221
General Assembly
Seventy-eighth session
Agenda item 71 (c)
Promotion and protection of human rights: human rights situations and reports of special rapporteurs and representatives

Resolution adopted by the General Assembly on 19 December 2023

[on the report of the Third Committee (A/78/481/Add.3, para. 33)]

78/221. Situation of human rights in the temporarily occupied territories of Ukraine, including the Autonomous Republic of Crimea and the city of Sevastopol

The General Assembly,

Guided by the purposes and principles of the Charter of the United Nations, and recalling the Universal Declaration of Human Rights,[1] international human rights treaties and other relevant international instruments and declarations,

Recalling the International Convention on the Elimination of All Forms of Racial Discrimination,[2] the Convention against Torture and Other Cruel, Inhuman or Degrading Treatment or

---

1 Resolution 217 A (III).
2 United Nations, *Treaty Series*, vol. 660, No. 9464.

Punishment,[3] the International Covenant on Civil and Political Rights,[4] the Convention on the Rights of the Child[5] and the Convention on the Rights of Persons with Disabilities,[6] as well as the United Nations Declaration on the Rights of Indigenous Peoples,[7]

Recalling also the Geneva Conventions of 12 August 1949[8] and Additional Protocol I thereto, of 1977,[9] as applicable, as well as relevant customary international law,

Confirming the primary responsibility of States to respect, protect and fulfil human rights,

Reaffirming the responsibility of States to respect international law, including the principle that all States shall refrain from the threat or use of force against the territorial integrity or political independence of any State and from acting in any other manner inconsistent with the purposes of the United Nations, recalling its resolution 2625 (XXV) of 24 October 1970, in which it approved the Declaration on Principles of International Law concerning Friendly Relations and Cooperation among States in accordance with the Charter of the United Nations, and reaffirming the principles contained therein,

Recalling its resolution 3314 (XXIX) of 14 December 1974, entitled "Definition of aggression", in which it states that no territorial acquisition or special advantage resulting from aggression is or shall be recognized as lawful,

Recalling also its resolution 68/262 of 27 March 2014 on the territorial integrity of Ukraine, in which it affirmed its commitment to the sovereignty, political independence, unity and territorial integrity of Ukraine within its internationally recognized borders and called upon all States, international organizations and specialized agencies not to recognize any alteration to the status of the Autonomous Republic of Crimea and the city of Sevastopol and to refrain

---

3   Ibid., vol. 1465, No. 24841.
4   See resolution 2200 A (XXI), annex.
5   United Nations, *Treaty Series*, vol. 1577, No. 27531.
6   Ibid., vol. 2515, No. 44910.
7   Resolution 61/295, annex.
8   United Nations, *Treaty Series*, vol. 75, Nos. 970–973.
9   Ibid., vol. 1125, No. 17512.

from any action or dealing that might be interpreted as recognizing any such altered status,

Recalling further its resolution ES-11/4 of 12 October 2022, entitled "Territorial integrity of Ukraine: defending the principles of the Charter of the United Nations",

Recalling its resolutions 71/205 of 19 December 2016, 72/190 of 19 December 2017, 73/263 of 22 December 2018, 74/168 of 18 December 2019, 75/192 of 16 December 2020, 76/179 of 16 December 2021 and 77/229 of 15 December 2022 on the situation of human rights in the temporarily occupied Autonomous Republic of Crimea and the city of Sevastopol, Ukraine, its resolutions 73/194 of 17 December 2018, 74/17 of 9 December 2019, 75/29 of 7 December 2020 and 76/70 of 9 December 2021 on the problem of the militarization of the Autonomous Republic of Crimea and the city of Sevastopol, Ukraine, as well as parts of the Black Sea and the Sea of Azov, and relevant decisions of international organizations, specialized agencies and bodies within the United Nations system,

Recalling also its resolutions ES-11/1 of 2 March 2022 on the aggression against Ukraine, ES-11/2 of 24 March 2022 on the humanitarian consequences of the aggression against Ukraine and ES-11/6 of 23 February 2023 on the principles of the Charter of the United Nations underlying a comprehensive, just and lasting peace in Ukraine, and Human Rights Council resolutions 49/1 of 4 March 2022[10] and 52/32 of 4 April 2023[11] on the situation of human rights in Ukraine stemming from the Russian aggression and S-34/1 of 12 May 2022 on the deteriorating human rights situation in Ukraine stemming from the Russian aggression,[12]

Gravely concerned that the provisions of these resolutions and relevant decisions of international organizations, specialized agencies and bodies within the United Nations system have not been implemented by the Russian Federation,

Condemning the ongoing temporary control or occupation by the Russian Federation of part of the territory of Ukraine, including

---

10 See *Official Records of the General Assembly, Seventy-seventh Session, Supplement No. 53* (A/77/53), chap. VI, sect. A.
11 Ibid., *Seventy-eighth Session, Supplement No. 53* (A/78/53), chap. V, sect. A.
12 Ibid., *Seventy-seventh Session, Supplement No. 53* (A/77/53), chap. VII.

the Autonomous Republic of Crimea and the city of Sevastopol (hereinafter "Crimea"), and certain areas of the Kherson, Zaporizhzhia, Donetsk and Luhansk regions (hereinafter "temporarily controlled or occupied territories of Ukraine"), and reaffirming the non-recognition of its annexation,

Condemning also the unprovoked aggression against Ukraine by the Russian Federation in violation of Article 2 (4) of the Charter, and the use of Crimea for this aim and to support the attempted illegal annexation of the Kherson, Zaporizhzhia, Donetsk and Luhansk regions,

Supporting the commitment by Ukraine to adhering to international law in its efforts to put an end to the temporary Russian occupation of Crimea, and welcoming the commitments by Ukraine to respecting, protecting and fulfilling the human rights and fundamental freedoms of all persons, including Indigenous Peoples, and its cooperation with human rights treaty bodies and international institutions,

Recalling that organs and officials of the Russian Federation established in the temporarily occupied territories of Ukraine are illegitimate and should be referred to as "occupying authorities of the Russian Federation",

Concerned that applicable international human rights obligations and treaties, to which Ukraine is a party, are not upheld by the occupying Power, thus significantly decreasing the ability of residents of the temporarily controlled or occupied territories of Ukraine to exercise their human rights and fundamental freedoms,

Reaffirming the obligation of States to ensure that persons belonging to national or ethnic, religious and linguistic minorities, and Indigenous Peoples may exercise fully and effectively all human rights and fundamental freedoms without any discrimination and in full equality before the law,

Welcoming the reports of the Office of the United Nations High Commissioner for Human Rights on the human rights situation in Ukraine, of the Commissioner for Human Rights of the Council of Europe and of the missions of experts under the Moscow Mechanism of the Organization for Security and Cooperation in Europe, in which they stated that violations and abuses of human rights continued to take place in Ukrainian territory affected by aggression by the Russian Federation,

Welcoming also the reports of the Office of the United Nations High Commissioner for Human Rights on the situation of human rights in the temporarily occupied Autonomous Republic of Crimea and the city of Sevastopol, Ukraine, submitted pursuant to resolutions 71/205[13] and 72/190,[14] and the reports of the Secretary-General submitted pursuant to resolutions 73/263,[15] 74/168,[16] 75/192,[17] 76/179[18] and 77/229,[19] and the reports of 18 October 2022,[20] 15 March 2023[21] and 19 October 2023[22] of the Independent International Commission of Inquiry on Ukraine pursuant to Human Rights Council resolution 49/1,

Condemning the imposition and retroactive application of the legal system of the Russian Federation, and its negative impact on the human rights situation in the temporarily controlled or occupied territories of Ukraine, the imposition of automatic citizenship of the Russian Federation on protected persons, which is contrary to international humanitarian law, including the Geneva Conventions and customary international law, and the deportation, regressive effects on the enjoyment of human rights and effective restriction of land ownership of those who have rejected that citizenship,

Deeply concerned about continued reports that the law enforcement system of the Russian Federation conducts searches and raids of private homes, businesses and meeting places in the temporarily controlled or occupied territories of Ukraine, which disproportionally affect Crimean Tatars, and recalling that the International Covenant on Civil and Political Rights prohibits arbitrary or unlawful

---

13 See A/72/498.
14 See A/73/404.
15 A/74/276.
16 A/75/334 and A/HRC/44/21.
17 A/76/260 and A/HRC/47/58.
18 A/77/220 and A/HRC/50/65.
19 A/78/340 and A/HRC/53/64.
20 A/77/533.
21 A/HRC/52/62.
22 A/78/540.

interference with a person's privacy, family, home or correspondence,

Gravely concerned that, since 2014, torture has reportedly been used by the Russian authorities, and expressing deep concern about the ongoing reports of arbitrary detentions, arrests and sentencing by the Russian Federation of Ukrainian citizens and citizens of other countries, in particular for statements and actions in opposition to the aggression by the Russian Federation against Ukraine, including Emir-Usein Kuku, Halyna Dovhopola, Server Mustafayev, Vladyslav Yesypenko, Nariman Dzhelyal, Asan and Aziz Akhmetov, Iryna Danilovych, Bohdan Ziza, Enver Krosh, Vilen Temeryanov, Mariano García Calatayud and many others,

Deeply concerned about the serious continued restrictions on the right to freedom of movement of persons who have been previously arbitrarily detained and served sentences on politically motivated criminal charges,

Gravely concerned that the temporary control or occupation continues to affect the enjoyment of social, cultural and economic rights by residents, including children, women, older persons, persons with disabilities and other persons in vulnerable and marginalized situations,

Condemning the reported serious violations of international humanitarian law and violations and abuses of human rights committed against residents of the temporarily controlled or occupied territories of Ukraine, in particular extrajudicial killings, abductions, enforced disappearances, politically motivated prosecutions, discrimination, harassment, intimidation, violence, including sexual and genderbased violence, mass searches and raids, arbitrary detentions and arrests, torture and ill-treatment, in particular to extract confessions, subjecting detainees to special security regimes and involuntary placement in psychiatric institutions, as well as deplorable treatment and conditions in detention, and the forcible transfer or deportation of protected persons to the Russian Federation, as well as reported abuses of other fundamental freedoms, including the freedoms of expression, religion or belief and association and the right to peaceful assembly,

Seriously concerned about reports of arbitrary detention and the taking of civilian hostages by the Russian Federation in the temporarily controlled or occupied territories of Ukraine, which is strictly prohibited under international law,

Deeply concerned about restrictions faced by Ukrainians, including Indigenous Peoples of Crimea, in particular the Crimean Tatars, in exercising their economic, social and cultural rights, including the right to work and education, as well as the ability to maintain their identity and culture and to education in the Ukrainian and Crimean Tatar languages,

Condemning the reported destructions of cultural and natural heritage, illegal archaeological excavations and transfer of cultural property, discrimination of persons belonging to religious minorities and repression of religious traditions, thereby diminishing Ukrainian and Crimean Tatar culture in the ethnocultural landscape of the temporarily controlled or occupied territories of Ukraine,

Expressing concern about the militarization and assimilation of young people in the temporarily controlled or occupied territories of Ukraine by the Russian Federation, including combat training of children for military service in the Russian armed forces as well as the introduction of the "military-patriotic" education system, and its blocking of access to Ukrainian education,

Condemning the incitement of hatred against Ukraine and Ukrainians as well as the dissemination of disinformation justifying the war of aggression against Ukraine by the Russian Federation, including through the education system,

Gravely concerned by the above-mentioned policies and practices of the Russian Federation, which cause a continuing threat and have caused a large number of Ukrainians to flee from the temporarily controlled or occupied territories of Ukraine,

Recalling that individual or mass forcible transfers and deportations of protected persons from occupied territory to the territory of the occupying Power, or to that of any other country, occupied or not, and the deportation or transfer by an occupying Power of parts of its own civilian population into the territory that it occupies, are prohibited under international humanitarian law, and may amount to war crimes or crimes against humanity,

Deeply concerned by consistent reports that the Russian Federation promotes policies and conducts practices aimed at changing the demographic, including ethnic, structure in the temporarily controlled or occupied territories of Ukraine,

Concerned about the negative effects on the full and effective enjoyment of human rights by residents of the temporarily controlled or occupied territories of Ukraine, in particular in Crimea, resulting from disruptive activities of the occupying Power, including the expropriation of land, demolition of houses and depletion of natural and agricultural resources,

Reaffirming the right of return of all internally displaced persons and refugees affected by the temporary occupation by the Russian Federation to their homes in Ukraine,

Reaffirming its serious concern that, according to the decision of the so-called "Supreme Court of Crimea" of 26 April 2016 and the decision of the Supreme Court of the Russian Federation of 29 September 2016, the Mejlis of the Crimean Tatar People, the self-governing body of the Indigenous People of Crimea — the Crimean Tatars, continues to be declared an extremist organization and the ban on its activities has still not been repealed, and that the persecution of the leaders of the Mejlis of the Crimean Tatar People continues,

Condemning the ongoing pressure exerted upon persons belonging to religious minorities and their communities, including through frequent police raids, demolition of and eviction from buildings dedicated to religion, undue registration requirements that have affected legal status and property rights and threats against and persecution of those belonging to the Orthodox Church of Ukraine, Protestant churches, Muslim religious communities, Greek Catholics, Roman Catholics and Jehovah's Witnesses, and condemning also the baseless prosecution of dozens of peaceful Muslims for allegedly belonging to extremist organizations,

Gravely concerned about the constant use of military courts, including those located on the territory of the Russian Federation, to try civilian residents of the temporarily controlled or occupied territories of Ukraine and the failure of the occupying Power to respect fair trial standards,

Condemning the continuous widespread misuse of counter-terrorism and anti-extremism laws to suppress dissent, including through enforcing new Russian legislation with the intent to dissuade the residents of the temporarily controlled or occupied territories of Ukraine from peaceful protests, in accordance with their rights to freedom of expression and political opinion, following and during the unprovoked Russian war of aggression against Ukraine,

Strongly condemning, in this regard, the ongoing pressure and mass detentions on terrorism, extremism and espionage grounds and other forms of repression against journalists and other media workers, human rights defenders and civil rights activists, including against activists of the Crimean Solidarity civic initiative, which documents violations and provides humanitarian assistance to the families of victims of politically motivated prosecutions,

Recalling the order of the International Court of Justice of 19 April 2017 on provisional measures in the case concerning the *Application of the International Convention for the Suppression of the Financing of Terrorism and of the International Convention on the Elimination of All Forms of Racial Discrimination (Ukraine v. Russian Federation),*[23]

Recalling also the order of the International Court of Justice of 16 March 2022 on provisional measures in the case concerning *Allegations of Genocide under the Convention on the Prevention and Punishment of the Crime of Genocide (Ukraine v. Russian Federation),*[24]

Recalling further the prohibition under the Geneva Conventions of 12 August 1949 for the occupying Power to compel protected persons to serve in its armed or auxiliary forces, including medical staff, and strongly condemning the ongoing forced conscription and mobilization to the armed forces of the Russian Federation in the temporarily controlled or occupied territories of

---

[23] See *Official Records of the General Assembly, Seventy-second Session, Supplement No. 4* (A/72/4), chap. V, sect. A.

[24] Ibid., *Seventy-seventh Session, Supplement No. 4* (A/77/4), chap. V.

Ukraine against the backdrop of the unprovoked aggression against Ukraine,

Recalling that the safety of journalists, other media workers and a free press, or other media, are essential for the realization of the rights to freedom of expression and freedom to seek, receive and impart information and the enjoyment of other human rights and fundamental freedoms, concerned about reports that journalists, media workers and citizen journalists continue to face unjustified interference with their reporting activities in the temporarily controlled or occupied territories of Ukraine, and expressing deep concern that journalists, media workers and citizen journalists have been arbitrarily arrested, detained, prosecuted, harassed and intimidated as a direct result of their reporting activities, in particular for covering developments in the temporarily controlled or occupied territories of Ukraine as well as the unprovoked Russian war of aggression against Ukraine,

Condemning the blocking by the Russian Federation of Ukrainian websites and television channels and the seizure of Ukrainian transmission frequencies in the temporarily controlled or occupied territories of Ukraine, as well as the use of mass media controlled by the occupying Power to incite hatred against Ukrainians, the Orthodox Church of Ukraine, Crimean Tatars, Muslims, Jehovah's Witnesses and activists and to call for atrocities against Ukrainians,

Gravely concerned by the documented cases in which the Federal Security Service of the Russian Federation allegedly tortured or ill-treated Ukrainian citizens following their arrests, including by using beatings, electric shocks and suffocation against victims,

Reiterating its concern regarding military use of the temporarily controlled or occupied territories of Ukraine and their infrastructure, including civilian, in the unprovoked full-scale aggression by the Russian Federation against Ukraine, which entails considerable long-term negative environmental consequences in the region, impacting civilians' enjoyment of their human rights,

Recalling that the Russian Federation bears legal responsibility as the occupying Power for the occupied territory, and deploring the destruction of the Kakhovka hydroelectric power plant, which has had catastrophic long-term humanitarian, economic, agricultural and environmental consequences in the region, and severely impacts civilians' enjoyment of their human rights, and also strongly condemning the refusal of the request of the United Nations for humanitarian access across the Dnipro River to the affected residents in the areas under the temporary control of the Russian Federation,

Condemning the persistent violent actions of the Russian Federation at the Zaporizhzhia nuclear power plant, including forceful seizure of control of the site, the restrictions on Ukrainian operating personnel in violation of their human rights, the placing of anti-personnel mines in some areas around the site, and other violent actions in connection with the ongoing presence of Russian military and Rosatom personnel at the site, which continue to pose serious and direct threats to the safety and security of this nuclear facility and its civilian personnel, thereby significantly raising the risk of a nuclear accident or incident, which endangers the population of Ukraine, neighbouring States and the international community,

Condemning also the continuous use of the temporarily controlled or occupied territories of Ukraine for missile and drone strikes across Ukraine, causing numerous civilian casualties and impacting civilian objects, including deliberate attacks against medical facilities and critical energy infrastructure,

Gravely concerned that attacks on Ukrainian civilian port infrastructure, means of navigation and grain terminals and the intended blockade of the ports of Ukraine, as well as threats of use of force against civilian and merchant vessels in the Black Sea heading to and from the ports of Ukraine, undermine critical global food supply routes, in particular to the most vulnerable regions, thus threatening global food security and access to affordable, safe and nutritious food for all those in need,

Welcoming the continued efforts of the Secretary-General, the United Nations High Commissioner for Human Rights, the Organization for Security and Cooperation in Europe, the Council of Europe, the Independent International Commission of Inquiry on Ukraine and other international and regional organizations to support Ukraine in respecting, protecting and fulfilling human rights, and expressing concern over the lack of safe and unfettered access by established regional and international human rights monitoring mechanisms and human rights non-governmental organizations to the temporarily controlled or occupied territories of Ukraine,

Strongly condemning the forcible transfer of Ukrainian children and other civilians to the temporarily controlled or occupied territories of Ukraine and their deportation to the Russian Federation, and the separation of families and of children from legal guardians, and any subsequent change of children's personal status, adoption or placement in foster families, and efforts to indoctrinate them,

Noting the issuance of warrants of arrest by the International Criminal Court for Vladimir Putin, President of the Russian Federation, and Maria Lvova-Belova, Commissioner for Children's Rights in the Office of the President of the Russian Federation, on the basis that there are reasonable grounds to believe that they are responsible for the war crime of unlawful deportation of children and that of unlawful transfer of children from occupied areas of Ukraine to the Russian Federation,

Noting also the inclusion of the Russian armed forces and affiliated armed groups in the annex to the annual report of the Secretary-General on children and armed conflict, for killings of children and attacks on schools and hospitals in Ukraine,

Commending the efforts of the Special Representative of the Secretary-General on Sexual Violence in Conflict on the prevention of and response to conflict-related sexual violence in Ukraine,

Acknowledging the importance of the investigation conducted by the Independent International Commission of Inquiry on Ukraine and emphasizing the role played by the Office of the United Nations High Commissioner for Human Rights in contributing to an objective appraisal of the situation of human rights in Ukraine, and in this regard welcoming the investigation by the International Criminal Court,

Strongly condemning the continued arbitrary detentions in the temporarily controlled or occupied territories of Ukraine, the ongoing impunity in reported cases of enforced disappearances, as well as the so-called filtration procedures, in particular in relation to displaced persons,

Gravely concerned that the temporary occupation of Crimea became a blueprint for a grave human rights crisis in other territories of Ukraine under temporary control or occupation by the Russian Federation,

Affirming that the seizure of Crimea and other territories of Ukraine by force is illegal and a violation of international law, and affirming also that control of all of the territory of Ukraine must be immediately restored to Ukraine,

1. *Condemns* the failure of the Russian Federation to comply with the repeated requests and demands of the General Assembly, as well as with the orders of the International Court of Justice of 19 April 2017 on provisional measures in the case concerning the *Application of the International Convention for the Suppression of the Financing of Terrorism and of the International Convention on the Elimination of All Forms of Racial Discrimination (Ukraine v. Russian Federation)*, and of 16 March 2022 on provisional measures in the case concerning *Allegations of Genocide under the Convention on the Prevention and Punishment of the Crime of Genocide (Ukraine v. Russian Federation)*;

2. *Strongly condemns* the continuing and total disregard by the Russian Federation for its obligations under international law, including the Charter of the United Nations, regarding its legal responsibility for the occupied territory, including the responsibility to respect Ukrainian law and the rights of all civilians;

3. *Condemns in the strongest terms* the aggression by the Russian Federation against Ukraine in violation of Article 2 (4) of the Charter, and the use of Crimea for this aim and to support the attempted illegal annexation of the Kherson, Zaporizhzhia, Donetsk and Luhansk regions;

4. *Demands* that the Russian Federation immediately cease its war of aggression against Ukraine and unconditionally withdraw all of its military forces from the territory of Ukraine within its internationally recognized borders;

5. *Condemns* violations and abuses of human rights law and international humanitarian law perpetrated by the Russian occupying authorities and entailing discrimination against the residents of the temporarily controlled or occupied territories of Ukraine,

including Crimean Tatars, as well as Ukrainians and persons belonging to other ethnic and religious groups;

6. *Demands* that the Russian Federation respect obligations under international law with regard to respecting the Ukrainian legislation in force prior to the temporary occupation;

7. *Urges* the Russian Federation:

(a) To uphold all of its obligations under applicable international law;

(b) To fully and immediately comply with the orders of the International Court of Justice of 19 April 2017 and of 16 March 2022;

(c) To take all measures necessary to bring an immediate end to all violations and abuses of international human rights law and violations of international humanitarian law against residents of the temporarily controlled or occupied territories of Ukraine, in particular reported discriminatory measures and practices, arbitrary detentions and arrests, violations and abuses within the framework of the filtration procedures, enforced disappearances, torture and other cruel, inhuman or degrading treatment, sexual and gender-based violence, including to compel apprehended persons to self-incriminate or "cooperate" with law enforcement, ensure fair trial, revoke all discriminatory legislation and hold accountable those responsible for those violations and abuses by ensuring the independent, impartial and effective investigation of all allegations;

(d) To refrain from arresting or prosecuting residents of the temporarily controlled or occupied territories of Ukraine for non-criminal acts committed or opinions expressed, including in social media comments or posts, and release all residents who have been arrested or imprisoned for such acts;

(e) To respect the laws in force in Ukraine, repeal laws unlawfully imposed by the Russian Federation in the temporarily controlled or occupied territories of Ukraine that allow for forced evictions and the confiscation of private property, including land, in violation of applicable international law, and respect the property rights of all former owners affected by previous confiscations;

(f) To immediately release and allow the return to Ukraine, without preconditions, of Ukrainian citizens who were unlawfully detained, as well as those transferred or deported by the Russian Federation;

(g) To disclose the number and identity of individuals deported from the temporarily controlled or occupied territories of Ukraine to the Russian Federation and take immediate action to allow the voluntary return of such individuals to Ukraine;

(h) To end the practice of placing detainees in solitary confinement cells as a method of intimidation;

(i) To monitor and accommodate the medical needs of all Ukrainian citizens, including those unlawfully detained and convicted on politically motivated grounds in the temporarily controlled or occupied territories of Ukraine and the Russian Federation and allow the monitoring of those detainees' state of health and conditions of detention by independent international monitors and physicians from reputable international health organizations, including the European Committee for the Prevention of Torture and Inhuman or Degrading Treatment or Punishment and the International Committee of the Red Cross, and investigate effectively all deaths in detention;

(j) To uphold the rights, in accordance with international law and until their release, of Ukrainian prisoners and detainees in the temporarily controlled or occupied territories of Ukraine and in the Russian Federation, including those on hunger strike, and encourages it to respect the United Nations Standard Minimum Rules for the Treatment of Prisoners (the Nelson Mandela Rules)[25] and the United Nations Rules for the Treatment of Women Prisoners and Non-custodial Measures for Women Offenders (the Bangkok Rules);[26]

(k) To address ongoing impunity and ensure that those found to be responsible for violations and abuses of human rights law and violations of international humanitarian law are held accountable before an independent judiciary;

(l) To create and maintain a safe and enabling environment for journalists and media workers and citizen journalists, human rights

---

25 Resolution 70/175, annex.
26 Resolution 65/229, annex.

defenders and lawyers to perform their work independently and without undue interference, including by refraining from travel bans, deportations, arbitrary arrests, detention and prosecution, and other restrictions on the enjoyment of their rights;

(m) To respect, protect and fulfil freedom of opinion and expression, which includes the freedom to seek, receive and impart information and ideas through any media and regardless of frontiers, enable a safe and enabling environment for independent media pluralism and ensure a safe and enabling environment for civil society organizations;

(n) To respect freedom of opinion, association and peaceful assembly without discrimination on any grounds other than those permissible under international law, and freedom of thought, conscience and religion or belief, without discrimination on any grounds, to lift discriminatory regulatory barriers prohibiting or limiting the activities of religious groups in the temporarily controlled or occupied territories of Ukraine, including but not limited to parishioners of the Orthodox Church of Ukraine, Muslim Crimean Tatars and Jehovah's Witnesses, and to permit unimpeded access, without any undue restrictions, to places of worship as well as gatherings for prayer and other religious practices;

(o) To restore enjoyment of the rights of all individuals, without any discrimination based on origin or religion or belief, revoke the decisions that banned cultural and religious institutions, nongovernmental organizations, human rights organizations and media outlets and restore enjoyment of the rights of individuals belonging to ethnic communities in the temporarily controlled or occupied territories of Ukraine, in particular ethnic Ukrainians and Crimean Tatars, including the right to freely participate in the cultural life of the community;

(p) To respect, protect and fulfil the right to be free from arbitrary or unlawful interference with a person's privacy, family, home or correspondence;

(q) To ensure that the right to freedom of opinion and expression and the rights to peaceful assembly and freedom of association can be exercised by all residents of the temporarily controlled or occupied territories of Ukraine in any form, including single-person pickets, without any restrictions other than those permissible under international law, including international human rights law, and without discrimination on any grounds, and to end the practices of abusing requirements of prior authorization for peaceful assemblies and issuing warnings or threats to potential participants in those assemblies;

(r) To refrain from criminalizing the rights to hold opinions without interference and to freedom of expression and the right to peaceful assembly and quash all penalties imposed on residents of the temporarily controlled or occupied territories of Ukraine for expressing dissenting views, including regarding the status of temporarily controlled or occupied territories of Ukraine and the unprovoked Russian war of aggression against Ukraine;

(s) To ensure the availability of education in the Ukrainian and Crimean Tatar languages, and stop the blocking of access to Ukrainian education;

(t) To respect the rights of the Indigenous Peoples of Ukraine set out in the United Nations Declaration on the Rights of Indigenous Peoples, revoke immediately the decision declaring the Mejlis of the Crimean Tatar People an extremist organization and banning its activities, repeal the decision banning leaders of the Mejlis from entering Crimea, repeal the sentences, including in absentia, against Crimean Tatars and their leaders and immediately release those arbitrarily detained, including the leaders of the Mejlis of the Crimean Tatar People, and refrain from maintaining or imposing limitations on the ability of the Crimean Tatars to conserve their representative institutions;

(u) To stop the illegal drafting and mobilization of residents of the temporarily controlled or occupied territories of Ukraine into the armed forces of the Russian Federation, stop pressure aimed at compelling residents of the temporarily controlled or occupied territories of Ukraine to serve in the armed or auxiliary forces of the Russian Federation, as well as using propaganda, also targeted at children and through the education system, and ensure strict compliance with its international obligations as an occupying Power;

(v) To end also the practice of criminal prosecution of inhabitants who resist conscription and mobilization into the armed or auxiliary forces of the Russian Federation;

(w) To end the practice of deporting Ukrainian citizens from the temporarily controlled or occupied territories of Ukraine for not taking Russian citizenship, stop transferring its own civilian population to the temporarily controlled or occupied territories of Ukraine and end the practice of encouraging such transfers;

(x) To immediately and unconditionally reverse the decision to simplify the procedure for obtaining citizenship of the Russian Federation for Ukrainian orphans or children left without parental care;

(y) To provide to the relevant United Nations bodies and international organizations a comprehensive list of the names and whereabouts of all Ukrainian children who were forcibly transferred to the temporarily controlled or occupied territories of Ukraine or deported to the Russian Federation, including on those who were subsequently adopted or transferred to foster families, in order to ensure that these children are provided protection and care in accordance with international law;

(z) To cease forcible transfers or deportation of Ukraine's children and other civilians and take all necessary steps with a view to their safe return and family reunification in line with the best interests of the child and in accordance with international law;

(aa) To cooperate fully and immediately with the Office of the United Nations High Commissioner for Human Rights, the Organization for Security and Cooperation in Europe and the Independent International Commission of Inquiry on Ukraine, which must have safe, secure and unhindered access to the entire territory of Ukraine, including the temporarily occupied territories of Ukraine, and the Council of Europe on the situation of human rights in the territories of Ukraine under the control of or temporarily occupied by the Russian Federation;

(bb) To create the conditions, as well as provide the means, to allow for the voluntary, safe, dignified and unhindered return to their homes of all internally displaced persons and refugees affected by the temporary occupation of territories of Ukraine by the Russian Federation;

(cc) To stop the policy of forcibly changing the demographic, including ethnic, composition of the population and take the necessary measures aimed at halting the free migration to and settling of citizens of the Russian Federation in the temporarily occupied territories of Ukraine;

(dd) To ensure compliance with obligations under international law, including humanitarian law and the 1954 Convention for the Protection of Cultural Property in the Event of Armed Conflict,[27] regarding the preservation of monuments of the cultural heritage of Ukraine in the temporarily controlled or occupied territories of Ukraine, in particular regarding the Khan Palace in Bakhchysarai and the monument "The ancient city of Chersonese and its Chora", to prevent and stop reported illegal archaeological excavations in Crimea and other temporarily occupied territories of Ukraine, and the illicit transfer of cultural property of Ukraine outside the territory of Ukraine;

8. *Calls upon* the Russian Federation to address the substantive concerns and all recommendations highlighted in the reports of the Secretary-General and the Office of the United Nations High Commissioner for Human Rights on the situation of human rights in the temporarily occupied territories of Ukraine, including the Autonomous Republic of Crimea and the city of Sevastopol, as well as previous relevant recommendations from reports on the situation of human rights in Ukraine by the Office of the High Commissioner based on the work of the human rights monitoring mission in Ukraine established to prevent further deterioration of human rights in the temporarily occupied territories of Ukraine;

9. *Supports* the efforts of Ukraine to maintain economic, financial, political, social, informational, cultural and other ties with its citizens in the temporarily controlled or occupied territories of Ukraine in order to facilitate their access to democratic processes, economic opportunities and objective information;

---

27 United Nations, *Treaty Series*, vol. 249, No. 3511.

10. *Calls upon* all international organizations and specialized agencies of the United Nations system, when referring to the temporarily controlled or occupied territories of Ukraine, including the Autonomous Republic of Crimea and the city of Sevastopol, in their official documents, communications, publications, information and reports, including with regard to statistical data of the Russian Federation or provided by the Russian Federation, as well as those placed or used on official United Nations Internet resources and platforms, to refer to "the Autonomous Republic of Crimea and the city of Sevastopol, and certain areas of the Kherson, Zaporizhzhia, Donetsk and Luhansk regions, Ukraine, temporarily controlled or occupied by the Russian Federation", and to refer to bodies of the Russian Federation and their representatives in the temporarily occupied territories of Ukraine as "occupying authorities of the Russian Federation", and encourages all States and other international organizations to do the same;

11. *Calls upon* Member States to support human rights defenders in the temporarily controlled or occupied territories of Ukraine and across Ukraine and to continue advocacy for the respect of human rights, including by condemning the violations committed by the Russian Federation in the temporarily controlled or occupied territories of Ukraine at bilateral and multilateral forums;

12. *Also calls upon* Member States to engage constructively in concerted efforts, including within international frameworks and the International Crimea Platform, aimed at improving the human rights situation in the temporarily controlled or occupied territories of Ukraine, as well as to continue to use all diplomatic means to press and urge the Russian Federation to comply with its obligations under international human rights law and international humanitarian law and to grant unimpeded access to the temporarily controlled or occupied territories of Ukraine for established regional and international human rights monitoring mechanisms, in particular the human rights monitoring Mission in Ukraine and the Ukraine Monitoring Initiative of the Office for Democratic Institutions and Human Rights of the Organization for Security and Cooperation in Europe;

13. *Condemns* all attempts by the Russian Federation to legitimize or normalize its attempted illegal annexation of the territories of Ukraine, including the automatic imposition of citizenship of the Russian Federation, illegal election campaigns and voting, population census, forcible change of the demographic structure of the population and suppression of national identity;

14. *Calls upon* the international community to continue to support the work of the United Nations to uphold international human rights law and international humanitarian law in the territories of Ukraine temporarily controlled or occupied by the Russian Federation;

15. *Requests* the Secretary-General to continue to seek ways and means, including through consultations with the United Nations High Commissioner for Human Rights and relevant regional organizations, to ensure safe and unfettered access to Crimea and other territories of Ukraine temporarily controlled or occupied by the Russian Federation by established regional and international human rights monitoring mechanisms, in particular the human rights monitoring mission in Ukraine and the Independent International Commission of Inquiry on Ukraine, to enable them to carry out their mandates;

16. *Urges* the Russian Federation to ensure the proper and unimpeded access of international human rights monitoring missions and human rights non-governmental organizations to the temporarily controlled or occupied territories of Ukraine, including all places where persons may be deprived of their liberty, recognizing that the international presence and monitoring of compliance with international human rights law and international humanitarian law are of paramount importance in preventing further deterioration of the situation;

17. *Decides* to include the item entitled "The situation in the temporarily occupied territories of Ukraine" in the annual agenda of the General Assembly;

18. *Requests* the Secretary-General to remain actively seized of the matter, and to take all steps necessary, including within the Secretariat, to ensure the full and effective coordination of all United

Nations bodies with regard to the implementation of the present resolution;

19. *Also requests* the Secretary-General to continue to provide his good offices and pursue his discussions relating to the matter, involving all relevant stakeholders and including the concerns addressed in the present resolution;

20. *Further requests* the Secretary-General to report to the General Assembly at its seventy-ninth session on the progress made in the implementation of all provisions of the present resolution, including options and recommendations to improve its implementation, and to submit for consideration an interim report to the Human Rights Council at its fifty-sixth session, to be followed by an interactive dialogue, in accordance with Council resolution 53/30 of 14 July 2023;[28]

21. *Decides* to continue its consideration of the matter at its seventy-ninth session under the item entitled "Promotion and protection of human rights".

50th plenary meeting
19 December 2023

---

[28] See *Official Records of the General Assembly, Seventy-eighth Session, Supplement No. 53* (A/78/53), chap. VII, sect. A.

4. Aggression against Ukraine. Resolution ES-11/1 adopted by the General Assembly on 2 March 2022

United Nations
A/RES/ES-11/1
General Assembly
Eleventh emergency special session
Agenda item 5
Letter dated 28 February 2014 from the Permanent Representative of Ukraine to the United Nations addressed to the President of the Security Council (S/2014/136)

Resolution adopted by the General Assembly on 2 March 2022

[without reference to a Main Committee (A/ES-11/L.1 and A/ES-11/L.1/Add.1)]

ES-11/1. Aggression against Ukraine

The General Assembly,

Reaffirming the paramount importance of the Charter of the United Nations in the promotion of the rule of law among nations,

Recalling the obligation of all States under Article 2 of the Charter to refrain in their international relations from the threat or use of force against the territorial integrity or political independence of any State, or in any other manner inconsistent with the purposes of the United Nations, and to settle their international disputes by peaceful means,

Recalling also the obligation under Article 2 (2) of the Charter, that all Members, in order to ensure to all of them the rights and benefits resulting from membership, shall fulfil in good faith the obligations assumed by them in accordance with the Charter,

Taking note of Security Council resolution 2623 (2022) of 27 February 2022, in which the Council called for an emergency special session of the General Assembly to examine the question contained in document S/Agenda/8979,

Recalling General Assembly resolution 377 A (V) of 3 November 1950, entitled "Uniting for peace", and taking into account that the lack of unanimity of the permanent members of the Security Council at its 8979th meeting has prevented it from exercising its primary responsibility for the maintenance of international peace and security,

Recalling also its resolution 2625 (XXV) of 24 October 1970, in which it approved the Declaration on Principles of International Law concerning Friendly Relations and Cooperation among States in accordance with the Charter of the United Nations, and reaffirming the principles contained therein that the territory of a State shall not be the object of acquisition by another State resulting from the threat or use of force, and that any attempt aimed at the partial or total disruption of the national unity and territorial integrity of a State or country or at its political independence is incompatible with the purposes and principles of the Charter,

Recalling further its resolution 3314 (XXIX) of 14 December 1974, which defines aggression as the use of armed force by a State against the sovereignty, territorial integrity or political independence of another State, or in any other manner inconsistent with the Charter,

Bearing in mind the importance of maintaining and strengthening international peace founded upon freedom, equality, justice and respect for human rights and of developing friendly relations among nations irrespective of their political, economic and social systems or the levels of their development,

Recalling the Final Act of the Conference on Security and Cooperation in Europe, signed in Helsinki on 1 August 1975, and the Memorandum on Security Assurances in Connection with Ukraine's Accession to the Treaty on the Non-Proliferation of Nuclear Weapons (Budapest Memorandum) of 5 December 1994,

Condemning the 24 February 2022 declaration by the Russian Federation of a "special military operation" in Ukraine,

Reaffirming that no territorial acquisition resulting from the threat or use of force shall be recognized as legal,

Expressing grave concern at reports of attacks on civilian facilities such as residences, schools and hospitals, and of civilian casualties, including women, older persons, persons with disabilities, and children,

Recognizing that the military operations of the Russian Federation inside the sovereign territory of Ukraine are on a scale that the international community has not seen in Europe in decades and that urgent action is needed to save this generation from the scourge of war,

Endorsing the Secretary-General's statement of 24 February 2022 in which he recalled that the use of force by one country against another is the repudiation of the principles that every country has committed to uphold and that the present military offensive of the Russian Federation is against the Charter,

Condemning the decision of the Russian Federation to increase the readiness of its nuclear forces,

Expressing grave concern at the deteriorating humanitarian situation in and around Ukraine, with an increasing number of internally displaced persons and refugees in need of humanitarian assistance, Expressing concern also about the potential impact of the conflict on increased food insecurity globally, as Ukraine and the region are one of the world's most important areas for grain and agricultural exports, when millions of people are facing famine or the immediate risk of famine or are experiencing severe food insecurity in several regions of the world, as well as on energy security,

Welcoming the continued efforts by the Secretary-General and the Organization for Security and Cooperation in Europe and other international and regional organizations to support de-escalation of the situation with respect to Ukraine, and encouraging continued dialogue,

1. *Reaffirms its commitment* to the sovereignty, independence, unity and territorial integrity of Ukraine within its internationally recognized borders, extending to its territorial waters;

2. *Deplores in the strongest terms* the aggression by the Russian Federation against Ukraine in violation of Article 2 (4) of the Charter;

APPENDICES 209

3. *Demands* that the Russian Federation immediately cease its use of force against Ukraine and to refrain from any further unlawful threat or use of force against any Member State;

4. *Also demands* that the Russian Federation immediately, completely and unconditionally withdraw all of its military forces from the territory of Ukraine within its internationally recognized borders;

5. *Deplores* the 21 February 2022 decision by the Russian Federation related to the status of certain areas of the Donetsk and Luhansk regions of Ukraine as a violation of the territorial integrity and sovereignty of Ukraine and inconsistent with the principles of the Charter;

6. *Demands* that the Russian Federation immediately and unconditionally reverse the decision related to the status of certain areas of the Donetsk and Luhansk regions of Ukraine;

7. *Calls upon* the Russian Federation to abide by the principles set forth in the Charter and the Declaration on Friendly Relations;[1]

8. *Calls upon* the parties to abide by the Minsk agreements and to work constructively in relevant international frameworks, including in the Normandy format and Trilateral Contact Group, towards their full implementation;

9. *Demands* all parties to allow safe and unfettered passage to destinations outside of Ukraine and to facilitate the rapid, safe and unhindered access to humanitarian assistance for those in need in Ukraine, to protect civilians, including humanitarian personnel and persons in vulnerable situations, including women, older persons, persons with disabilities, indigenous peoples, migrants and children, and to respect human rights;

10. *Deplores* the involvement of Belarus in this unlawful use of force against Ukraine, and calls upon it to abide by its international obligations;

11. *Condemns* all violations of international humanitarian law and violations and abuses of human rights, and calls upon all parties to respect strictly the relevant provisions of international humanitarian law, including the Geneva Conventions of 1949[2] and

---

[1] Resolution 2625 (XXV), annex.
[2] United Nations, *Treaty Series*, vol. 75, Nos. 970–973.

Additional Protocol I thereto of 1977,[3] as applicable, and to respect international human rights law, and in this regard further demands that all parties ensure respect for and the protection of all medical personnel and humanitarian personnel exclusively engaged in medical duties, their means of transport and equipment, as well as hospitals and other medical facilities;

12. *Demands* that all parties fully comply with their obligations under international humanitarian law to spare the civilian population, and civilian objects, refraining from attacking, destroying, removing or rendering useless objects indispensable to the survival of the civilian population, and respecting and protecting humanitarian personnel and consignments used for humanitarian relief operations;

13. *Requests* the Emergency Relief Coordinator to provide, 30 days after the adoption of the present resolution, a report on the humanitarian situation in Ukraine and on the humanitarian response;

14. *Urges* the immediate peaceful resolution of the conflict between the Russian Federation and Ukraine through political dialogue, negotiations, mediation and other peaceful means;

15. *Welcomes and urges* the continued efforts by the Secretary-General, Member States, the Organization for Security and Cooperation in Europe and other international and regional organizations to support the de-escalation of the current situation, as well as the efforts of the United Nations, including of the United Nations Crisis Coordinator for Ukraine, and humanitarian organizations to respond to the humanitarian and refugee crisis that the aggression by the Russian Federation has created;

16. *Decides* to adjourn the eleventh emergency special session of the General Assembly temporarily and to authorize the President of the General Assembly to resume its meetings upon request from Member States.

1st plenary meeting
2 March 2022

---

3   Ibid., vol. 1125, No. 17512.

5. Humanitarian consequences of the aggression against Ukraine. Resolution ES-11/2 adopted by the General Assembly on 24 March 2022

United Nations
A/RES/ES-11/2
General Assembly
Eleventh emergency special session
Agenda item 5
Letter dated 28 February 2014 from the Permanent Representative of Ukraine to the United Nations addressed to the President of the Security Council (S/2014/136)

Resolution adopted by the General Assembly on 24 March 2022

[without reference to a Main Committee (A/ES-11/L.2 and A/ES-11/L.2 /Add.1)]

ES-11/2. Humanitarian consequences of the aggression against Ukraine

The General Assembly,

Reaffirming its determination to save succeeding generations from the scourge of war,

Reaffirming its resolutions 46/182 of 19 December 1991 and 76/124 of 10 December 2021,

Recalling the obligation of all States under Article 2 of the Charter of the United Nations to refrain in their international relations from the threat or use of force against the territorial integrity or political independence of any State, or in any other manner inconsistent with the purposes of the United Nations, and to settle their international disputes by peaceful means,

Reaffirming its commitment to the sovereignty, independence, unity and territorial integrity of Ukraine within its internationally recognized borders, extending to its territorial waters,

Recognizing that the military offensive of the Russian Federation inside the sovereign territory of Ukraine and its humanitarian consequences are on a scale that the international community has not seen in Europe in decades,

Reiterating the call of the Secretary-General to the Russian Federation to stop its military offensive, as well as his call to establish a ceasefire and to return to the path of dialogue and negotiations,

Recalling its demand that the Russian Federation immediately, completely and unconditionally withdraw all of its military forces from the territory of Ukraine within its internationally recognized borders,

Deploring the dire humanitarian consequences of the hostilities by the Russian Federation against Ukraine, including the besiegement of and shelling and air strikes in densely populated cities of Ukraine, in particular Mariupol, as well as attacks striking civilians, including journalists, and civilian objects, in particular schools and other educational institutions, water and sanitation systems, medical facilities and their means of transport and equipment, and the abduction of local officials, as well as attacks striking diplomatic premises and cultural sites,

Expressing grave concern at the deteriorating humanitarian situation in and around Ukraine, in particular at the high number of civilian casualties, including women and children, and the increasing number of internally displaced persons and refugees in need of humanitarian assistance,

Reaffirming the need to protect, without discrimination of any kind, the safety, dignity, human rights and fundamental freedoms of people fleeing the conflict and violence, regardless of their status, while promoting the security and prosperity of all communities, and condemning in this regard any acts, manifestations and expressions of racism, racial discrimination, xenophobia and related intolerance against people on the move, including refugees,

Strongly condemning any attacks directed against civilians as such and other protected persons and civilian objects, including civilian evacuation convoys, as well as indiscriminate and disproportionate attacks, including indiscriminate shelling and the indiscriminate use of explosive weapons, and further expressing concern about the long-term risks posed by damage to civilian infrastructure and unexploded ordnance to the civilian population,

Stressing the particular impact that armed conflict has on women and children, including as refugees and internally displaced persons, and other civilians who have specific needs, including persons with disabilities and older persons, and stressing also the need to ensure safe passage, as well as protection and assistance, to all affected civilian populations,

Expressing its deep appreciation for the significant and admirable efforts that have been made by neighbouring countries to accommodate refugees,

Expressing concern about the impact of the conflict on increased food insecurity globally, in particular in the least developed countries, as Ukraine and the region are one of the world's most important areas for grain and agricultural exports, when millions of people are facing famine or the immediate risk of famine or are experiencing severe food insecurity in several regions of the world, as well as on energy security,

Recalling the link between armed conflict and violence and conflict-induced food insecurity and the threat of famine, and stressing in this regard that armed conflict, violations of international humanitarian law and international human rights law, and food insecurity can be drivers of forced displacement and that, conversely, forced displacement in countries in armed conflict can have a devastating impact on agricultural production and livelihoods,

Expressing concern about the grave humanitarian consequences of a possible accident resulting from the bombing and shelling of the Ukrainian nuclear infrastructure, reiterating the obligation to ensure the safety and security of all nuclear infrastructure, and expressing concern about the impact of the conflict on the environment,

Recalling the obligation of all States and parties to an armed conflict to fully respect international humanitarian law, in particular the principles of distinction and proportionality and the obligation to take all feasible precautions to avoid and in any event minimize harm to civilians and damage to civilian objects, reiterating that sieges, the purpose of which is to starve the civilian populations, are a violation of international humanitarian law, and urging all States and parties to armed conflict to respect human rights, including with regard to those forcibly displaced, and the principle of non-refoulement,

Reiterating the call upon all parties to the armed conflict to comply with their obligations under international humanitarian law regarding the protection of civilians and civilian objects, and the environment, and to spare civilian objects, including those critical to the delivery of essential services to the civilian population, refraining from attacking, destroying, removing or rendering useless objects that are indispensable to the survival of the civilian population, and respecting and protecting humanitarian personnel and consignments used for humanitarian relief operations,

Reaffirming the principles of humanity, neutrality, impartiality and independence in the provision of humanitarian assistance, and reaffirming also the need for all actors engaged in the provision of humanitarian assistance in situations of complex emergencies to promote and fully respect these principles,

1. *Reiterates* the need for the full implementation of resolution ES-11/1 of 2 March 2022, entitled "Aggression against Ukraine";

2. *Demands* an immediate cessation of the hostilities by the Russian Federation against Ukraine, in particular of any attacks against civilians and civilian objects;

3. *Also demands* that civilians, including humanitarian personnel, journalists and persons in vulnerable situations, including women and children, be fully protected;

4. *Further demands* full respect for and protection of all medical personnel and humanitarian personnel exclusively engaged in medical duties, their means of transport and equipment, as well as hospitals and other medical facilities;

5. *Demands* full respect for and protection of objects indispensable to the survival of the civilian population and civilian infrastructure that is critical to the delivery of essential services in armed conflict;

6. *Also demands* that all parties protect civilians fleeing armed conflict and violence, including foreign nationals, notably students,

without discrimination, to allow voluntary, safe and unhindered passage;

7. *Further demands* that the parties comply with their obligation to ensure the safe and unhindered humanitarian access of humanitarian personnel as well as their means of transport, supplies and equipment to those in need in Ukraine and its neighbouring countries;

8. *Stresses* that the sieges of cities in Ukraine, in particular the city of Mariupol, further aggravate the humanitarian situation for the civilian population and hamper evacuation efforts, and therefore demands to put an end to these sieges;

9. *Condemns* all violations of international humanitarian law and violations and abuses of human rights, and calls upon all parties to the armed conflict to strictly respect international humanitarian law, including the Geneva Conventions of 1949[1] and Additional Protocol I thereto, of 1977,[2] and to respect international human rights law and international refugee law, including the principle of non-refoulement, as applicable;

10. *Calls upon* Member States to fully fund the United Nations Humanitarian Response Plan 2022, the flash appeal launched by the United Nations for the humanitarian response in Ukraine, as well as the regional refugee response plan for Ukraine and its neighbouring countries, and notes with concern the findings in the *Global Humanitarian Overview 2022*, including its February 2022 update;

11. *Welcomes and urges* the continued efforts by the Secretary-General, Member States, entities of the United Nations system and the international community to deliver humanitarian assistance as well as assistance and protection for refugees, and also welcomes the appointment by the Secretary-General of a United Nations Crisis Coordinator for Ukraine;

12. *Reiterates its request* to the Emergency Relief Coordinator to provide a report on the humanitarian situation in Ukraine and on the humanitarian response, in accordance with its resolution ES-11/1, and requests the Secretary-General to brief the General

---

1 United Nations, *Treaty Series*, vol. 75, Nos. 970–973.
2 Ibid., vol. 1125, No. 17512.

Assembly, on a regular basis, on the implementation of the present resolution;

13. *Strongly encourages* the continued negotiations between all parties, and again urges the immediate peaceful resolution of the conflict between the Russian Federation and Ukraine through political dialogue, negotiations, mediation and other peaceful means in accordance with international law;

14. *Decides* to adjourn the eleventh emergency special session of the General Assembly temporarily and to authorize the President of the General Assembly to resume its meetings upon request from Member States.

9th plenary meeting
24 March 2022

6. Territorial integrity of Ukraine: defending the principles of the Charter of the United Nations. Resolution ES-11/4 adopted by the General Assembly on 12 October 2022

United Nations
A/RES/ES-11/4
General Assembly
Eleventh emergency special session
Agenda item 5
Letter dated 28 February 2014 from the Permanent Representative of Ukraine to the United Nations addressed to the President of the Security Council (S/2014/136)

Resolution adopted by the General Assembly on 12 October 2022

[without reference to a Main Committee (A/ES-11/L.5)]

ES-11/4. Territorial integrity of Ukraine: defending the principles of the Charter of the United Nations

The General Assembly,

Recalling the obligation of all States under Article 2 of the Charter of the United Nations to refrain in their international relations from the threat or use of force against the territorial integrity or political independence of any State, or in any other manner inconsistent with the purposes of the United Nations, and to settle their international disputes by peaceful means in such a manner that international peace and security and justice are not endangered,

Reaffirming the principle of customary international law, as restated in its resolution 2625 (XXV) of 24 October 1970, entitled "Declaration on Principles of International Law concerning Friendly Relations and Cooperation among States in accordance with the Charter of the United Nations", that no territorial acquisition resulting from the threat or use of force shall be recognized as legal,

Recalling its resolutions 68/262 of 27 March 2014, entitled "Territorial integrity of Ukraine", ES-11/1 of 2 March 2022, entitled "Aggression against Ukraine", and ES-11/2 of 24 March 2022, entitled "Humanitarian consequences of the aggression against Ukraine",

Noting that the Donetsk, Kherson, Luhansk and Zaporizhzhia regions of Ukraine are areas that, in part, are or have been under the temporary military control of the Russian Federation, as a result of aggression, in violation of the sovereignty, political independence and territorial integrity of Ukraine,

Noting also that the decisions of 21 February and 29 September 2022 by the Russian Federation related to the status of the Donetsk, Kherson, Luhansk and Zaporizhzhia regions of Ukraine are a violation of the territorial integrity and sovereignty of Ukraine and inconsistent with the principles of the Charter,

Noting with concern that the illegal so-called referendums were organized from 23 to 27 September 2022 in these regions as attempts to modify the internationally recognized borders of Ukraine,

Noting the Secretary-General's statement of 29 September 2022 in which he recalled that any annexation of a State's territory by another State resulting from the threat or use of force is a violation of the principles of the Charter and international law,

1. *Reaffirms its commitment* to the sovereignty, independence, unity and territorial integrity of Ukraine within its internationally recognized borders, extending to its territorial waters;

2. *Condemns* the organization by the Russian Federation of illegal so-called referendums in regions within the internationally recognized borders of Ukraine and the attempted illegal annexation of the Donetsk, Kherson, Luhansk and Zaporizhzhia regions of Ukraine, following the organization of the above-mentioned referendums;

3. *Declares* that the unlawful actions of the Russian Federation with regard to the illegal so-called referendums held from 23 to 27 September 2022 in parts of the Donetsk, Kherson, Luhansk and Zaporizhzhia regions of Ukraine that, in part, are or have been under the temporary military control of the Russian Federation, and the

subsequent attempted illegal annexation of these regions, have no validity under international law and do not form the basis for any alteration of the status of these regions of Ukraine;

4. *Calls upon* all States, international organizations and United Nations specialized agencies not to recognize any alteration by the Russian Federation of the status of any or all of the Donetsk, Kherson, Luhansk or Zaporizhzhia regions of Ukraine, and to refrain from any action or dealing that might be interpreted as recognizing any such altered status;

5. *Demands* that the Russian Federation immediately and unconditionally reverse its decisions of 21 February and 29 September 2022 related to the status of certain areas of the Donetsk, Kherson, Luhansk and Zaporizhzhia regions of Ukraine, as they are a violation of the territorial integrity and sovereignty of Ukraine and inconsistent with the principles of the Charter of the United Nations, and immediately, completely and unconditionally withdraw all of its military forces from the territory of Ukraine within its internationally recognized borders;

6. *Welcomes* the efforts of the United Nations, Member States and humanitarian organizations to respond to the humanitarian and refugee crisis;

7. *Welcomes and expresses its strong support* for the continued efforts by the Secretary-General and Member States, and calls upon Member States and international organizations, including the Organization for Security and Cooperation in Europe and other international and regional organizations, to support the de-escalation of the current situation and a peaceful resolution of the conflict through political dialogue, negotiation, mediation and other peaceful means, with respect for the sovereignty and territorial integrity of Ukraine within its internationally recognized borders and in accordance with the principles of the Charter;

8. *Decides* to adjourn the eleventh emergency special session of the General Assembly temporarily and to authorize the President of the General Assembly to resume its meetings upon request from Member States.

14th plenary meeting
12 October 2022

7. Furtherance of remedy and reparation for aggression against Ukraine. Resolution ES-11/5 adopted by the General Assembly on 14 November 2022

United Nations
A/RES/ES-11/5
General Assembly
Eleventh emergency special session
Agenda item 5
Letter dated 28 February 2014 from the Permanent Representative of Ukraine to the United Nations addressed to the President of the Security Council (S/2014/136)

Resolution adopted by the General Assembly on 14 November 2022

[without reference to a Main Committee (A/ES-11/L.6)]

ES-11/5. Furtherance of remedy and reparation for aggression against Ukraine

The General Assembly,

Reaffirming the paramount importance of the Charter of the United Nations in the promotion of the rule of law among nations,

Recalling the obligations of all States under Article 2 of the Charter, including the obligation to refrain in their international relations from the threat or use of force against the territorial integrity or political independence of any State, or in any other manner inconsistent with the purposes of the United Nations, and to settle their international disputes by peaceful means,

Recalling also the obligation under Article 33 (1) of the Charter that Members which are parties to any dispute shall, first of all, seek a solution by negotiation, inquiry, mediation, conciliation, arbitration, judicial settlement, resort to regional agencies or arrangements, or other peaceful means of their own choice,

Taking note of Security Council resolution 2623 (2022) of 27 February 2022,

Recalling its right under Article 14 of the Charter to recommend measures for the peaceful adjustment of any situation which it deems likely to impair the general welfare or friendly relations among nations, including situations resulting from a violation of the provisions of the Charter,

Recalling also its resolutions ES-11/1 of 2 March 2022, entitled "Aggression against Ukraine", ES-11/2 of 24 March 2022, entitled "Humanitarian consequences of the aggression against Ukraine", and ES-11/4 of 12 October 2022, entitled "Territorial integrity of Ukraine: defending the principles of the Charter of the United Nations", in which, among other things, it reaffirmed its commitment to the sovereignty, independence, unity and territorial integrity of Ukraine,

Recalling further the order of the International Court of Justice of 16 March 2022 on the indication of provisional measures in the case concerning *Allegations of Genocide under the Convention on the Prevention and Punishment of the Crime of Genocide (Ukraine v. Russian Federation)*,[1]

Bearing in mind the importance of maintaining and strengthening international peace founded upon freedom, equality, justice and respect for human rights, and of developing friendly relations among nations irrespective of their political, economic and social systems or the levels of their development,

Expressing grave concern at the loss of life, civilian displacement, destruction of infrastructure and natural resources, loss of public and private property, and economic calamity caused by the aggression by the Russian Federation against Ukraine,

Recalling its resolution 60/147 of 16 December 2005, the annex to which contains the Basic Principles and Guidelines on the Right to a Remedy and Reparation for Victims of Gross Violations of International Human Rights Law and Serious Violations of International Humanitarian Law,

---

[1] See *Official Records of the General Assembly, Seventy-seventh Session, Supplement No. 4* (A/77/4), paras. 189–197.

1. *Reaffirms* its commitment to the sovereignty, independence, unity and territorial integrity of Ukraine and its demand that the Russian Federation immed iately cease its use of force against Ukraine and that the Russian Federation immediately, completely and unconditionally withdraw all of its military forces from the territory of Ukraine within its internationally recognized borders, extending to its territorial waters;

2. *Recognizes* that the Russian Federation must be held to account for any violations of international law in or against Ukraine, including its aggression in violation of the Charter of the United Nations, as well as any violations of international humanitarian law and international human rights law, and that it must bear the legal consequences of all of its internationally wrongful acts, including making reparation for the injury, including any damage, caused by such acts;

3. *Recognizes also* the need for the establishment, in cooperation with Ukraine, of an international mechanism for reparation for damage, loss or injury, and arising from the internationally wrongful acts of the Russian Federation in or against Ukraine;

4. *Recommends* the creation by Member States, in cooperation with Ukraine, of an international register of damage to serve as a record, in documentary form, of evidence and claims information on damage, loss or injury to all natural and legal persons concerned, as well as the State of Ukraine, caused by internationally wrongful acts of the Russian Federation in or against Ukraine, as well as to promote and coordinate evidence-gathering;

5. *Decides* to adjourn the eleventh emergency special session of the General Assembly temporarily and to authorize the President of the General Assembly to resume its meetings upon request from Member States.

15th plenary meeting
14 November 2022

8. Principles of the Charter of the United Nations underlying a comprehensive, just and lasting peace in Ukraine. Resolution ES-11/6 adopted by the General Assembly on 23 February 2023

United Nations
A/RES/ES-11/6
General Assembly
Eleventh emergency special session
Agenda item 5
Letter dated 28 February 2014 from the Permanent Representative of Ukraine to the United Nations addressed to the President of the Security Council (S/2014/136)

Resolution adopted by the General Assembly on 23 February 2023

[without reference to a Main Committee (A/ES-11/L.7)]

ES-11/6. Principles of the Charter of the United Nations underlying a comprehensive, just and lasting peace in Ukraine

The General Assembly,

Recalling the purposes and principles enshrined in the Charter of the United Nations,

Recalling also the obligation of all States under Article 2 of the Charter of the United Nations to refrain in their international relations from the threat or use of force against the territorial integrity or political independence of any State, or in any other manner inconsistent with the purposes of the United Nations, and to settle their international disputes by peaceful means,

Reaffirming that no territorial acquisition resulting from the threat or use of force shall be recognized as legal,

Recalling its relevant resolutions adopted at its eleventh emergency special session and its resolution 68/262 of 27 March 2014,

Stressing, one year into the full-scale invasion of Ukraine, that the achievement of a comprehensive, just and lasting peace would constitute a significant contribution to strengthening international peace and security,

Recalling the order of the International Court of Justice of 16 March 2022,[1]

Deploring the dire human rights and humanitarian consequences of the aggression by the Russian Federation against Ukraine, including the continuous attacks against critical infrastructure across Ukraine with devastating consequences for civilians, and expressing grave concern at the high number of civilian casualties, including women and children, the number of internally displaced persons and refugees in need of humanitarian assistance, and violations and abuses committed against children,

Noting with deep concern the adverse impact of the war on global food security, energy, nuclear security and safety and the environment,

1. *Underscores* the need to reach, as soon as possible, a comprehensive, just and lasting peace in Ukraine in line with the principles of the Charter of the United Nations;

2. *Welcomes and expresses strong support* for the efforts of the Secretary-General and Member States to promote a comprehensive, just and lasting peace in Ukraine, consistent with the Charter, including the principles of sovereign equality and territorial integrity of States;

3. *Calls upon* Member States and international organizations to redouble support for diplomatic efforts to achieve a comprehensive, just and lasting peace in Ukraine, consistent with the Charter;

4. *Reaffirms its commitment* to the sovereignty, independence, unity and territorial integrity of Ukraine within its internationally recognized borders, extending to its territorial waters;

5. *Reiterates its demand* that the Russian Federation immediately, completely and unconditionally withdraw all of its military

---

1 See *Official Records of the General Assembly, Seventy-seventh Session, Supplement No. 4* (A/77/4), paras. 189–197.

forces from the territory of Ukraine within its internationally recognized borders, and calls for a cessation of hostilities;

6. *Demands* that the treatment by the parties to the armed conflict of all prisoners of war be in accordance with the provisions of the Geneva Convention relative to the Treatment of Prisoners of War of 12 August 1949[2] and Additional Protocol I to the Geneva Conventions of 1949,[3] and calls for the complete exchange of prisoners of war, the release of all unlawfully detained persons and the return of all internees and of civilians forcibly transferred and deported, including children;

7. *Calls for* full adherence by the parties to the armed conflict to their obligations under international humanitarian law to take constant care to spare the civilian population and civilian objects, to ensure safe and unhindered humanitarian access to those in need, and to refrain from attacking, destroying, removing or rendering useless objects indispensable to the survival of the civilian population;

8. *Also calls for* an immediate cessation of the attacks on the critical infrastructure of Ukraine and any deliberate attacks on civilian objects, including those that are residences, schools and hospitals;

9. *Emphasizes* the need to ensure accountability for the most serious crimes under international law committed on the territory of Ukraine through appropriate, fair and independent investigations and prosecutions at the national or international level, and ensure justice for all victims and the prevention of future crimes;

10. *Urges* all Member States to cooperate in the spirit of solidarity to address the global impacts of the war on food security, energy, finance, the environment and nuclear security and safety, underscores that arrangements for a comprehensive, just and lasting peace in Ukraine should take into account these factors, and calls upon Member States to support the Secretary-General in his efforts to address these impacts;

---

2   United Nations, *Treaty Series*, vol. 75, No. 972.
3   Ibid., vol. 1125, No. 17512.

11. *Decides* to adjourn the eleventh emergency special session of the General Assembly temporarily and to authorize the President of the General Assembly to resume its meetings upon request from Member States.

19th plenary meeting
23 February 2023

SOVIET AND POST-SOVIET POLITICS AND SOCIETY
Edited by Dr. Andreas Umland | ISSN 1614-3515

1   Андреас Умланд (ред.) | Воплощение Европейской конвенции по правам человека в России. Философские, юридические и эмпирические исследования | ISBN 3-89821-387-0

2   *Christian Wipperfürth* | Russland – ein vertrauenswürdiger Partner? Grundlagen, Hintergründe und Praxis gegenwärtiger russischer Außenpolitik | Mit einem Vorwort von Heinz Timmermann | ISBN 3-89821-401-X

3   *Manja Hussner* | Die Übernahme internationalen Rechts in die russische und deutsche Rechtsordnung. Eine vergleichende Analyse zur Völkerrechtsfreundlichkeit der Verfassungen der Russländischen Föderation und der Bundesrepublik Deutschland | Mit einem Vorwort von Rainer Arnold | ISBN 3-89821-438-9

4   *Matthew Tejada* | Bulgaria's Democratic Consolidation and the Kozloduy Nuclear Power Plant (KNPP). The Unattainability of Closure | With a foreword by Richard J. Crampton | ISBN 3-89821-439-7

5   *Марк Григорьевич Меерович* | Квадратные метры, определяющие сознание. Государственная жилищная политика в СССР. 1921 – 1941 гг | ISBN 3-89821-474-5

6   *Andrei P. Tsygankov, Pavel A. Tsygankov (Eds.)* | New Directions in Russian International Studies | ISBN 3-89821-422-2

7   *Марк Григорьевич Меерович* | Как власть народ к труду приучала. Жилище в СССР – средство управления людьми. 1917 – 1941 гг. | С предисловием Елены Осокиной | ISBN 3-89821-495-8

8   *David J. Galbreath* | Nation-Building and Minority Politics in Post-Socialist States. Interests, Influence and Identities in Estonia and Latvia | With a foreword by David J. Smith | ISBN 3-89821-467-2

9   *Алексей Юрьевич Безугольный* | Народы Кавказа в Вооруженных силах СССР в годы Великой Отечественной войны 1941-1945 гг. | С предисловием Николая Бугая | ISBN 3-89821-475-3

10   *Вячеслав Лихачев и Владимир Прибыловский (ред.)* | Русское Национальное Единство, 1990-2000. В 2-х томах | ISBN 3-89821-523-7

11   *Николай Бугай (ред.)* | Народы стран Балтии в условиях сталинизма (1940-е – 1950-е годы). Документированная история | ISBN 3-89821-525-3

12   *Ingmar Bredies (Hrsg.)* | Zur Anatomie der Orange Revolution in der Ukraine. Wechsel des Elitenregimes oder Triumph des Parlamentarismus? | ISBN 3-89821-524-5

13   *Anastasia V. Mitrofanova* | The Politicization of Russian Orthodoxy. Actors and Ideas | With a foreword by William C. Gay | ISBN 3-89821-481-8

14   *Nathan D. Larson* | Alexander Solzhenitsyn and the Russo-Jewish Question | ISBN 3-89821-483-4

15   *Guido Houben* | Kulturpolitik und Ethnizität. Staatliche Kunstförderung im Russland der neunziger Jahre | Mit einem Vorwort von Gert Weisskirchen | ISBN 3-89821-542-3

16   *Leonid Luks* | Der russische „Sonderweg"? Aufsätze zur neuesten Geschichte Russlands im europäischen Kontext | ISBN 3-89821-496-6

17   *Евгений Мороз* | История «Мёртвой воды» – от страшной сказки к большой политике. Политическое неоязычество в постсоветской России | ISBN 3-89821-551-2

18   *Александр Верховский и Галина Кожевникова (ред.)* | Этническая и религиозная интолерантность в российских СМИ. Результаты мониторинга 2001-2004 гг. | ISBN 3-89821-569-5

19   *Christian Ganzer* | Sowjetisches Erbe und ukrainische Nation. Das Museum der Geschichte des Zaporoger Kosakentums auf der Insel Chortycja | Mit einem Vorwort von Frank Golczewski | ISBN 3-89821-504-0

20   *Эльза-Баир Гучинова* | Помнить нельзя забыть. Антропология депортационной травмы калмыков | С предисловием Кэролайн Хамфри | ISBN 3-89821-506-7

21   *Юлия Лидерман* | Мотивы «проверки» и «испытания» в постсоветской культуре. Советское прошлое в российском кинематографе 1990-х годов | С предисловием Евгения Марголита | ISBN 3-89821-511-3

22   *Tanya Lokshina, Ray Thomas, Mary Mayer (Eds.)* | The Imposition of a Fake Political Settlement in the Northern Caucasus. The 2003 Chechen Presidential Election | ISBN 3-89821-436-2

23   *Timothy McCajor Hall, Rosie Read (Eds.)* | Changes in the Heart of Europe. Recent Ethnographies of Czechs, Slovaks, Roma, and Sorbs | With an afterword by Zdeněk Salzmann | ISBN 3-89821-606-3

24 *Christian Autengruber* | Die politischen Parteien in Bulgarien und Rumänien. Eine vergleichende Analyse seit Beginn der 90er Jahre | Mit einem Vorwort von Dorothée de Nève | ISBN 3-89821-476-1

25 *Annette Freyberg-Inan with Radu Cristescu* | The Ghosts in Our Classrooms, or: John Dewey Meets Ceaușescu. The Promise and the Failures of Civic Education in Romania | ISBN 3-89821-416-8

26 *John B. Dunlop* | The 2002 Dubrovka and 2004 Beslan Hostage Crises. A Critique of Russian Counter-Terrorism | With a foreword by Donald N. Jensen | ISBN 3-89821-608-X

27 *Peter Koller* | Das touristische Potenzial von Kam''janec'–Podil's'kyj. Eine fremdenverkehrsgeographische Untersuchung der Zukunftsperspektiven und Maßnahmenplanung zur Destinationsentwicklung des „ukrainischen Rothenburg" | Mit einem Vorwort von Kristiane Klemm | ISBN 3-89821-640-3

28 *Françoise Daucé, Elisabeth Sieca-Kozlowski (Eds.)* | Dedovshchina in the Post-Soviet Military. Hazing of Russian Army Conscripts in a Comparative Perspective | With a foreword by Dale Herspring | ISBN 3-89821-616-0

29 *Florian Strasser* | Zivilgesellschaftliche Einflüsse auf die Orange Revolution. Die gewaltlose Massenbewegung und die ukrainische Wahlkrise 2004 | Mit einem Vorwort von Egbert Jahn | ISBN 3-89821-648-9

30 *Rebecca S. Katz* | The Georgian Regime Crisis of 2003-2004. A Case Study in Post-Soviet Media Representation of Politics, Crime and Corruption | ISBN 3-89821-413-3

31 *Vladimir Kantor* | Willkür oder Freiheit. Beiträge zur russischen Geschichtsphilosophie | Ediert von Dagmar Herrmann sowie mit einem Vorwort versehen von Leonid Luks | ISBN 3-89821-589-X

32 *Laura A. Victoir* | The Russian Land Estate Today. A Case Study of Cultural Politics in Post-Soviet Russia | With a foreword by Priscilla Roosevelt | ISBN 3-89821-426-5

33 *Ivan Katchanovski* | Cleft Countries. Regional Political Divisions and Cultures in Post-Soviet Ukraine and Moldova | With a foreword by Francis Fukuyama | ISBN 3-89821-558-X

34 *Florian Mühlfried* | Postsowjetische Feiern. Das Georgische Bankett im Wandel | Mit einem Vorwort von Kevin Tuite | ISBN 3-89821-601-2

35 *Roger Griffin, Werner Loh, Andreas Umland (Eds.)* | Fascism Past and Present, West and East. An International Debate on Concepts and Cases in the Comparative Study of the Extreme Right | With an afterword by Walter Laqueur | ISBN 3-89821-674-8

36 *Sebastian Schlegel* | Der „Weiße Archipel". Sowjetische Atomstädte 1945-1991 | Mit einem Geleitwort von Thomas Bohn | ISBN 3-89821-679-9

37 *Vyacheslav Likhachev* | Political Anti-Semitism in Post-Soviet Russia. Actors and Ideas in 1991-2003 | Edited and translated from Russian by Eugene Veklerov | ISBN 3-89821-529-6

38 *Josette Baer (Ed.)* | Preparing Liberty in Central Europe. Political Texts from the Spring of Nations 1848 to the Spring of Prague 1968 | With a foreword by Zdeněk V. David | ISBN 3-89821-546-6

39 *Михаил Лукьянов* | Российский консерватизм и реформа, 1907-1914 | С предисловием Марка Д. Стейнберга | ISBN 3-89821-503-2

40 *Nicola Melloni* | Market Without Economy. The 1998 Russian Financial Crisis | With a foreword by Eiji Furukawa | ISBN 3-89821-407-9

41 *Dmitrij Chmelnizki* | Die Architektur Stalins | Bd. 1: Studien zu Ideologie und Stil | Bd. 2: Bilddokumentation | Mit einem Vorwort von Bruno Flierl | ISBN 3-89821-515-6

42 *Katja Yafimava* | Post-Soviet Russian-Belarussian Relationships. The Role of Gas Transit Pipelines | With a foreword by Jonathan P. Stern | ISBN 3-89821-655-1

43 *Boris Chavkin* | Verflechtungen der deutschen und russischen Zeitgeschichte. Aufsätze und Archivfunde zu den Beziehungen Deutschlands und der Sowjetunion von 1917 bis 1991 | Ediert von Markus Edlinger sowie mit einem Vorwort versehen von Leonid Luks | ISBN 3-89821-756-6

44 *Anastasija Grynenko in Zusammenarbeit mit Claudia Dathe* | Die Terminologie des Gerichtswesens der Ukraine und Deutschlands im Vergleich. Eine übersetzungswissenschaftliche Analyse juristischer Fachbegriffe im Deutschen, Ukrainischen und Russischen | Mit einem Vorwort von Ulrich Hartmann | ISBN 3-89821-691-8

45 *Anton Burkov* | The Impact of the European Convention on Human Rights on Russian Law. Legislation and Application in 1996-2006 | With a foreword by Françoise Hampson | ISBN 978-3-89821-639-5

46 *Stina Torjesen, Indra Overland (Eds.)* | International Election Observers in Post-Soviet Azerbaijan. Geopolitical Pawns or Agents of Change? | ISBN 978-3-89821-743-9

47 *Taras Kuzio* | Ukraine – Crimea – Russia. Triangle of Conflict | ISBN 978-3-89821-761-3

48 *Claudia Šabić* | „Ich erinnere mich nicht, aber L'viv!" Zur Funktion kultureller Faktoren für die Institutionalisierung und Entwicklung einer ukrainischen Region | Mit einem Vorwort von Melanie Tatur | ISBN 978-3-89821-752-1

49 *Marlies Bilz* | Tatarstan in der Transformation. Nationaler Diskurs und Politische Praxis 1988-1994 | Mit einem Vorwort von Frank Golczewski | ISBN 978-3-89821-722-4

50 *Марлен Ларюэль (ред.)* | Современные интерпретации русского национализма | ISBN 978-3-89821-795-8

51 *Sonja Schüler* | Die ethnische Dimension der Armut. Roma im postsozialistischen Rumänien | Mit einem Vorwort von Anton Sterbling | ISBN 978-3-89821-776-7

52 *Галина Кожевникова* | Радикальный национализм в России и противодействие ему. Сборник докладов Центра «Сова» за 2004-2007 гг. | С предисловием Александра Верховского | ISBN 978-3-89821-721-7

53 *Галина Кожевникова и Владимир Прибыловский* | Российская власть в биографиях I. Высшие должностные лица РФ в 2004 г. | ISBN 978-3-89821-796-5

54 *Галина Кожевникова и Владимир Прибыловский* | Российская власть в биографиях II. Члены Правительства РФ в 2004 г. | ISBN 978-3-89821-797-2

55 *Галина Кожевникова и Владимир Прибыловский* | Российская власть в биографиях III. Руководители федеральных служб и агентств РФ в 2004 г.| ISBN 978-3-89821-798-9

56 *Ileana Petroniu* | Privatisierung in Transformationsökonomien. Determinanten der Restrukturierungs-Bereitschaft am Beispiel Polens, Rumäniens und der Ukraine | Mit einem Vorwort von Rainer W. Schäfer | ISBN 978-3-89821-790-3

57 *Christian Wipperfürth* | Russland und seine GUS-Nachbarn. Hintergründe, aktuelle Entwicklungen und Konflikte in einer ressourcenreichen Region| ISBN 978-3-89821-801-6

58 *Togzhan Kassenova* | From Antagonism to Partnership. The Uneasy Path of the U.S.-Russian Cooperative Threat Reduction | With a foreword by Christoph Bluth | ISBN 978-3-89821-707-1

59 *Alexander Höllwerth* | Das sakrale eurasische Imperium des Aleksandr Dugin. Eine Diskursanalyse zum postsowjetischen russischen Rechtsextremismus | Mit einem Vorwort von Dirk Uffelmann | ISBN 978-3-89821-813-9

60 *Олег Рябов* | «Россия-Матушка». Национализм, гендер и война в России XX века | С предисловием Елены Гощило | ISBN 978-3-89821-487-2

61 *Ivan Maistrenko* | Borot'bism. A Chapter in the History of the Ukrainian Revolution | With a new Introduction by Chris Ford | Translated by George S. N. Luckyj with the assistance of Ivan L. Rudnytsky | Second, Revised and Expanded Edition ISBN 978-3-8382-1107-7

62 *Maryna Romanets* | Anamorphosic Texts and Reconfigured Visions. Improvised Traditions in Contemporary Ukrainian and Irish Literature | ISBN 978-3-89821-576-3

63 *Paul D'Anieri and Taras Kuzio (Eds.)* | Aspects of the Orange Revolution I. Democratization and Elections in Post-Communist Ukraine | ISBN 978-3-89821-698-2

64 *Bohdan Harasymiw in collaboration with Oleh S. Ilnytzkyj (Eds.)* | Aspects of the Orange Revolution II. Information and Manipulation Strategies in the 2004 Ukrainian Presidential Elections | ISBN 978-3-89821-699-9

65 *Ingmar Bredies, Andreas Umland and Valentin Yakushik (Eds.)* | Aspects of the Orange Revolution III. The Context and Dynamics of the 2004 Ukrainian Presidential Elections | ISBN 978-3-89821-803-0

66 *Ingmar Bredies, Andreas Umland and Valentin Yakushik (Eds.)* | Aspects of the Orange Revolution IV. Foreign Assistance and Civic Action in the 2004 Ukrainian Presidential Elections | ISBN 978-3-89821-808-5

67 *Ingmar Bredies, Andreas Umland and Valentin Yakushik (Eds.)* | Aspects of the Orange Revolution V. Institutional Observation Reports on the 2004 Ukrainian Presidential Elections | ISBN 978-3-89821-809-2

68 *Taras Kuzio (Ed.)* | Aspects of the Orange Revolution VI. Post-Communist Democratic Revolutions in Comparative Perspective | ISBN 978-3-89821-820-7

69 *Tim Bohse* | Autoritarismus statt Selbstverwaltung. Die Transformation der kommunalen Politik in der Stadt Kaliningrad 1990-2005 | Mit einem Geleitwort von Stefan Troebst | ISBN 978-3-89821-782-8

70 *David Rupp* | Die Rußländische Föderation und die russischsprachige Minderheit in Lettland. Eine Fallstudie zur Anwaltspolitik Moskaus gegenüber den russophonen Minderheiten im „Nahen Ausland" von 1991 bis 2002 | Mit einem Vorwort von Helmut Wagner | ISBN 978-3-89821-778-1

71 *Taras Kuzio* | Theoretical and Comparative Perspectives on Nationalism. New Directions in Cross-Cultural and Post-Communist Studies | With a foreword by Paul Robert Magocsi | ISBN 978-3-89821-815-3

72 *Christine Teichmann* | Die Hochschultransformation im heutigen Osteuropa. Kontinuität und Wandel bei der Entwicklung des postkommunistischen Universitätswesens | Mit einem Vorwort von Oskar Anweiler | ISBN 978-3-89821-842-9

73 *Julia Kusznir* | Der politische Einfluss von Wirtschaftseliten in russischen Regionen. Eine Analyse am Beispiel der Erdöl- und Erdgasindustrie, 1992-2005 | Mit einem Vorwort von Wolfgang Eichwede | ISBN 978-3-89821-821-4

74 *Alena Vysotskaya* | Russland, Belarus und die EU-Osterweiterung. Zur Minderheitenfrage und zum Problem der Freizügigkeit des Personenverkehrs | Mit einem Vorwort von Katlijn Malfliet | ISBN 978-3-89821-822-1

75 *Heiko Pleines (Hrsg.)* | Corporate Governance in post-sozialistischen Volkswirtschaften | ISBN 978-3-89821-766-8

76 *Stefan Ihrig* | Wer sind die Moldawier? Rumänismus versus Moldowanismus in Historiographie und Schulbüchern der Republik Moldova, 1991-2006 | Mit einem Vorwort von Holm Sundhaussen | ISBN 978-3-89821-466-7

77 *Galina Kozhevnikova in collaboration with Alexander Verkhovsky and Eugene Veklerov* | Ultra-Nationalism and Hate Crimes in Contemporary Russia. The 2004-2006 Annual Reports of Moscow's SOVA Center | With a foreword by Stephen D. Shenfield | ISBN 978-3-89821-868-9

78 *Florian Küchler* | The Role of the European Union in Moldova's Transnistria Conflict | With a foreword by Christopher Hill | ISBN 978-3-89821-850-4

79 *Bernd Rechel* | The Long Way Back to Europe. Minority Protection in Bulgaria | With a foreword by Richard Crampton | ISBN 978-3-89821-863-4

80 *Peter W. Rodgers* | Nation, Region and History in Post-Communist Transitions. Identity Politics in Ukraine, 1991-2006 | With a foreword by Vera Tolz | ISBN 978-3-89821-903-7

81 *Stephanie Solywoda* | The Life and Work of Semen L. Frank. A Study of Russian Religious Philosophy | With a foreword by Philip Walters | ISBN 978-3-89821-457-5

82 *Vera Sokolova* | Cultural Politics of Ethnicity. Discourses on Roma in Communist Czechoslovakia | ISBN 978-3-89821-864-1

83 *Natalya Shevchik Ketenci* | Kazakhstani Enterprises in Transition. The Role of Historical Regional Development in Kazakhstan's Post-Soviet Economic Transformation | ISBN 978-3-89821-831-3

84 *Martin Malek, Anna Schor-Tschudnowskaja (Hgg.)* | Europa im Tschetschenienkrieg. Zwischen politischer Ohnmacht und Gleichgültigkeit | Mit einem Vorwort von Lipchan Basajewa | ISBN 978-3-89821-676-0

85 *Stefan Meister* | Das postsowjetische Universitätswesen zwischen nationalem und internationalem Wandel. Die Entwicklung der regionalen Hochschule in Russland als Gradmesser der Systemtransformation | Mit einem Vorwort von Joan DeBardeleben | ISBN 978-3-89821-891-7

86 *Konstantin Sheiko in collaboration with Stephen Brown* | Nationalist Imaginings of the Russian Past. Anatolii Fomenko and the Rise of Alternative History in Post-Communist Russia | With a foreword by Donald Ostrowski | ISBN 978-3-89821-915-0

87 *Sabine Jenni* | Wie stark ist das „Einige Russland"? Zur Parteibindung der Eliten und zum Wahlerfolg der Machtpartei im Dezember 2007 | Mit einem Vorwort von Klaus Armingeon | ISBN 978-3-89821-961-7

88 *Thomas Borén* | Meeting-Places of Transformation. Urban Identity, Spatial Representations and Local Politics in Post-Soviet St Petersburg | ISBN 978-3-89821-739-2

89 *Aygul Ashirova* | Stalinismus und Stalin-Kult in Zentralasien. Turkmenistan 1924-1953 | Mit einem Vorwort von Leonid Luks | ISBN 978-3-89821-987-7

90 *Leonid Luks* | Freiheit oder imperiale Größe? Essays zu einem russischen Dilemma | ISBN 978-3-8382-0011-8

91 *Christopher Gilley* | The 'Change of Signposts' in the Ukrainian Emigration. A Contribution to the History of Sovietophilism in the 1920s | With a foreword by Frank Golczewski | ISBN 978-3-89821-965-5

92 *Philipp Casula, Jeronim Perovic (Eds.)* | Identities and Politics During the Putin Presidency. The Discursive Foundations of Russia's Stability | With a foreword by Heiko Haumann | ISBN 978-3-8382-0015-6

93 *Marcel Viëtor* | Europa und die Frage nach seinen Grenzen im Osten. Zur Konstruktion ‚europäischer Identität' in Geschichte und Gegenwart | Mit einem Vorwort von Albrecht Lehmann | ISBN 978-3-8382-0045-3

94 *Ben Hellman, Andrei Rogachevskii* | Filming the Unfilmable. Casper Wrede's 'One Day in the Life of Ivan Denisovich' | Second, Revised and Expanded Edition | ISBN 978-3-8382-0044-6

95 *Eva Fuchslocher* | Vaterland, Sprache, Glaube. Orthodoxie und Nationenbildung am Beispiel Georgiens | Mit einem Vorwort von Christina von Braun | ISBN 978-3-89821-884-9

96 *Vladimir Kantor* | Das Westlertum und der Weg Russlands. Zur Entwicklung der russischen Literatur und Philosophie | Ediert von Dagmar Herrmann | Mit einem Beitrag von Nikolaus Lobkowicz | ISBN 978-3-8382-0102-3

97 *Kamran Musayev* | Die postsowjetische Transformation im Baltikum und Südkaukasus. Eine vergleichende Untersuchung der politischen Entwicklung Lettlands und Aserbaidschans 1985-2009 | Mit einem Vorwort von Leonid Luks | Ediert von Sandro Henschel | ISBN 978-3-8382-0103-0

98 *Tatiana Zhurzhenko* | Borderlands into Bordered Lands. Geopolitics of Identity in Post-Soviet Ukraine | With a foreword by Dieter Segert | ISBN 978-3-8382-0042-2

99 *Кирилл Галушко, Лидия Смола (ред.)* | Пределы падения – варианты украинского будущего. Аналитико-прогностические исследования | ISBN 978-3-8382-0148-1

100 *Michael Minkenberg (Ed.)* | Historical Legacies and the Radical Right in Post-Cold War Central and Eastern Europe | With an afterword by Sabrina P. Ramet | ISBN 978-3-8382-0124-5

101 *David-Emil Wickström* | Rocking St. Petersburg. Transcultural Flows and Identity Politics in the St. Petersburg Popular Music Scene | With a foreword by Yngvar B. Steinholt | Second, Revised and Expanded Edition | ISBN 978-3-8382-0100-9

102 *Eva Zabka* | Eine neue „Zeit der Wirren"? Der spät- und postsowjetische Systemwandel 1985-2000 im Spiegel russischer gesellschaftspolitischer Diskurse | Mit einem Vorwort von Margareta Mommsen | ISBN 978-3-8382-0161-0

103 *Ulrike Ziemer* | Ethnic Belonging, Gender and Cultural Practices. Youth Identitites in Contemporary Russia | With a foreword by Anoop Nayak | ISBN 978-3-8382-0152-8

104 *Ksenia Chepikova* | ‚Einiges Russland' - eine zweite KPdSU? Aspekte der Identitätskonstruktion einer postsowjetischen „Partei der Macht" | Mit einem Vorwort von Torsten Oppelland | ISBN 978-3-8382-0311-9

105 *Леонид Люкс* | Западничество или евразийство? Демократия или идеократия? Сборник статей об исторических дилеммах России | С предисловием Владимира Кантора | ISBN 978-3-8382-0211-2

106 *Anna Dost* | Das russische Verfassungsrecht auf dem Weg zum Föderalismus und zurück. Zum Konflikt von Rechtsnormen und -wirklichkeit in der Russländischen Föderation von 1991 bis 2009 | Mit einem Vorwort von Alexander Blankenagel | ISBN 978-3-8382-0292-1

107 *Philipp Herzog* | Sozialistische Völkerfreundschaft, nationaler Widerstand oder harmloser Zeitvertreib? Zur politischen Funktion der Volkskunst im sowjetischen Estland | Mit einem Vorwort von Andreas Kappeler | ISBN 978-3-8382-0216-7

108 *Marlène Laruelle (Ed.)* | Russian Nationalism, Foreign Policy, and Identity Debates in Putin's Russia. New Ideological Patterns after the Orange Revolution | ISBN 978-3-8382-0325-6

109 *Michail Logvinov* | Russlands Kampf gegen den internationalen Terrorismus. Eine kritische Bestandsaufnahme des Bekämpfungsansatzes | Mit einem Geleitwort von Hans-Henning Schröder und einem Vorwort von Eckhard Jesse | ISBN 978-3-8382-0329-4

110 *John B. Dunlop* | The Moscow Bombings of September 1999. Examinations of Russian Terrorist Attacks at the Onset of Vladimir Putin's Rule | Second, Revised and Expanded Edition | ISBN 978-3-8382-0388-1

111 *Андрей А. Ковалёв* | Свидетельство из-за кулис российской политики I. Можно ли делать добро из зла? (Воспоминания и размышления о последних советских и первых послесоветских годах) | With a foreword by Peter Reddaway | ISBN 978-3-8382-0302-7

112 *Андрей А. Ковалёв* | Свидетельство из-за кулис российской политики II. Угроза для себя и окружающих (Наблюдения и предостережения относительно происходящего после 2000 г.) | ISBN 978-3-8382-0303-4

113 *Bernd Kappenberg* | Zeichen setzen für Europa. Der Gebrauch europäischer lateinischer Sonderzeichen in der deutschen Öffentlichkeit | Mit einem Vorwort von Peter Schlobinski | ISBN 978-3-89821-749-1

114 *Ivo Mijnssen* | The Quest for an Ideal Youth in Putin's Russia I. Back to Our Future! History, Modernity, and Patriotism according to Nashi, 2005-2013 | With a foreword by Jeronim Perović | Second, Revised and Expanded Edition | ISBN 978-3-8382-0368-3

115 *Jussi Lassila* | The Quest for an Ideal Youth in Putin's Russia II. The Search for Distinctive Conformism in the Political Communication of Nashi, 2005-2009 | With a foreword by Kirill Postoutenko | Second, Revised and Expanded Edition | ISBN 978-3-8382-0415-4

116 *Valerio Trabandt* | Neue Nachbarn, gute Nachbarschaft? Die EU als internationaler Akteur am Beispiel ihrer Demokratieförderung in Belarus und der Ukraine 2004-2009 | Mit einem Vorwort von Jutta Joachim | ISBN 978-3-8382-0437-6

117 *Fabian Pfeiffer* | Estlands Außen- und Sicherheitspolitik I. Der estnische Atlantizismus nach der wiedererlangten Unabhängigkeit 1991-2004 | Mit einem Vorwort von Helmut Hubel | ISBN 978-3-8382-0127-6

118 *Jana Podßuweit* | Estlands Außen- und Sicherheitspolitik II. Handlungsoptionen eines Kleinstaates im Rahmen seiner EU-Mitgliedschaft (2004-2008) | Mit einem Vorwort von Helmut Hubel | ISBN 978-3-8382-0440-6

119 *Karin Pointner* | Estlands Außen- und Sicherheitspolitik III. Eine gedächtnispolitische Analyse estnischer Entwicklungskooperation 2006-2010 | Mit einem Vorwort von Karin Liebhart | ISBN 978-3-8382-0435-2

120 *Ruslana Vovk* | Die Offenheit der ukrainischen Verfassung für das Völkerrecht und die europäische Integration | Mit einem Vorwort von Alexander Blankenagel | ISBN 978-3-8382-0481-9

121 *Mykhaylo Banakh* | Die Relevanz der Zivilgesellschaft bei den postkommunistischen Transformationsprozessen in mittel- und osteuropäischen Ländern. Das Beispiel der spät- und postsowjetischen Ukraine 1986-2009 | Mit einem Vorwort von Gerhard Simon | ISBN 978-3-8382-0499-4

122 *Michael Moser* | Language Policy and the Discourse on Languages in Ukraine under President Viktor Yanukovych (25 February 2010–28 October 2012) | ISBN 978-3-8382-0497-0 (Paperback edition) | ISBN 978-3-8382-0507-6 (Hardcover edition)

123 *Nicole Krome* | Russischer Netzwerkkapitalismus Restrukturierungsprozesse in der Russischen Föderation am Beispiel des Luftfahrtunternehmens „Aviastar" | Mit einem Vorwort von Petra Stykow | ISBN 978-3-8382-0534-2

124 *David R. Marples* | 'Our Glorious Past'. Lukashenka's Belarus and the Great Patriotic War | ISBN 978-3-8382-0574-8 (Paperback edition) | ISBN 978-3-8382-0675-2 (Hardcover edition)

125 *Ulf Walther* | Russlands „neuer Adel". Die Macht des Geheimdienstes von Gorbatschow bis Putin | Mit einem Vorwort von Hans-Georg Wieck | ISBN 978-3-8382-0584-7

126 *Simon Geissbühler (Hrsg.)* | Kiew – Revolution 3.0. Der Euromaidan 2013/14 und die Zukunftsperspektiven der Ukraine | ISBN 978-3-8382-0581-6 (Paperback edition) | ISBN 978-3-8382-0681-3 (Hardcover edition)

127 *Andrey Makarychev* | Russia and the EU in a Multipolar World. Discourses, Identities, Norms | With a foreword by Klaus Segbers | ISBN 978-3-8382-0629-5

128 *Roland Scharff* | Kasachstan als postsowjetischer Wohlfahrtsstaat. Die Transformation des sozialen Schutzsystems | Mit einem Vorwort von Joachim Ahrens | ISBN 978-3-8382-0622-6

129 *Katja Grupp* | Bild Lücke Deutschland. Kaliningrader Studierende sprechen über Deutschland | Mit einem Vorwort von Martin Schulz | ISBN 978-3-8382-0552-6

130 *Konstantin Sheiko, Stephen Brown* | History as Therapy. Alternative History and Nationalist Imaginings in Russia, 1991-2014 | ISBN 978-3-8382-0665-3

131 *Elisa Kriza* | Alexander Solzhenitsyn: Cold War Icon, Gulag Author, Russian Nationalist? A Study of the Western Reception of his Literary Writings, Historical Interpretations, and Political Ideas | With a foreword by Andrei Rogatchevski | ISBN 978-3-8382-0589-2 (Paperback edition) | ISBN 978-3-8382-0690-5 (Hardcover edition)

132 *Serghei Golunov* | The Elephant in the Room. Corruption and Cheating in Russian Universities | ISBN 978-3-8382-0570-0

133 *Manja Hussner, Rainer Arnold (Hgg.)* | Verfassungsgerichtsbarkeit in Zentralasien I. Sammlung von Verfassungstexten | ISBN 978-3-8382-0595-3

134 *Nikolay Mitrokhin* | Die „Russische Partei". Die Bewegung der russischen Nationalisten in der UdSSR 1953-1985 | Aus dem Russischen übertragen von einem Übersetzerteam unter der Leitung von Larisa Schippel | ISBN 978-3-8382-0024-8

135 *Manja Hussner, Rainer Arnold (Hgg.)* | Verfassungsgerichtsbarkeit in Zentralasien II. Sammlung von Verfassungstexten | ISBN 978-3-8382-0597-7

136 *Manfred Zeller* | Das sowjetische Fieber. Fußballfans im poststalinistischen Vielvölkerreich | Mit einem Vorwort von Nikolaus Katzer | ISBN 978-3-8382-0757-5

137 *Kristin Schreiter* | Stellung und Entwicklungspotential zivilgesellschaftlicher Gruppen in Russland. Menschenrechtsorganisationen im Vergleich | ISBN 978-3-8382-0673-8

138 *David R. Marples, Frederick V. Mills (Eds.)* | Ukraine's Euromaidan. Analyses of a Civil Revolution | ISBN 978-3-8382-0660-8

139 *Bernd Kappenberg* | Setting Signs for Europe. Why Diacritics Matter for European Integration | With a foreword by Peter Schlobinski | ISBN 978-3-8382-0663-9

140 *René Lenz* | Internationalisierung, Kooperation und Transfer. Externe bildungspolitische Akteure in der Russischen Föderation | Mit einem Vorwort von Frank Ettrich | ISBN 978-3-8382-0751-3

141 *Juri Plusnin, Yana Zausaeva, Natalia Zhidkevich, Artemy Pozanenko* | Wandering Workers. Mores, Behavior, Way of Life, and Political Status of Domestic Russian Labor Migrants | Translated by Julia Kazantseva | ISBN 978-3-8382-0653-0

142 *David J. Smith (Eds.)* | Latvia – A Work in Progress? 100 Years of State- and Nation-Building | ISBN 978-3-8382-0648-6

143 *Инна Чувычкина (ред.)* | Экспортные нефте- и газопроводы на постсоветском пространстве. Анализ трубопроводной политики в свете теории международных отношений | ISBN 978-3-8382-0822-0

144 *Johann Zajaczkowski* | Russland – eine pragmatische Großmacht? Eine rollentheoretische Untersuchung russischer Außenpolitik am Beispiel der Zusammenarbeit mit den USA nach 9/11 und des Georgienkrieges von 2008 | Mit einem Vorwort von Siegfried Schieder | ISBN 978-3-8382-0837-4

145 *Boris Popivanov* | Changing Images of the Left in Bulgaria. The Challenge of Post-Communism in the Early 21st Century | ISBN 978-3-8382-0667-7

146 *Lenka Krátká* | A History of the Czechoslovak Ocean Shipping Company 1948-1989. How a Small, Landlocked Country Ran Maritime Business During the Cold War | ISBN 978-3-8382-0666-0

147 *Alexander Sergunin* | Explaining Russian Foreign Policy Behavior. Theory and Practice | ISBN 978-3-8382-0752-0

148 *Darya Malyutina* | Migrant Friendships in a Super-Diverse City. Russian-Speakers and their Social Relationships in London in the 21st Century | With a foreword by Claire Dwyer | ISBN 978-3-8382-0652-3

149 *Alexander Sergunin, Valery Konyshev* | Russia in the Arctic. Hard or Soft Power? | ISBN 978-3-8382-0753-7

150 *John J. Maresca* | Helsinki Revisited. A Key U.S. Negotiator's Memoirs on the Development of the CSCE into the OSCE | With a foreword by Hafiz Pashayev | ISBN 978-3-8382-0852-7

151 *Jardar Østbø* | The New Third Rome. Readings of a Russian Nationalist Myth | With a foreword by Pål Kolstø | ISBN 978-3-8382-0870-1

152 *Simon Kordonsky* | Socio-Economic Foundations of the Russian Post-Soviet Regime. The Resource-Based Economy and Estate-Based Social Structure of Contemporary Russia | With a foreword by Svetlana Barsukova | ISBN 978-3-8382-0775-9

153 *Duncan Leitch* | Assisting Reform in Post-Communist Ukraine 2000–2012. The Illusions of Donors and the Disillusion of Beneficiaries | With a foreword by Kataryna Wolczuk | ISBN 978-3-8382-0844-2

154 *Abel Polese* | Limits of a Post-Soviet State. How Informality Replaces, Renegotiates, and Reshapes Governance in Contemporary Ukraine | With a foreword by Colin Williams | ISBN 978-3-8382-0845-9

155 *Mikhail Suslov (Ed.)* | Digital Orthodoxy in the Post-Soviet World. The Russian Orthodox Church and Web 2.0 | With a foreword by Father Cyril Hovorun | ISBN 978-3-8382-0871-8

156 *Leonid Luks* | Zwei „Sonderwege"? Russisch-deutsche Parallelen und Kontraste (1917-2014). Vergleichende Essays | ISBN 978-3-8382-0823-7

157 *Vladimir V. Karacharovskiy, Ovsey I. Shkaratan, Gordey A. Yastrebov* | Towards a New Russian Work Culture. Can Western Companies and Expatriates Change Russian Society? | With a foreword by Elena N. Danilova | Translated by Julia Kazantseva | ISBN 978-3-8382-0902-9

158 *Edmund Griffiths* | Aleksandr Prokhanov and Post-Soviet Esotericism | ISBN 978-3-8382-0963-0

159 *Timm Beichelt, Susann Worschech (Eds.)* | Transnational Ukraine? Networks and Ties that Influence(d) Contemporary Ukraine | ISBN 978-3-8382-0944-9

160 *Mieste Hotopp-Riecke* | Die Tataren der Krim zwischen Assimilation und Selbstbehauptung. Der Aufbau des krimtatarischen Bildungswesens nach Deportation und Heimkehr (1990-2005) | Mit einem Vorwort von Swetlana Czerwonnaja | ISBN 978-3-89821-940-2

161 *Olga Bertelsen (Ed.)* | Revolution and War in Contemporary Ukraine. The Challenge of Change | ISBN 978-3-8382-1016-2

162 *Natalya Ryabinska* | Ukraine's Post-Communist Mass Media. Between Capture and Commercialization | With a foreword by Marta Dyczok | ISBN 978-3-8382-1011-7

163 *Alexandra Cotofana, James M. Nyce (Eds.)* | Religion and Magic in Socialist and Post-Socialist Contexts. Historic and Ethnographic Case Studies of Orthodoxy, Heterodoxy, and Alternative Spirituality | With a foreword by Patrick L. Michelson | ISBN 978-3-8382-0989-0

164 *Nozima Akhrarkhodjaeva* | The Instrumentalisation of Mass Media in Electoral Authoritarian Regimes. Evidence from Russia's Presidential Election Campaigns of 2000 and 2008 | ISBN 978-3-8382-1013-1

165 *Yulia Krasheninnikova* | Informal Healthcare in Contemporary Russia. Sociographic Essays on the Post-Soviet Infrastructure for Alternative Healing Practices | ISBN 978-3-8382-0970-8

166 *Peter Kaiser* | Das Schachbrett der Macht. Die Handlungsspielräume eines sowjetischen Funktionärs unter Stalin am Beispiel des Generalsekretärs des Komsomol Aleksandr Kosarev (1929-1938) | Mit einem Vorwort von Dietmar Neutatz | ISBN 978-3-8382-1052-0

167 *Oksana Kim* | The Effects and Implications of Kazakhstan's Adoption of International Financial Reporting Standards. A Resource Dependence Perspective | With a foreword by Svetlana Vlady | ISBN 978-3-8382-0987-6

168 *Anna Sanina* | Patriotic Education in Contemporary Russia. Sociological Studies in the Making of the Post-Soviet Citizen | With a foreword by Anna Oldfield | ISBN 978-3-8382-0993-7

169 *Rudolf Wolters* | Spezialist in Sibirien Faksimile der 1933 erschienenen ersten Ausgabe | Mit einem Vorwort von Dmitrij Chmelnizki | ISBN 978-3-8382-0515-1

170 *Michal Vít, Magdalena M. Baran (Eds.)* | Transregional versus National Perspectives on Contemporary Central European History. Studies on the Building of Nation-States and Their Cooperation in the 20th and 21st Century | With a foreword by Petr Vágner | ISBN 978-3-8382-1015-5

171 *Philip Gamaghelyan* | Conflict Resolution Beyond the International Relations Paradigm. Evolving Designs as a Transformative Practice in Nagorno-Karabakh and Syria | With a foreword by Susan Allen | ISBN 978-3-8382-1057-5

172 *Maria Shagina* | Joining a Prestigious Club. Cooperation with Europarties and Its Impact on Party Development in Georgia, Moldova, and Ukraine 2004–2015 | With a foreword by Kataryna Wolczuk | ISBN 978-3-8382-1084-1

173 *Alexandra Cotofana, James M. Nyce (Eds.)* | Religion and Magic in Socialist and Post-Socialist Contexts II. Baltic, Eastern European, and Post-USSR Case Studies | With a foreword by Anita Stasulane | ISBN 978-3-8382-0990-6

174 *Barbara Kunz* | Kind Words, Cruise Missiles, and Everything in Between. The Use of Power Resources in U.S. Policies towards Poland, Ukraine, and Belarus 1989–2008 | With a foreword by William Hill | ISBN 978-3-8382-1065-0

175 *Eduard Klein* | Bildungskorruption in Russland und der Ukraine. Eine komparative Analyse der Performanz staatlicher Antikorruptionsmaßnahmen im Hochschulsektor am Beispiel universitärer Aufnahmeprüfungen | Mit einem Vorwort von Heiko Pleines | ISBN 978-3-8382-0995-1

176 *Markus Soldner* | Politischer Kapitalismus im postsowjetischen Russland. Die politische, wirtschaftliche und mediale Transformation in den 1990er Jahren | Mit einem Vorwort von Wolfgang Ismayr | ISBN 978-3-8382-1222-7

177 *Anton Oleinik* | Building Ukraine from Within. A Sociological, Institutional, and Economic Analysis of a Nation-State in the Making | ISBN 978-3-8382-1150-3

178 *Peter Rollberg, Marlene Laruelle (Eds.)* | Mass Media in the Post-Soviet World. Market Forces, State Actors, and Political Manipulation in the Informational Environment after Communism | ISBN 978-3-8382-1116-9

179 *Mikhail Minakov* | Development and Dystopia. Studies in Post-Soviet Ukraine and Eastern Europe | With a foreword by Alexander Etkind | ISBN 978-3-8382-1112-1

180 *Aijan Sharshenova* | The European Union's Democracy Promotion in Central Asia. A Study of Political Interests, Influence, and Development in Kazakhstan and Kyrgyzstan in 2007–2013 | With a foreword by Gordon Crawford | ISBN 978-3-8382-1151-0

181 *Andrey Makarychev, Alexandra Yatsyk (Eds.)* | Boris Nemtsov and Russian Politics. Power and Resistance | With a foreword by Zhanna Nemtsova | ISBN 978-3-8382-1122-0

182 *Sophie Falsini* | The Euromaidan's Effect on Civil Society. Why and How Ukrainian Social Capital Increased after the Revolution of Dignity | With a foreword by Susann Worschech | ISBN 978-3-8382-1131-2

183 *Valentyna Romanova, Andreas Umland (Eds.)* | Ukraine's Decentralization. Challenges and Implications of the Local Governance Reform after the Euromaidan Revolution | ISBN 978-3-8382-1162-6

184 *Leonid Luks* | A Fateful Triangle. Essays on Contemporary Russian, German and Polish History | ISBN 978-3-8382-1143-5

185 *John B. Dunlop* | The February 2015 Assassination of Boris Nemtsov and the Flawed Trial of his Alleged Killers. An Exploration of Russia's "Crime of the 21st Century" | ISBN 978-3-8382-1188-6

186 *Vasile Rotaru* | Russia, the EU, and the Eastern Partnership. Building Bridges or Digging Trenches? | ISBN 978-3-8382-1134-3

187 *Marina Lebedeva* | Russian Studies of International Relations. From the Soviet Past to the Post-Cold-War Present | With a foreword by Andrei P. Tsygankov | ISBN 978-3-8382-0851-0

188 *Tomasz Stępniewski, George Soroka (Eds.)* | Ukraine after Maidan. Revisiting Domestic and Regional Security | ISBN 978-3-8382-1075-9

189 *Petar Cholakov* | Ethnic Entrepreneurs Unmasked. Political Institutions and Ethnic Conflicts in Contemporary Bulgaria | ISBN 978-3-8382-1189-3

190 *A. Salem, G. Hazeldine, D. Morgan (Eds.)* | Higher Education in Post-Communist States. Comparative and Sociological Perspectives | ISBN 978-3-8382-1183-1

191 *Igor Torbakov* | After Empire. Nationalist Imagination and Symbolic Politics in Russia and Eurasia in the Twentieth and Twenty-First Century | With a foreword by Serhii Plokhy | ISBN 978-3-8382-1217-3

192 *Aleksandr Burakovskiy* | Jewish-Ukrainian Relations in Late and Post-Soviet Ukraine. Articles, Lectures and Essays from 1986 to 2016 | ISBN 978-3-8382-1210-4

193 *Natalia Shapovalova, Olga Burlyuk (Eds.)* | Civil Society in Post-Euromaidan Ukraine. From Revolution to Consolidation | With a foreword by Richard Youngs | ISBN 978-3-8382-1216-6

194 *Franz Preissler* | Positionsverteidigung, Imperialismus oder Irredentismus? Russland und die „Russischsprachigen", 1991–2015 | ISBN 978-3-8382-1262-3

195 *Marian Madeła* | Der Reformprozess in der Ukraine 2014-2017. Eine Fallstudie zur Reform der öffentlichen Verwaltung | Mit einem Vorwort von Martin Malek | ISBN 978-3-8382-1266-1

196 *Anke Giesen* | „Wie kann denn der Sieger ein Verbrecher sein?" Eine diskursanalytische Untersuchung der russlandweiten Debatte über Konzept und Verstaatlichungsprozess der Lagergedenkstätte „Perm'-36" im Ural | ISBN 978-3-8382-1284-5

197 *Victoria Leukavets* | The Integration Policies of Belarus and Ukraine vis-à-vis the EU and Russia. A Comparative Analysis Through the Prism of a Two-Level Game Approach | ISBN 978-3-8382-1247-0

198 *Oksana Kim* | The Development and Challenges of Russian Corporate Governance I. The Roles and Functions of Boards of Directors | With a foreword by Sheila M. Puffer | ISBN 978-3-8382-1287-6

199 *Thomas D. Grant* | International Law and the Post-Soviet Space I. Essays on Chechnya and the Baltic States | With a foreword by Stephen M. Schwebel | ISBN 978-3-8382-1279-1

200 *Thomas D. Grant* | International Law and the Post-Soviet Space II. Essays on Ukraine, Intervention, and Non-Proliferation | ISBN 978-3-8382-1280-7

201 *Slavomír Michálek, Michal Štefansky* | The Age of Fear. The Cold War and Its Influence on Czechoslovakia 1945–1968 | ISBN 978-3-8382-1285-2

202 *Iulia-Sabina Joja* | Romania's Strategic Culture 1990–2014. Continuity and Change in a Post-Communist Country's Evolution of National Interests and Security Policies | With a foreword by Heiko Biehl | ISBN 978-3-8382-1286-9

203 *Andrei Rogatchevski, Yngvar B. Steinholt, Arve Hansen, David-Emil Wickström* | War of Songs. Popular Music and Recent Russia-Ukraine Relations | With a foreword by Artemy Troitsky | ISBN 978-3-8382-1173-2

204 *Maria Lipman (Ed.)* | Russian Voices on Post-Crimea Russia. An Almanac of Counterpoint Essays from 2015–2018 | ISBN 978-3-8382-1251-7

205 *Ksenia Maksimovtsova* | Language Conflicts in Contemporary Estonia, Latvia, and Ukraine. A Comparative Exploration of Discourses in Post-Soviet Russian-Language Digital Media | With a foreword by Ammon Cheskin | ISBN 978-3-8382-1282-1

206 *Michal Vit* | The EU's Impact on Identity Formation in East-Central Europe between 2004 and 2013. Perceptions of the Nation and Europe in Political Parties of the Czech Republic, Poland, and Slovakia | With a foreword by Andrea Pető | ISBN 978-3-8382-1275-3

207 *Per A. Rudling* | Tarnished Heroes. The Organization of Ukrainian Nationalists in the Memory Politics of Post-Soviet Ukraine | ISBN 978-3-8382-0999-9

208 *Kaja Gadowska, Peter Solomon (Eds.)* | Legal Change in Post-Communist States. Progress, Reversions, Explanations | With a foreword by Nils Muižnieks | ISBN 978-3-8382-1312-5

209 *Pawel Kowal, Georges Mink, Iwona Reichardt (Eds.)* | Three Revolutions: Mobilization and Change in Contemporary Ukraine I. Theoretical Aspects and Analyses on Religion, Memory, and Identity | ISBN 978-3-8382-1321-7

210 *Pawel Kowal, Georges Mink, Adam Reichardt, Iwona Reichardt (Eds.)* | Three Revolutions: Mobilization and Change in Contemporary Ukraine II. An Oral History of the Revolution on Granite, Orange Revolution, and Revolution of Dignity | ISBN 978-3-8382-1323-1

211 *Li Bennich-Björkman, Sergiy Kurbatov (Eds.)* | When the Future Came. The Collapse of the USSR and the Emergence of National Memory in Post-Soviet History Textbooks | ISBN 978-3-8382-1335-4

212 *Olga R. Gulina* | Migration as a (Geo-)Political Challenge in the Post-Soviet Space. Border Regimes, Policy Choices, Visa Agendas | With a foreword by Nils Muižnieks | ISBN 978-3-8382-1338-5

213 *Sanna Turoma, Kaarina Aitamurto, Slobodanka Vladiv-Glover (Eds.)* | Religion, Expression, and Patriotism in Russia. Essays on Post-Soviet Society and the State. ISBN 978-3-8382-1346-7

214 *Vasif Huseynov* | Geopolitical Rivalries in the "Common Neighborhood". Russia's Conflict with the West, Soft Power, and Neoclassical Realism | With a foreword by Nicholas Ross Smith | ISBN 978-3-8382-1277-7

215 *Mikhail Suslov* | Geopolitical Imagination. Ideology and Utopia in Post-Soviet Russia | With a foreword by Mark Bassin | ISBN 978-3-8382-1361-3

216 *Alexander Etkind, Mikhail Minakov (Eds.)* | Ideology after Union. Political Doctrines, Discourses, and Debates in Post-Soviet Societies | ISBN 978-3-8382-1388-0

217 *Jakob Mischke, Oleksandr Zabirko (Hgg.)* | Protestbewegungen im langen Schatten des Kreml. Aufbruch und Resignation in Russland und der Ukraine | ISBN 978-3-8382-0926-5

218 *Oksana Huss* | How Corruption and Anti-Corruption Policies Sustain Hybrid Regimes. Strategies of Political Domination under Ukraine's Presidents in 1994-2014 | With a foreword by Tobias Debiel and Andrea Gawrich | ISBN 978-3-8382-1430-6

219 *Dmitry Travin, Vladimir Gel'man, Otar Marganiya* | The Russian Path. Ideas, Interests, Institutions, Illusions | With a foreword by Vladimir Ryzhkov | ISBN 978-3-8382-1421-4

220 *Gergana Dimova* | Political Uncertainty. A Comparative Exploration | With a foreword by Todor Yalamov and Rumena Filipova | ISBN 978-3-8382-1385-9

221 *Torben Waschke* | Russland in Transition. Geopolitik zwischen Raum, Identität und Machtinteressen | Mit einem Vorwort von Andreas Dittmann | ISBN 978-3-8382-1480-1

222 *Steven Jobbitt, Zsolt Bottlik, Marton Berki (Eds.)* | Power and Identity in the Post-Soviet Realm. Geographies of Ethnicity and Nationality after 1991 | ISBN 978-3-8382-1399-6

223 *Daria Buteiko* | Erinnerungsort. Ort des Gedenkens, der Erholung oder der Einkehr? Kommunismus-Erinnerung am Beispiel der Gedenkstätte Berliner Mauer sowie des Soloveckij-Klosters und -Museumsparks | ISBN 978-3-8382-1367-5

224 *Olga Bertelsen (Ed.)* | Russian Active Measures. Yesterday, Today, Tomorrow | With a foreword by Jan Goldman | ISBN 978-3-8382-1529-7

225 *David Mandel* | "Optimizing" Higher Education in Russia. University Teachers and their Union "Universitetskaya solidarnost'" | ISBN 978-3-8382-1519-8

226 *Mikhail Minakov, Gwendolyn Sasse, Daria Isachenko (Eds.)* | Post-Soviet Secessionism. Nation-Building and State-Failure after Communism | ISBN 978-3-8382-1538-9

227 *Jakob Hauter (Ed.)* | Civil War? Interstate War? Hybrid War? Dimensions and Interpretations of the Donbas Conflict in 2014–2020 | With a foreword by Andrew Wilson | ISBN 978-3-8382-1383-5

228 *Tima T. Moldogaziev, Gene A. Brewer, J. Edward Kellough (Eds.)* | Public Policy and Politics in Georgia. Lessons from Post-Soviet Transition | With a foreword by Dan Durning | ISBN 978-3-8382-1535-8

229 *Oxana Schmies (Ed.)* | NATO's Enlargement and Russia. A Strategic Challenge in the Past and Future | With a foreword by Vladimir Kara-Murza | ISBN 978-3-8382-1478-8

230 *Christopher Ford* | Ukapisme – Une Gauche perdue. Le marxisme anti-colonial dans la révolution ukrainienne 1917-1925 | Avec une préface de Vincent Présumey | ISBN 978-3-8382-0899-2

231 *Anna Kutkina* | Between Lenin and Bandera. Decommunization and Multivocality in Post-Euromaidan Ukraine | With a foreword by Juri Mykkänen | ISBN 978-3-8382-1506-1

232 *Lincoln E. Flake* | Defending the Faith. The Russian Orthodox Church and the Demise of Religious Pluralism | With a foreword by Peter Martland | ISBN 978-3-8382-1378-1

233 *Nikoloz Samkharadze* | Russia's Recognition of the Independence of Abkhazia and South Ossetia. Analysis of a Deviant Case in Moscow's Foreign Policy | With a foreword by Neil MacFarlane | ISBN 978-3-8382-1414-6

234 *Arve Hansen* | Urban Protest. A Spatial Perspective on Kyiv, Minsk, and Moscow | With a foreword by Julie Wilhelmsen | ISBN 978-3-8382-1495-5

235 *Eleonora Narvselius, Julie Fedor (Eds.)* | Diversity in the East-Central European Borderlands. Memories, Cityscapes, People | ISBN 978-3-8382-1523-5

236 *Regina Elsner* | The Russian Orthodox Church and Modernity. A Historical and Theological Investigation into Eastern Christianity between Unity and Plurality | With a foreword by Mikhail Suslov | ISBN 978-3-8382-1568-6

237 *Bo Petersson* | The Putin Predicament. Problems of Legitimacy and Succession in Russia | With a foreword by J. Paul Goode | ISBN 978-3-8382-1050-6

238 *Jonathan Otto Pohl* | The Years of Great Silence. The Deportation, Special Settlement, and Mobilization into the Labor Army of Ethnic Germans in the USSR, 1941–1955 | ISBN 978-3-8382-1630-0

239 *Mikhail Minakov (Ed.)* | Inventing Majorities. Ideological Creativity in Post-Soviet Societies | ISBN 978-3-8382-1641-6

240 *Robert M. Cutler* | Soviet and Post-Soviet Foreign Policies I. East-South Relations and the Political Economy of the Communist Bloc, 1971–1991 | With a foreword by Roger E. Kanet | ISBN 978-3-8382-1654-6

241 *Izabella Agardi* | On the Verge of History. Life Stories of Rural Women from Serbia, Romania, and Hungary, 1920–2020 | With a foreword by Andrea Pető | ISBN 978-3-8382-1602-7

242 *Sebastian Schäffer (Ed.)* | Ukraine in Central and Eastern Europe. Kyiv's Foreign Affairs and the International Relations of the Post-Communist Region | With a foreword by Pavlo Klimkin and Andreas Umland| ISBN 978-3-8382-1615-7

243 *Volodymyr Dubrovskyi, Kalman Mizsei, Mychailo Wynnyckyj (Eds.)* | Eight Years after the Revolution of Dignity. What Has Changed in Ukraine during 2013–2021? | With a foreword by Yaroslav Hrytsak | ISBN 978-3-8382-1560-0

244 *Rumena Filipova* | Constructing the Limits of Europe Identity and Foreign Policy in Poland, Bulgaria, and Russia since 1989 | With forewords by Harald Wydra and Gergana Yankova-Dimova | ISBN 978-3-8382-1649-2

245 *Oleksandra Keudel* | How Patronal Networks Shape Opportunities for Local Citizen Participation in a Hybrid Regime A Comparative Analysis of Five Cities in Ukraine | With a foreword by Sabine Kropp | ISBN 978-3-8382-1671-3

246 *Jan Claas Behrends, Thomas Lindenberger, Pavel Kolar (Eds.)* | Violence after Stalin Institutions, Practices, and Everyday Life in the Soviet Bloc 1953–1989 | ISBN 978-3-8382-1637-9

247 *Leonid Luks* | Macht und Ohnmacht der Utopien Essays zur Geschichte Russlands im 20. und 21. Jahrhundert | ISBN 978-3-8382-1677-5

248 *Iuliia Barshadska* | Brüssel zwischen Kyjiw und Moskau Das auswärtige Handeln der Europäischen Union im ukrainisch-russischen Konflikt 2014-2019 | Mit einem Vorwort von Olaf Leiße | ISBN 978-3-8382-1667-6

249 *Valentyna Romanova* | Decentralisation and Multilevel Elections in Ukraine Reform Dynamics and Party Politics in 2010–2021 | With a foreword by Kimitaka Matsuzato | ISBN 978-3-8382-1700-0

250 *Alexander Motyl* | National Questions. Theoretical Reflections on Nations and Nationalism in Eastern Europe | ISBN 978-3-8382-1675-1

251 *Marc Dietrich* | A Cosmopolitan Model for Peacebuilding. The Ukrainian Cases of Crimea and the Donbas | With a foreword by Rémi Baudouï | ISBN 978-3-8382-1687-4

252 *Eduard Baidaus* | An Unsettled Nation. Moldova in the Geopolitics of Russia, Romania, and Ukraine | With forewords by John-Paul Himka and David R. Marples | ISBN 978-3-8382-1582-2

253 *Igor Okunev, Petr Oskolkov (Eds.)* | Transforming the Administrative Matryoshka. The Reform of Autonomous Okrugs in the Russian Federation, 2003–2008 | With a foreword by Vladimir Zorin | ISBN 978-3-8382-1721-5

254 *Winfried Schneider-Deters* | Ukraine's Fateful Years 2013–2019. Vol. I: The Popular Uprising in Winter 2013/2014 | ISBN 978-3-8382-1725-3

255 *Winfried Schneider-Deters* | Ukraine's Fateful Years 2013–2019. Vol. II: The Annexation of Crimea and the War in Donbas | ISBN 978-3-8382-1726-0

256 *Robert M. Cutler* | Soviet and Post-Soviet Russian Foreign Policies II. East-West Relations in Europe and the Political Economy of the Communist Bloc, 1971–1991 | With a foreword by Roger E. Kanet | ISBN 978-3-8382-1727-7

257 *Robert M. Cutler* | Soviet and Post-Soviet Russian Foreign Policies III. East-West Relations in Europe and Eurasia in the Post-Cold War Transition, 1991–2001 | With a foreword by Roger E. Kanet | ISBN 978-3-8382-1728-4

258 *Paweł Kowal, Iwona Reichardt, Kateryna Pryshchepa (Eds.)* | Three Revolutions: Mobilization and Change in Contemporary Ukraine III. Archival Records and Historical Sources on the 1990 Revolution on Granite | ISBN 978-3-8382-1376-7

259 *Mikhail Minakov (Ed.)* | Philosophy Unchained. Developments in Post-Soviet Philosophical Thought. | With a foreword by Christopher Donohue | ISBN 978-3-8382-1768-0

260 *David Dalton* | The Ukrainian Oligarchy After the Euromaidan. How Ukraine's Political Economy Regime Survived the Crisis | With a foreword by Andrew Wilson | ISBN 978-3-8382-1740-6

261 *Andreas Heinemann-Grüder (Ed.)* | Who Are the Fighters? Irregular Armed Groups in the Russian-Ukrainian War since 2014 | ISBN 978-3-8382-1777-2

262 *Taras Kuzio (Ed.)* | Russian Disinformation and Western Scholarship. Bias and Prejudice in Journalistic, Expert, and Academic Analyses of East European, Russian and Eurasian Affairs | ISBN 978-3-8382-1685-0

263 *Darius Furmonavicius* | LithuaniaTransforms the West. Lithuania's Liberation from Soviet Occupation and the Enlargement of NATO (1988–2022) | With a foreword by Vytautas Landsbergis | ISBN 978-3-8382-1779-6

264 *Dirk Dalberg* | Politisches Denken im tschechoslowakischen Dissens. Egon Bondy, Miroslav Kusý, Milan Šimečka und Petr Uhl (1968-1989) | ISBN 978-3-8382-1318-7

265 *Леонид Люкс* | К столетию «философского парохода». Мыслители «первой» русской эмиграции о русской революции и о тоталитарных соблазнах XX века | ISBN 978-3-8382-1775-8

266 *Daviti Mtchedlishvili* | The EU and the South Caucasus. European Neighborhood Policies between Eclecticism and Pragmatism, 1991-2021 | With a foreword by Nicholas Ross Smith | ISBN 978-3-8382-1735-2

267 *Bohdan Harasymiw* | Post-Euromaidan Ukraine. Domestic Power Struggles and War of National Survival in 2014–2022 | ISBN 978-3-8382-1798-7

268 *Nadiia Koval, Denys Tereshchenko (Eds.)* | Russian Cultural Diplomacy under Putin. Rossotrudnichestvo, the "Russkiy Mir" Foundation, and the Gorchakov Fund in 2007–2022 | ISBN 978-3-8382-1801-4

269 *Izabela Kazejak* | Jews in Post-War Wrocław and L'viv. Official Policies and Local Responses in Comparative Perspective, 1945-1970s | ISBN 978-3-8382-1802-1

270 *Jakob Hauter* | Russia's Overlooked Invasion. The Causes of the 2014 Outbreak of War in Ukraine's Donbas | With a foreword by Hiroaki Kuromiya | ISBN 978-3-8382-1803-8

271 *Anton Shekhovtsov* | Russian Political Warfare. Essays on Kremlin Propaganda in Europe and the Neighbourhood, 2020-2023 | With a foreword by Nathalie Loiseau | ISBN 978-3-8382-1821-2

272 *Андреа Пето* | Насилие и Молчание. Красная армия в Венгрии во Второй Мировой войне | ISBN 978-3-8382-1636-2

273 *Winfried Schneider-Deters* | Russia's War in Ukraine. Debates on Peace, Fascism, and War Crimes, 2022–2023 | With a foreword by Klaus Gestwa | ISBN 978-3-8382-1876-2

274 *Rasmus Nilsson* | Uncanny Allies. Russia and Belarus on the Edge, 2012-2024 | ISBN 978-3-8382-1288-3

275 *Anton Grushetskyi, Volodymyr Paniotto* | War and the Transformation of Ukrainian Society (2022–23). Empirical Evidence | ISBN 978-3-8382-1944-8

276 *Christian Kaunert, Alex MacKenzie, Adrien Nonjon (eds.)* | In the Eye of the Storm. Origins, Ideology, and Controversies of the Azov Brigade, 2014–23 | ISBN 978-3-8382-1750-5

277 *Gian Marco Moisé* | The House Always Wins. The Corrupt Strategies that Shaped Kazakh Oil Politics and Business in the Nazarbayev Era | With a foreword by Alena Ledeneva | ISBN 978-3-8382-1917-2

278 *Mikhail Minakov* | The Post-Soviet Human | Philosophical Reflections on Social History after the End of Communism | ISBN 978-3-8382-1943-1

279 *Natalia Kudriavtseva, Debra A. Friedman (eds.)* | Language and Power in Ukraine and Kazakhstan. Essays on Education, Ideology, Literature, Practice, and the Media | With a foreword by Laada Bilaniuk | ISBN 978-3-8382-1949-3

280 *Paweł Kowal, Georges Mink, Iwona Reichardt (eds.)* | The End of the Soviet World? Essays on Post-Communist Political and Social Change | With a foreword by Richard Butterwick-Pawlikowski | ISBN 978-3-8382-1961-5

281 *Kateryna Zarembo, Michèle Knodt, Maksym Yakovlyev (eds.)* | Teaching IR in Wartime. Experiences of University Lecturers during Russia's Full-Scale Invasion of Ukraine | ISBN 978-3-8382-1954-7

282 *Oleksiy V. Kresin* | The United Nations General Assembly Resolutions. Their Nature and Significance in the Context of the Russian War Against Ukraine | Edited by William E. Butler | ISBN 978-3-8382-1967-7